GRAMMAR WARS

Dedicated to Lawrence D. Green

Grammar Wars
Language as cultural battlefield in 17th and 18th century England

LINDA C. MITCHELL
San José State University, USA

LONDON AND NEW YORK

First published 2001 by Ashgate Publishing

Reissued 2018 by Routledge
2 Park Square, Milton Park, Abingdon, Oxon OX14 4RN
711 Third Avenue, New York, NY 10017, USA

Routledge is an imprint of the Taylor & Francis Group, an informa business

Copyright © Linda C. Mitchell 2001

All rights reserved. No part of this book may be reprinted or reproduced or utilised in any form or by any electronic, mechanical, or other means, now known or hereafter invented, including photocopying and recording, or in any information storage or retrieval system, without permission in writing from the publishers.

Notice:
Product or corporate names may be trademarks or registered trademarks, and are used only for identification and explanation without intent to infringe.

Publisher's Note
The publisher has gone to great lengths to ensure the quality of this reprint but points out that some imperfections in the original copies may be apparent.

Disclaimer
The publisher has made every effort to trace copyright holders and welcomes correspondence from those they have been unable to contact.

A Library of Congress record exists under LC control number: 2001046420

ISBN 13: 978-1-138-70209-7 (hbk)
ISBN 13: 978-0-415-79379-7 (pbk)
ISBN 13: 978-1-315-20984-5 (ebk)

Contents

List of Figures *vi*
Acknowledgements *vii*

Introduction 1

1   Vernacular Claims Victory   17
   English and Latin Models
   Inversion of Linguistic Authority

2   "Reformation of Schooles": Hartlib, Comenius, Milton   46
   Architectural Metaphors
   Comenius and Hartlib
   Reception of Comenius's Ideas
   Less Grammar, More Reading and Writing

3   The Battle: Good Grammar or Good Writing   73
   Putting Grammar to Work
   Rhetoric Subsumes Grammar: Grammar Texts as Rhetoric Handbooks
   Grammar Texts and Composition in the Schoolroom

4   Repairing Babel: Battles in Universal Language and   108
       Universal Grammar
   Language Acquisition: Descartes and Locke
   Universal Schemes in Seventeenth-Century England
   Universal Language in Eighteenth-Century England

5   Regulating Social Position   133
   Grammar for Foreigners: A Moral and National Identity
   Grammar for the "Weaker Sex": How Much is Morally Appropriate?
   Self-Generated Identity: The Middle Class and Birth of the
      "Language Police"

Afterword   165
Bibliography   168
Index   208

List of Figures

2.1	Tower of Knowledge, *Margarita Philosophica* (1504). Library of Congress	47
2.2	Johann Romberch, *Congestorium Artificiose Memorie* (1533). Department of Rare Books and Special Collections, Princeton University Library	49
2.3	Johann Amos Comenius, *Orbis sensualium pictus* (1658). William Andrews Clark Memorial Library, University of California, Los Angeles	60
2.4	Johann Amos Comenius, *Orbis sensualium pictus* (1658). William Andrews Clark Memorial Library, University of California, Los Angeles	61
4.1	Francis Lodowyck *A Common Writing* (1647). William Andrews Clark Memorial Library, University of California, Los Angeles	112
4.2	George Dalgarno, *Ars signorum* (1661). William Andrews Clark Memorial Library, University of California, Los Angeles	116
4.3	George Dalgarno, *Ars signorum* (1661). William Andrews Clark Memorial Library, University of California, Los Angeles	117
4.4	John Wilkins, *Essay Towards a Real Character and a Philosophical Language* (1668). William Andrews Clark Memorial Library, University of California, Los Angeles	119
4.5	John Wilkins, *Essay Towards a Real Character and a Philosophical Language* (1668). William Andrews Clark Memorial Library, University of California, Los Angeles	120
4.6	John Wilkins, *Essay Towards a Real Character and a Philosophical Language* (1668). William Andrews Clark Memorial Library, University of California, Los Angeles	122

Acknowledgements

I am indebted to my family and friends for supporting me while I wrote this book, especially to Christopher Mitchell, John Jason Mitchell, John P. Mitchell, Carrie Campion, E. J. Smith, Judith A. Sipple, Mary Antoinette Smith, B. Kaye Watson, and Carol Poster. I am also grateful to the students who encouraged me during the writing process, especially Rigoberto Palacios, Abir Ward Richani, and Erma Jackson. Thanks also for support received from the faculties and staffs of Pepperdine University, University of Southern California, and San José State University. Most of all, I wish to thank my friend and fellow scholar Jameela Lares for her valuable advice, daily support, and endless patience.

I owe many thanks to those who guided me through the original dissertation and its subsequent revision into this book: John Bidwell, Thomas M. Conley, Walter Fisher, Thomas Gustafson, Stanley R. Hauer, James J. Murphy, John M. Steadman, and Paul M. Zall. Special thanks to Joseph A. Dane who served *ex officio* on the dissertation committee and to Dagmar Čapková (Charles University, Prague) for being my mentor and friend. Victoria May gave generously of her talents in graphics and design, and she worked closely with both Ashgate Publishing and rare book libraries. Leo P. Fishman made valuable final corrections on the typescript. Several assistants helped me through the most rigorous stages of the book. Christine Peek eliminated many residual errors in the formatted copy. Andrea Cruz was a matchless detective in her bibliographic work. E. D. "Sweeney" Schragg believed in the book, read drafts tirelessly, and made insightful directions; his energy was contagious. Thanks also to Erika Gaffney, editor, at Ashgate Publishing, for her support and advice. All residual errors are mine.

I could not have done this project without the help of Suzanne Tatian, Bruce Whiteman and the staff of the William Andrews Clark Memorial Library (Los Angeles), and of Virginia Renner, Romaine Ahlstrom, and the Readers Services of the Henry E. Huntington Library. I wish to thank those who made arrangements for illustrations: AnnaLee Pauls, Charles Greene and Ben Primer, Princeton University; Jennifer Schaffner, William Andrews Clark Memorial Library; Jamie Jamison, UCLA Library; and the Library of Congress. Graham Parry, University of York, kindly gave permission to use a privately owned illustration for the book jacket. Thanks also to the friendly and helpful rare book staffs of the Bancroft Library (Berkeley), Bibliothèque Nationale (Paris), British Library, Bodleian Library, Cambridge University Library, Charles University Library (Prague), John Rylands Library, Lily Library (Indiana University), New

York Public Library, Newberry Library, Scottish National Library, Stanford Library, Trinity College Library (Dublin), University of Notre Dame Library, University of Sheffield Library, Vrije Universiteit Library (Amsterdam) and University of York Library. I benefited from funding from University of Southern California and Pepperdine University. I am also grateful to Paul Douglass, chair of the Department of English at San José State University, for his continual support and kindness. In particular, I want to thank Dean Carmen Sigler and Associate Dean Lucius Eastman in the College of the Humanities and The Arts for the grants and travel funds that made it possible for me to complete this project.

My deepest appreciation goes to Lawrence D. Green who has served as a model scholar, teacher, mentor, and friend. Professor Green served as my faculty adviser at USC, chaired my dissertation committee, invested many hours as my mentor, involved me in research projects in primary materials, and encouraged me to present papers at national and international conferences. Without him, this book would never have been written.

Introduction

Grammar is a natural battlefield for the intellect. It represents common mental ground, one of the few intellectual competencies that each of us attains. A linguistically static culture may take "grammar" for granted. In times of linguistic change or innovation, however, grammar becomes a hotly contested issue. Thus, during the seventeenth and eighteenth centuries, we find not only marked linguistic change but also numerous conflicts over what is called "grammar." The language theorists of this period claimed they were fighting battles to correct errors in grammar and to preserve language from corruption. More significantly, however, these combatants were choosing grammar as a place to contest issues that went far beyond grammar.

The diversity of subject, organization, and formats in seventeenth- and eighteenth-century materials cannot be understood in terms of a specified number of examples. Grammar books start to make sense only when we view them as argumentative statements in controversies of the time. Grammar texts functioned as cultural statements because of the diversity of material and approaches. The terms "grammar" and "grammar texts" were ambiguous concepts that fueled the controversies over grammar. In order for twentieth-century researchers to discuss seventeenth- and eighteenth-century grammar texts, they have to define grammar. In these centuries-old texts, "grammar" can mean anything from parts of speech to spelling and punctuation. In order to investigate what "grammar" meant to seventeenth- and eighteenth-century grammarians, scholars *must* examine the prefaces and introductions to grammar books where grammarians carried on disputes with fellow grammarians and linguists about such topics as religion, politics, linguistics, women, foreigners, social status, and even science. Without those treatises, we would not know as much about how "grammar" was conceived during this period.

I. Riotous Definitions of Grammar and Grammar Texts

Previous scholarly definitions of what grammar meant to the writers of these texts have failed to account for their riotous diversity, primarily because such definitions have stated our modern concerns rather than those of the period. I will instead try to make sense out of the diversity of grammar texts by examining their changing definitions of grammar. According to Ian Michael in *English Grammatical Categories* (1970), "grammar" was an "elastic and ambiguous term," and it could mean the study of the vernacular or of a foreign language, parts of speech, language use, language itself, or even translation (199). To understand what seventeenth- and eighteenth-century grammarians mean by "grammar," we have to look at the sheer diversity of definitions. If an author chooses to define grammar, he does so on the first page of his text, thus providing possible clues as to how he will approach his material. For centuries grammarians traditionally offered a conventional formula, such as grammar is "the art of speaking and writing correctly."[1] As for English grammarians in the seventeenth century, about one-third offer no definition of grammar because the formula is so well known that it is not worth including it in the book, Michael claims (189). He also discovered that of those who do use a definition, two-thirds use a formula, such as Charles Butler's definition in *English Grammar* (1633): grammar is the "art of writing and speaking well" (1). Michael shows that until 1740 only about one-half of the grammarians use definitions. After 1740, according to his research, most grammarians do use a definition, possibly because the texts were becoming more uniform and they could easily borrow a definition.

My interest, however, lies in the grammarians who are not conventional. Those grammarians who deviate from the norm tell us the most about the issues being fought in the name of grammar in the seventeenth and eighteenth centuries. These grammarians try to change language paradigms by attempting to change ideas about grammar. Grammar texts are in fact argumentative statements about controversial issues. I could begin by saying that in the late seventeenth and early eighteenth centuries, grammarians tended to write concrete, systematic definitions, while in the eighteenth century they wrote definitions that centered on literacy skills, yet even these two generalizations do not hold true. I am going to attempt to look at definitions of grammar in five categories (standardization, pedagogy, writing instruction, universal language, and social position), although the distinctions blur.

Definitions mask controversial issues over standardization. Some grammarians implied in their definitions a possibility of certainty and consistency of rules in the search for a doctrine of correctness. The desire for orthographical and syntactic certainty is reflected in the move to prescriptive, uniform grammar texts in the eighteenth century. Grammarians view correctness by what is proper, according to rules and custom. In *An Essay Towards a Practical English Grammar* (1722) James Greenwood defines grammar as "the Art of Speaking and Writing truly and properly," that is, he believes that following rules lead to standardization (2). In *A Practical Guide to the Latin Tongue* (1729) John Milner defines grammar as a "collection of Rules, for speaking and writing properly, according to the custom of *that* Nation whose language we learn," thus adding custom to Greenwood's definition (2). Thomas Dyche addresses idiom in his *A New General English Dictionary* (1735) where he called grammar "the art of adjusting words according to the idiom and flexion of any language" (3). Habit of speaking, to some grammarians, became one of the measuring devices for correct grammar, although to other grammarians it is a thorny, explosive issue. Benjamin Martin in *Bibliotheca Technologica* (1737) defines grammar as "the Art of expressing the Relation of Things by Words in Construction, with due Accent in speaking and Orthography in Writing, according to the Custom of those, whose Language we learn" (xvii). Grammars are also becoming prescriptive and rule-based in order to standardize language, such as in Ellin Devis's *The Accidence* (1775): grammar is "the art of using words according to certain established rules" (1). Bishop Robert Lowth's definition of grammar in Short Introduction to Grammar (1763) is the "Art of rightly expressing our thoughts by Words" in which the user can "judge of every phrase and form of construction, whether it be right or not" (x).

Second, definitions of grammar also reflect controversies in pedagogy. Grammarians word their definitions to describe their methodologies for teaching grammar, methodologies that were exceptionally diverse. Some grammarians thought they could actually avoid controversy by not being original, such as repeating the formula that grammar is "the art of speaking and writing correctly" and "the art of writing and speaking well." But they were subscribing, whether they admitted it or not, to Quintilian's pedagogy: "*Grammatica est recte scribendi et loquendi ars*" (I.V.41). William Lily's copycat definition in *Royal Grammar* (1540) that grammar is the art of speaking correctly is also an attempt to follow a traditional method of pedagogy. Charles Hoole uses Lily's definition to his advantage by changing it slightly in *The Latine Grammar* (1651) and arguing that grammar is the "Art of Writing and Speaking aright" (2). Hoole manipulates Lily's definition to argue that Lily's text was pedagogically sound and that he, Hoole, should publish the grammar as a bilingual text, thus making Lily more accessible yet upholding the classical tradition. Another traditional practice for grammarians is teaching grammar through translation and literature. James Howell connects grammar with literature in *The New English Grammar* (1662): in the days of antiquity grammar meant reading literature, as in "the Art of Letters" (2).

Some grammarians identify their pedagogy by defining grammar with terms of logic.[2] The book that introduces the concept of defining grammar with logic is the first foreign grammar used in English schools, *The Latine Grammar of P. Ramus* (1585), and it manages to overturn Lily's definition of grammar (Book I, chapter 1). Lily defines grammar in four parts (*orthographia, etymologia, syntaxis, prosodia*), but Ramus defines grammar in two parts: etymology and syntax. Ramus argued that grammar could be learned more efficiently if it were part of logic, and thus he sets up a system marked by his own binary divisions throughout. Numerous English grammarians followed Ramus in using schematized logic to teach grammar: Paul Greaves's *Grammatica Anglicana* (1594), Thomas Granger's *Syntagma Grammaticum* (1616), Ben Jonson's *English Grammar* (1640), John Evelyn's *The English Grammar* (1650), and Alexander Richardson's *The Logicians School-Master: or, a comment upon Ramus Logicke* (1657), and John Milton's *Accedence Commenc't Grammar* (1669).[3] In *The Construction of the Westminster-*

Grammar (1712) Nicholas Brady, the Younger, defines grammar as being taught from the foundation or in increments: "Art that teaches four elements of human speech: a Letter, a Syllable, a Word, and a Sentence" (2).

Third, writing instruction makes its appearance in definitions. *Royal Grammar of [William Lily]* (1695) defines grammar as an "art of expressing the thoughts by proper words aptly joined in true writing and speaking" (3). In *Right Spelling Very Much Improved* (1704), expressing oneself is important: "Grammar teacheth how to express our Minds by words in Speaking, or by Letters or Characters in Writing" (25). Charles Gildon stresses propriety in *A Grammar of the English Tongue* (1712) (often referred to as "Brightland's Grammar") in his definition: "Grammar is the Knowledge or Sentences according to the Use, Form and Propriety of every Tongue either in speaking or Writing" (3). Gildon also praised Richard Johnson in *Grammatical Commentaries* (1704) for defining the qualities of both speaking and writing in grammar as "the Art of Expressing the Relations of Things in Construction" (ii). Thomas Bowles sees grammar in *Aristarchus* (1748) as the "Art of expressing properly the Relations of Things by Construction of Words" (Preface). William Ward states in *An Essay on Grammar* (1765) that grammar is "the art of applying [articulate] sounds and letters consistently for the purpose of communicating the thoughts of one man to another" (v).

Fourth, definitions reflect controversial issues in universal grammar and universal language. The concept of "universal language" appears in definitions aiming to discover a single system of grammar that everyone could learn. Such an easily learned language could overcome semantic confusion and repair the results of Babel. Usually, universal language definitions would begin with letters, syllables, words, and sentences (which grammarians called "components"), starting out at a basic linguistic level and working to a more complex one. In *A Rational and Speedy Method of Attaining to the Latin Tongue* (1695) Archibald Lane wanted to be the first English grammarian after Wilkins to make universal claims for his work: "the true End and Use of Grammar is to teach us how to speak and write well and learnedly in a Language already known, according to the unalterable Rules of right Reason, which are the same in all Languages how different soever they be" (Introduction). And later, Lane states in *Key to the Art of Letters* (1700) that universal grammar is the "Art that Teaches the Right Way of Speaking and Writing, according to the particular Form of every Language" (1). In *A New General English Dictionary* (1735) Thomas Dyche and William Pardon define grammar according to its components: grammar is the "Art or Science that teaches Persons the true and proper Use of Letters, Syllables, Words and Sentences, in any Language whatever" (A4). Another text to define grammar by emphasizing the formal linguistic structure of language is *A Vocabulary, or Pocket Dictionary* (1765): "Unless the Grammarian fix the Meaning and Use of Words (which is reasonably expected from every Dictionary) he has nothing left him belonging to the Language, but the Inflections, which are extremely few; and the Order in which Words are placed in a Sentence" (A1).

Definitions in grammar also identify a fifth issue, that of social position. Language is a reflection of a person's character and competency, and the focus of grammar books projected that goal in opening statements. Edmund Coote in the *English School-Master* (1596), which was used throughout the seventeenth century, writes that he is directing the text "to the unskilled sort," the trades people, who will use this knowledge in commercial establishments (Title page). This book is one of the first annotated teacher's editions. Its marginalia are intended to assist the schoolmaster in his teaching techniques, and indicate that public instruction was changing to meet the needs of a more diverse group of students. Ralph Johnson's *Scholar's Guide* (1679) stresses the importance for the children of the aspiring classes to learn to speak well in their mother tongue so that they can communicate in their vocations (Preface). In *Tutor to True English* (1699) Henry Care also entreats vocational students of the rising classes to learn the mother tongue for good communication rather than to slave over Latin (Preface). Care demonstrates his social awareness when he defines grammar as the art of being able to write and speak in relation to others. In the *Supplement to Dr. Harris's Dictionary* (1744), the author defines grammar as "the Art of Speaking and Writing Correctly and Properly" (54). He calls grammar the "most essential Bond of human Society" and is disappointed that it does not get more emphasis. A less scholarly text, but one that emphasizes communication skills for social position is George Brown's *The New English Letter-Writer* (1779): Grammar is the "art of one human creature speaking to another, so as to be understood" (17).

Grammar seems to be a simple subject, but the term itself is devilishly hard to define. Even in the seventeenth century, grammar was considered dry and boring, yet even then, this so-called dull subject was quick to spark a heated argument about its definition and its goals. The definitions of grammar on the battlefield of standardization, pedagogy, writing instruction, universal language, and social position are diverse, yet they are a reflection of what grammarians believed to be the most important goal, be it vocational skills, universal language, social discourse, or educational reform. By mid-eighteenth century, the emphasis had shifted from social communication to codifying the English language, exemplifying an anxiety as to linguistic certainty.

II. Review of Scholarship

Modern scholars of seventeenth- and eighteenth-century grammar agree that the putatively boring subject of grammar is always at the heart of controversy. They do not, however, agree about the reasons, and they are not all talking about the same controversies. Each scholar focuses on different aspects, examining a fraction that cannot represent the whole. The very strengths of an approach to one area will slight the other areas. Consequently, the controversies over grammar still remain obscure and unappreciated. The field is too rich and still too unexplored to yield to broad theses.

Standardization Modern research recognizes that some grammarians of the seventeenth and eighteenth centuries thought that language should reflect "custom" and "usage," allowing that even the "best authors" made grammatical mistakes, while other grammarians acted as individual champions of a preferred orthography and grammar, and yet a third group of grammarians declared a truce on trying to codify grammar by combining custom and usage with preferred forms.

In *On the History of Some Problems of English Grammar Before 1800* (1948), Ivan Poldauf focuses on the ways grammarians try to reach some form of standardization of the vernacular. He starts with the grammar texts of the late sixteenth century that led to the prescriptive grammars of the late eighteenth century. Poldauf distinguishes between Ben Jonson's "common speech" in *English Grammar* (1640) and Alexander Gill's "proper speech" in *Logonomia Anglica* (1619). Poldauf claims that John Wallis is influential in helping to standardize grammar because Wallis takes an empirical and rational approach to grammar (82). Poldauf also credits Wallis with the first significant grammatical description of the English language and for being the first grammarian to engage in serious modern linguistic study.[4] According to Poldauf, Wallis's *Grammatica linguae Anglicanae* (1653) is the "first description of the sounds of a language that can claim to be scientific" (79). Wallis, like Gill, tries to break from the Latin tradition, and concentrates on standardizing the word formation of the vernacular by systemizing rules. Although Poldauf says that Wallis was a major influence on the linguistic theory of grammar, he does not mention the other influences on the development of grammar texts themselves.

In an overview of the grammar books Poldauf chooses, for example, two grammars of "practical aims" most similar to Wallis's demonstrate some of the first attempts at standardizing the English language. The two texts, Guy Miège's *The English Grammar* (1688) and Christopher Cooper's *The English Teacher* (1687), argued that there was only one correct form of usage. Poldauf also describes the codification of English grammar by relating stories such as the "grammar war" in which John Brightland, Michael Maittaire, and James Greenwood all participated. Poldauf does not, however, mention other issues of importance like the recognition of women in grammar texts, the differences between 1711 and 1712 editions of Gildon's grammar, the addition of a compendium of grammar to dictionaries, and the addition of logic and rhetoric to grammar texts.

Pedagogy In modern research on the history of grammar, scholars often ignore the relations between language activities and pedagogical practices. The peripheral issues surrounding the teaching of language are central to understanding the evolution of grammar texts. Why did seventeenth- and eighteenth-century grammarians argue over whether Latin grammar should be taught in Latin or in the vernacular, in translation, or in bilingual texts? Why did some grammarians argue that the elite should get a classical education and the lower classes a vocational one? Why did some grammarians visualize educational reform as a repairing of the old foundation, while others saw reform in terms of tearing out the old foundation and putting in a new one?

The scholar who has done the most comprehensive work on the pedagogy of teaching in grammar texts is Ian Michael.[5] In his brief overview of the history of grammar he lists 273 texts, arranged topically. Michael traces the changing definitions of grammar and shows how those changes reflect the teaching of grammar. In a later study, Michael focuses on how pedagogy relates to the teaching of grammar.[6] In this second book he not only pinpoints issues in the teaching of grammar, but he also explains how seventeenth-century grammarians taught reading, writing, and speaking, and describes how these disciplines were taught over centuries amidst changing social and economic conditions.[7]

Dagmar Čapková, a prolific scholar at Charles University (Prague), focuses on pedagogical issues as they relate to the teaching of language to youth. For example, she looks at the "visible language" methods that Comenius used to teach grammar and vocabulary. She points out that Comenius not only wanted students to acquire literacy but also to learn moral and religious values. He connected the soul with the mind for a total being. Čapková also emphasizes that Comenius, an educator and reformer, wanted language instruction to speak to the vocational interests of students and to nourish the soul. She is especially thorough in describing Comenius's commitment to "pansophy," a call for a child to love God, fill his soul with light, and learn a language that would take him through a "universal gate." But Comenius and his teachings need to be placed in a broader context than Čapková provides, especially because the seventeenth century is a period of much experimentation with language, and Comenius is only one part of the picture. Even though Čapková herself is clearly aware of the extent to which these language activities were taking place, she still takes time to provide sufficient background for the reader to understand what she is explaining.

Writing Instruction Not much scholarly work has been done on the writing instruction that appears in grammar texts in the seventeenth and eighteenth centuries. James Murphy's *A Short History of Writing Instruction: From Ancient Greece to Twentieth-Century America* (1990) touches upon some writing instruction, but the essay does not speak directly to what was being taught from grammar texts.

Universal Language On the subject of grammar, most modern research concentrates on the theoretical linguistic issues that dominated the works of grammarians. Linguistic questions have been of the most interest because they are the most obvious ones to ask about language. For example, modern scholars who have done research on seventeenth- and eighteenth-century universal grammar want to isolate what grammarians claimed were the underpinnings of language. How a modern scholar assesses "universal grammar" in the seventeenth and eighteenth centuries varies according to the goals of the research. Vivian Salmon, for instance, looks at language problems that grammarians tried to find solutions to, including thorny issues in pedagogical practices.[8] Significant figures and works in her study are George Dalgarno's *Ars Signorum* (1661), Cave Beck's *Universal Character* (1657), and John Wilkins's *An Essay Towards a Real Character, and a Philosophical Language* (1668). Those grammarians, she argues, illustrate innovative attempts to construct an artificial language and put it into actual practice. In an article on Francis Lodowyck, Salmon describes how well Lodowyck classifies cognitive acts in order to determine how such an artificial language should be constructed.[9] She also analyzes the relations that are possible among cognitive acts. Finally, she looks at the written and spoken symbols that are used to express the acts and their relations. She also assesses the contributions to artificial language schemes by the Samuel Hartlib circle, especially Comenius. Salmon recognizes that school grammars were, in fact, profoundly affected by grammar practices in cases like John Brinsley and Joseph Webbe.[10] She does not, however, explain fully how practices like learning grammar by sentence patterns or by memorization affected the production of school grammars. Moreover, although she evaluates the strengths and weaknesses of universal language schemes, she does not indicate that the meaning of the term "universal language" goes through significant changes by the end of the century. Of all the modern historians, Vivian Salmon has constructed the most detailed picture of language planning in the seventeenth century in *The Study of Language in Seventeenth-Century England* (1988). Salmon's more recent book, *Language and Society in Early Modern England* (1996) continues to examine sixteenth- and seventeenth-century linguistic scholarship, this time touching more on rhetorical issues and grammar.

In *Universal Language Schemes in England and France 1600–1800* (1975) James Knowlson details the linguistic struggle of seventeenth-century grammarians in England and on the Continent to find a universal language. Knowlson examines the various schemes, particularly that of "secret language" (e.g., codes, hieroglyphics, symbols) and sign systems, that linguists proposed to use for different types of communication among peoples of the world. Seventeenth-century linguists, he says, regard artificial or "real character" languages as a mirror of reality.[11] John Wilkins (1668), for example, invents an ideal character scheme that will not only support a proposed universal language, but will also lend itself to a theory of grammar. A minor problem in Knowlson's presentation is that he focuses on secret languages at the expense of showing how grammarians developed other universal grammars. Even though he promises in the title of his book to discuss universal language schemes in England and in France, he concentrates on the Continent rather than on England.

Benjamin DeMott, another modern scholar, also focuses on linguistic issues. DeMott argues that the Czech educator Johann Amos Comenius was instrumental in moving philosophical language from lists and strange alphabets to more developed concepts of universal language. DeMott also claims that Comenius brought the idea of universal language to England through his publication of *Via Lucis* in the 1630s, and that Comenius's visit to England in 1641 afforded him the opportunity to explain his language plan. DeMott also demonstrates that Wilkins's *Essay* (1668) shows the influence of Comenius's *Janua linguarum reserata* (1652) and *Orbis sensualium pictus* (1659). He identifies the two periods in the development of universal and philosophical language projects: the first period (ca. 1635–47) shows the effort to devise a *universal* language that would function as an easily-learned substitute for existing language, whereas the second period (ca. 1650–68) shows the attempt to devise a universal *and* philosophical language that would be adapted to the exact and perfect representation of things. DeMott does a thorough job of looking at the actual language planning in the seventeenth century, but at the expense of overlooking how the systems themselves worked. Like other modern scholars, he dismisses the eighteenth century without looking into the significant changes in definitions of "universal language."

Modern scholars also inquire into other linguistic issues in their research. Gerald A. Padley focuses on the theories of grammar and the development of universal language on the Continent. In *Grammatical Theory in Western Europe: 1500–1700: the Latin Tradition* (1976), *Grammatical Theory in Western Europe: 1500–1700: Trends in Vernacular Grammar I* (1985), and *Grammatical Theory in Western Europe: 1500–1700: Trends in Vernacular Grammar II* (1988), Padley looks at grammarians whose systems are driven by such philosophies as ramistic methodology or German mysticism. He particularly examines the developments in five major vernaculars (English, French, German, Spanish, and Italian). For the linguist who is making a detailed study of the evolution of grammar in England and on the Continent, Padley's two volumes are indispensable. The scholar studying the history of ideas in grammar texts may find Padley's work is not quite so helpful in that it provides little information about seventeenth- and eighteenth-century British grammar books. Padley does not set out to focus on pedagogical or social issues in his discussion on the evolution of grammar, and thus he omits these influences on grammar texts.

Herbert E. Brekle summarizes linguistic issues in the work done by modern scholars of seventeenth and eighteenth-century grammar, work that has been under-recognized. He looks at the controversies described by linguists researching grammar and the theory of language in the seventeenth century. Brekle not only evaluates scholars, but he also comments on the contributions of seventeenth- and eighteenth-century grammarians. Brekle surveys an impressive range of linguistic data for England, Germany, Italy, Spain, France. His extensive bibliography of primary and secondary sources, which includes a supplement from Hans Aarsleff's studies, is thorough and comprehensive.[12]

Brekle outlines several important issues that many modern scholars overlook. He explains, for example, that the debate about "patterns" versus "judgment" began in the sixteenth century because of the need to teach both the vernaculars and Latin. Grammarians became involved in a "grammar war" over whether to teach Latin through pattern drills or by rules. Two grammarians involved in this dispute were Joseph Webbe and John Brooke. Joseph Webbe obtained a patent (1626) and published textbooks on the pattern-drill method of teaching language; John Brooke (1627) defended the rule-governed method of teaching language and evaluated Webbe's method.[13] Another issue that Brekle traces is the development of universal and philosophical languages. His detailed outline of Wilkins's *Essay* (1668) shows that Wilkins was doing prelinguistic work. In both the discussions on Webbe and universal languages, Brekle refers to the significance of Vivian Salmon's work. As thorough as Brekle is, he concentrates on Continental material. In addition, although he looks at related areas such as language philosophy and semiotics, he limits his discussion to grammar books and treatises. He ignores, for example, the separation at the end of the seventeenth century of the philosophy of grammar from the practice of grammar, thus making it difficult for the reader to put some of his information into the appropriate context.

Another source overlooked in the study of grammar books is Tetsuro Hayashi's (1978) effort to account for anomalies that influence thinking about language and that helped shape dictionaries. He offers a comprehensive commentary about the role that grammar began to assume in dictionaries in the eighteenth century. His book is important because no other scholar has connected the role of lexicography to the evolution of grammar texts, but unfortunately it has only a limited discussion of how the dictionaries embraced grammar. Another important aspect of his study is his survey of dictionaries for women, children, foreigners, and the working class. His study raises questions about the foreigners and their use of grammar books and dictionaries.

Social Position The role of grammar with respect to social position engendered the fifth area of controversy, but relatively little scholarly work has been done on this aspect. Grammarians had the power to assign identities, or encoded behavior, appropriate to marginal groups like foreigners, women, and the aspiring classes. Moreover, because many or most handbooks were directed to the teaching of children, they were nakedly ideological in motive. Emma Vorlat (1975) has reviewed later sixteenth- and early seventeenth-century grammar texts in their social context and has detailed how grammarians such as William Bullokar (1586) and John Wallis (1653) were writing texts to respond to larger groups of readers. Next, she moves to the independent development of English grammar, that is, from John Wallis to William Loughton's *A Practical Grammar of the*

English Tongue (1734). Grammarians, she notes, include instruction for women, foreigners, and unskilled workers and teach people how to read English so that they can understand religious material. Vorlat, however, stops at the beginning of the seventeenth century, just when grammar texts are beginning to evolve into the next phase of diverse, philosophical grammars. Vorlat rightly connects the learning of grammar with social position, but she does not provide the evidence to support that assertion, and while she claims that literacy becomes an issue as early as the end of the sixteenth century, she does not tell us why and how grammarians tried to resolve the problem.

Murray Cohen in *Sensible Words: Linguistic Practice in England 1640–1785* (1977) argues social implications for the move in grammar texts from a small audience of academic readers to a wider public audience. According to Cohen, texts began to meet special needs in society by teaching manners, morals, and religion. The strongest section of Cohen's book (for my present purposes) is his description of the increasing demand for competence in social discourse. He shows that grammar books began teaching skills like reading, writing, and speaking because people needed to be able to communicate effectively in a rapidly changing society. Cohen begins his study with that instruction which first recognizes the vernacular as an academic and intellectual subject. He concludes with the writers who accept the basic assumptions of what we would recognize as modern schoolroom grammar. Cohen's discussion ranges over visual grammars, shorthand systems, theories of signs, and universal languages during the middle of the seventeenth century, and he argues that the seventeenth century posits an isomorphic relationship between language and nature, whereas the eighteenth century thinks that language reflects the structure of the mind. Cohen provides a valuable broad survey of authors and issues from 1640 to 1785, but even so, the gaps in his study are still significant. For example, from 1640 to 1700 he focuses on philosophical grammars that incorporated universal language schemes, omitting other significant texts of the period that might have changed his discussion, such as Thomas Farnaby's *Systema Grammaticum* (1641), E. Young's *The Compleat English Scholar* (1680), William Mather's *The Young Man's Companion* (1695), and Henry Care's *The Tutor to True English* (1699). He does not talk about the addition of compendia of grammar to dictionaries in the eighteenth century, and he ignores rhetoric subsuming grammar and logic in handbooks. He lists many grammarians but does not give enough background information to allow the reader to put them into a context. James Howell, for example, contributed significantly to teaching English to foreigners, but Cohen does not explain what motivated Howell to do it. A knowledgeable Cohen has written a survey of issues surrounding grammar texts, a study that no one else has done, but the frustrated reader is left wishing there were more to it.[14]

Other publications offer excellent social histories of English. Dick Leith's *A Social History of English* (1983, rpt. 1997) highlights changing patterns of usage from both social and linguistic perspectives. Another worthwhile book is Keith Wrightson's *English Society 1580–1680* (1982, rpt. 1998) which provides a necessary social history background for looking at language. Important reading is Rosemary O'Day's *Education and Society 1500–1800: The Social Foundations of Education in Early Modern Britain* (1982). O'Day meticulously describes and documents educational practices for all classes. A bibliography on marginalized groups should include *Attending to Women in Early Modern England.* (Travitsky and Seeff 1994); *An Ordered Society: Gender and Class in Early Modern England* (Amussen 1988); *The Patriarch's Wife: Literary Evidence and the History of the Family* (Ezell 1987) and *Writing Women's Literary History* (Ezell 1993); *Renaissance Feminism: Literary Texts and Political Models* (Constance Jordan 1990); *Writing, gender and state in early modern England: Identity formation and the female subject* (Matchinske 1998); *Women in Early Modern England* (Mendelson and Crawford 1998).

III. Overview of Grammar Texts

Modern scholars have specific goals and interests, and in the pursuit of their various intentions it is reasonable that they should focus on particular aspects, texts, and problems while ignoring others. Despite the individuality of their approaches, however, they do share a number of assumptions and procedures, and those commonalities provide the starting point for my own study and interests.

First, all of these researchers conflate the term "grammar" with the phenomenon of the "grammar text." They are not the same. When we conflate the term "grammar" with "grammar text," we lose sight of the innovations and advances grammarians made in the teaching of language and the separation of independent subjects from grammar itself. We also do not take into account the social, political, and economic factors that influence the content of those books. If we try to define grammar synonymously with grammar books, we overlook such things as the emergence and final separation of "rhetoric" from "grammar," not as these two terms had been defined for centuries, but as they were understood at the time in terms of theory and practice. We also lose sight of the important merger of communication skills with the discipline of grammar, a merger that becomes significant in the eighteenth century. It is easy to overlook the riches of seventeenth and eighteenth century textbooks.

Second, modern researchers have been interested in how theories of universal language affected grammar and the teaching of grammar. Although their research has been helpful and informative in understanding universal language activities, scholars have not looked at all the implications of what they have found, such as the reasons for the change in the definition of universal grammar. They also have not looked at how the concepts of universal grammar influenced the teaching of reading, writing, and speaking. Tied into these questions is how the changing social and economic conditions encouraged or discouraged the research and teaching of universal language in the seventeenth and eighteenth centuries.

Third, researchers focus on the "grammar" in these texts rather than on the evolution of grammar texts, and so lose sight of differences in content, form, and point of view. It is not that scholars purposely ignore diversity (Cohen, for example, discusses cultural issues in grammar texts), but rather that they are interested in linguistic issues. It is easier to trace verb forms and noun changes than explain why grammar books had such a wide variety of subjects like punctuation, rhetoric, literature, spelling and pronunciation, devotional and moral lessons, bad-English exercises, history and geography, linguistics, logic, letter-writing, book making, medicine, and etiquette. One of the reasons may be that modern grammarians do not feel comfortable venturing out into this unknown territory when they are not trained as social historians, cultural critics, or rhetoricians.

And last, grammarians do not try to explain the extensive variety of grammar books because it is difficult to determine what is meant by "grammar," or even by "grammar book." The staggering variety of grammar texts makes sorting them into neat classifications nearly impossible because some defy categorization. Authors of many of these early grammar texts wrote on agricultural subjects, such as irrigation and cattle. Samuel Hartlib published detailed accounts on farming and bee-keeping. The Royal Society and a "scientific" approach are represented by John Wallis and John Wilkins. Some authors like Michael Maittaire and Ralph Johnson were schoolmasters. Literary figures are Ben Jonson, a playwright; Samuel Johnson, an educator, biographer, and literary arbiter; Jonathan Swift, a clergyman, poet, novelist, phamphleter, and political activist; Cave Beck and Robert Lowth, who held religious positions; and Joseph Priestley, a leisured researcher in chemistry. Regardless of the diversity of material, authors of these early texts all had the common goal of writing a grammar book that codified spelling, pronunciation, vocabulary, and parts of speech.

With the introduction of printing into England, the number of grammar texts at first proliferated, next declined, and then again proliferated until the period of the present study. There were twenty-four major authors of Latin grammar texts from 1481 to 1542, the year in which a royal monopoly was granted to William Lily.[15] The royal edict granting this monopoly stated that all schoolchildren had to use Lily's Latin text, *Short Introduction to Grammar* (1527). The royal monopoly reduced the number of grammar texts to twelve between the years 1542 and 1612. The publication rates, however, rose after that until 1669, resulting in some 169 editions of Latin grammars. The demand for education among rising social classes, the Puritan interest in schooling, and the weakening of the royal monopoly all contributed to the increase in texts.

IV. Plan of the Study

Any given grammar text was almost always engaged in one of five controversies of the time: standardization, pedagogy, writing instruction, universal language, and social position. In the following chapters I will look at a variety of theoretical issues raised by language on the cultural battleground, and I will look at the manifestation of these same controversies in the practical implementation and application of competing ideas about grammar.

In chapter one I look at the various issues of standardization. In the seventeenth and early eighteenth centuries several changes occurred in how grammar was understood and how it was perceived to relate to other disciplines. I am interested in three changes that determined who held linguistic authority. Chapter two is a discussion on how grammarians used the metaphor of architecture to develop a pedagogy using *incremental competence*.

In chapter three I examine how grammar books served the utilitarian needs of the middle class in the seventeenth and eighteenth centuries by teaching vocational writing skills. Chapter four describes how the definition of universal language in the seventeenth century changes in the eighteenth century. In chapter five I show that grammar created and maintained an identity for marginal groups.

In the chapters which follow I will avoid the temptation to offer yet another premature and reductive thesis, and instead describe some of the variety which I have found, organized under a series of lesser theses which relate the vigor and diversity of the materials, and which outline the five major battle fields I perceive: standardization, pedagogy, writing instruction, universal language, and social position.

Some of the material in this book appeared in considerably different form in the following publications: "Pedagogical Practices of Lexicographers in Seventeenth- and Eighteenth-Century England," *Actes EURALEX '98 Proceedings*; "Anne Fisher and Literacy Training in 18th-Century England." ERIC (Educational Resources Information Center), 1999; "The Use of Rhetoric in Seventeenth-Century Writing Pedagogy," in *Proceedings of the Canadian Society for the Study of Rhetoric 94–97*; "Comenius: A Redefinition of a Seventeenth-Century European Mind and the Quest for Education Identity," *Studies in Early Modern Philosophy*; and "Inversion of Grammar Books and Dictionaries in 17th- and 18th-Century England," in *Actes EURALEX '94 Proceedings*.

I have attempted to use the original texts whenever possible and to stay with the original spelling. I have made silent corrections on some words and have normalized *i, j, u,* and *v*. When I have used more than one edition of a work, I list the editions.

Notes

1 Per Michael (1970:189), these early definitions appear as early as Diomedes in the fourth century A.D.
2 More than do other scholars, Gordon Campbell explains in detail how grammarians used logic to define and teach grammar (1976:41–48).
3 J. Milton French (1961:647–57).
4 Subbiondo (1992:184) argues that Wallis was the "first to analyze English grammar by framing and testing hypotheses which were based on formal criteria derived from his observations of English structure".
5 Michael (1970:1–81, 147–200).
6 Michael (1987:14–134, 317–371).
7 See Houston (1988:56–75) for a discussion of the methods of teaching in the lower grades.
8 Salmon 1961, 1966, 1964, 1972, 1979.
9 Salmon (1972:12).
10 Salmon (1961:325).
11 Knowlson (1975:27).
12 Brekle 1975.
13 Webbe (1622), Salmon 1979. See Webster (1970:18–21) for an informative discussion about the conflict between Webbe and Brooke.
14 Some of Cohen's informative endnotes (e.g., notes 1, 25, and 26 in chapter two) would have been worthwhile additions to the text itself.
15 David P. French (1953–82:65).

Chapter One
Vernacular Claims Victory

We assume that a book about grammar is one that records the standardized, codified language used by educated people. In the seventeenth and eighteenth centuries, however, "grammar" was an elastic term, one that varied from textbook to textbook. In *A Social History of English* Dick Leith states, "there are probably more misconceptions about the term 'grammar' than any other term in the popular vocabulary of linguistics."[1] Several of these misconceptions have been byproducts of the evolution of grammar. These include the notions that some people are automatically equipped with grammar while others are not, that grammar is an integral part of the written language but not of the spoken language, that the use of the term "grammar" refers to a written account of language rules, that grammar is good or bad, and that some languages have more complicated grammars than others.[2]

In the seventeenth and eighteenth centuries, several changes occurred in the way grammar was understood and the way it was perceived to relate to other disciplines. Some of these changes manifested themselves in battlefields that were centered on the relationship between English grammar and Latin grammar. Another battle was fought between two growing factions in the eighteenth century: the prescriptivists, who wanted language to remain unchanged, and the descriptivists, who recognized that language changes and custom and habit determine how people speak. And finally, a much subtler change took place: the linguistic authority held by grammarians in the seventeenth century was transferred in the eighteenth century to lexicographers. This chapter will look at some of these changes, in hopes of coming to a greater understanding of why we force illogical Latinate rules onto English grammar, why people resist language change, and why dictionaries carry the burden of maintaining the integrity of language.

I. English and Latin Models

In the seventeenth and early eighteenth centuries, several controversies centered on the relationships between English grammar and Latin grammar. One thing decided by mid-seventeenth century was that the vernacular should be taught in schools as a way to prepare students to learn Latin. Pedagogues who promoted this idea had won the argument, but one hold out was Thomas Farnaby. He argues in the preface of *Systema grammaticum* (1641) that Latin should be taught in Latin and claims that bilingual translations make schoolboys lazy. Farnaby objects to using English models of grammar to teach Latin on the grounds that the elements are not transferable and that English examples keep schoolboys from learning Latin (Preface). A "model of grammar" is used here to mean a grammatical construction in one language that can be used as an analogy to teach a similar construction in another language. By the end of the seventeenth century, the vernacular had won the battle to become the language of the learned. Acceptance of and victory for the vernacular gave rise to four separate schools of thought: using English as a way to get to Latin; promoting English for its own merit; using Latin as a way to "fix" or legitimize English; and acknowledging language that cannot be "fixed."

English as a Way to Get to Latin (or Other Languages)

Many grammarians argued that children should learn the grammar of their mother tongue first because they could apply that knowledge to Latin or another foreign language.[3] Schoolmasters agreed that learning the native tongue was pedagogically sound.[4] In arguing for mastering English, however, grammarians were motivated by additional issues. It was a matter of national pride to give the mother tongue priority. Grammarians were engaged in a battle of breaking the traditional dependence on Latin as the language of the educated. In *Ludus Literarius* (1612) John Brinsley argues that English is a separate subject from Latin. In this text Brinsley has two schoolmasters talk about their teaching of English and Latin. Spoudeus teaches Latin and then has trouble finding time to teach his students English, which they consequently do not learn. "I have sometimes beene so abashed and ashamed, that I have not knowne what to say, when some being a little discontented, or taking occasion to quarrel about paying my stipend, have cast this in my teeth, that their children have been under me sixe or seven yeeres, and yet have not learned to reade English well" (14). The other schoolmaster Philoponus, however, has had success with his students learning English and Latin, and he explains why, making a forceful early statement about the value of English when Latin was still the language of the education: "There is no care had in respect, to traine up schollers so, as they may be able to express their minds purely and readily in our owne tongue, and to increase in the practice of it...because that language which all sorts and conditions of men amongst us are to have most use of, both in speech and writing, is our owne native tongue" (22). Brinsley suggests through the voice of Philoponus that students can learn English separately from Latin and then apply that knowledge to Latin. Students were to follow the method Roger Ascham describes in *The Scholemaster* (1570) of translating Latin into English, and then, their English back into Latin (23). What is interesting here is that grammarians like Brinsley referred to William Lily's *Introduction to Grammar* (1567), a Latin grammar in English, to argue for teaching grammar skills first in English and then in Latin, an indication that English skills would take on increasing priority as the century progressed.

In *Latine Grammar* (1651) Charles Hoole used English models on the left side of the page and Latin models on the right side. It is possible that Hoole came up with the bilingual text as a way of publishing his own school grammar without breaking the royal edict of 1542 that only William Lily's text could be used in schools. Nonetheless, the bilingual method proved to be a practical system for learning a foreign language insofar as it built on old knowledge (the vernacular) before introducing new knowledge (Latin grammar). The bilingual edition worked especially well for those students who did not intend to study the classics and who would be apprenticed to a trade. Hoole also translated Johann Amos Comenius's *Orbis sensualium pictus* (1658) as a means for children to use their mother tongue and pictures of those words to learn Latin and English.

John Wallis writes in *Grammatica lingua Anglicanae* (1653) that people should learn first their native language and that they should not have to make it conform to Latin (A7v). He states in the *Praefatio ad Lectorem* that grammarians like Alexander Gill's *Logonomia Anglica* (1619) and Ben Jonson's *English Grammar* (1640) had written grammars in English but did not accomplish what they set out to do. He argues "none of the [grammarians] proceeded on the way which is more suitable to the undertaking; for all of them have forced our tongue too much into the pattern of Latin (an error shared by nearly all teachers of other modern languages)" (Praefatio). He continues to describe the inadequate grammar texts of grammarians: they "have taught many useless things about the cases of Nouns, Genders and Declensions, and about the Tenses, Moods, and Conjugations of Verbs, about the government of nouns and verbs, etc., matters absolutely foreign to our language, producing confusion and obscurity rather than serving as explanations[5] (Praefatio).

Wallis further ponders the futility of using English to learn Latin and calls for a new method, "one not so much adapted to Latin as to the logic of our own tongue" (Praefatio):

> Even in Latin there are some nouns and adjectives such as ... *instar, sat, frugi, neguam, præsto*, etc., which are quite indeclinable and which are supposed to have cases and genders on the analogy of other words, but which remain absolutely invariable: if all Nouns and Adjectives had been so, it is more than certain that there would have been a deep silence about cases and genders and a good deal of the syntax of the Noun would never be heeded. And so with the Moods and Tenses of the Verb if they were expressed by circumlocutions (Praefatio).

Wallis questions the logic of using English to get into Latin: "Why should we introduce a fictitious and quite foolish collection of Cases, Genders, Moods and Tenses, without any need, and for which there is no reason in the basis of the language itself?" (Praefatio). Wallis's opinion differs from other scholars. Educational reformer Samuel Hartlib argues in *The True and Readie Way To Learne the Latine*

Tongue (1654) that a student learns by using what is familiar to him. Teachers, he believed, have to build a foundation by referring to a student's native language and comparing the common elements to the new ones of the foreign language. Hartlib warned grammarians that they must understand both languages they are teaching, English as the mother tongue and Latin as the foreign one, in order to point out the common elements and the disparities and lay a "good Foundation of the first" (A1). Many grammarians complained that schoolmasters were not well grounded in the grammar of either language.

In *English Grammar* (1654), Jeremiah Wharton states that his grammar will be a good model and preparation to learn other languages: "Upon the sight of any Englished-Latine-Word, pertaining to the rules of Derivation set down herein, hee shall bee able presently to turn it into Latine; though before hee never saw or heard of it before" (A5r–A5v). Wharton claims that if a student learns English grammar first and then transfers the knowledge to Latin, he can be accurate in both languages. He explains that it is "more especially profitable for the youth of this Nation immediately before their Entrance into the Rudiments of the Latine tongue: becaus the knowledg of their mother-tongue is most necessarie, both for the understanding of what they hear or read therein, as also the expressing of their conceit, in what they understand" (A5v). Wharton cites analogy as a good reason to learn English first because "Lastly, it will bee a notable Preparative to the learning of the Latine, or any other Grammatized language; becaus the Rules in this, for the most part may bee applied unto that" (A6r). Still concerned with using English as a preparation for Latin, Wharton states that one needs to have a "warrantable rule or reason of their own, as of a forrein tongue ... Besides they will more easily comprehend the Rules and Terms of Art in that tongue, wherein they have been accustomed from their infancie, then in the Latine, whereof they are altogether ignorant" (A5v–A6r).

Throughout the seventeenth century, grammarians continued to be critical about how grammar was taught to children and foreigners. Grammarians used common elements in languages, their "universal" aspects, to teach by analogy.[6] Teachers found, for example, that it was easier to explain the subjunctive in a familiar language before explaining it in a foreign language.[7] In *Syncrisis, Or The Most Natural and Easie Method of Learning Latin* (1675), Elisha Coles argues that "the whole Mother-Tongue ... assists ... in the introducing [of] any other that is foreign" (A1v). Using analogy, he urges schoolmasters to look at one language that "may assist us in the Learning of the other" (A1v).

In *A Rational and Speedy Method Attaining to the Latin Tongue* (1695), Archibald Lane believes that by using analogy one can better learn idioms and other eccentric practices in a language. The purpose of English models to learn a foreign language brings us to the "true End and Use of Grammar ... to teach us how to speak and write well and learnedly in a Language already known, according to the unalterable Rules of right Reason, which are the same in all Languages how different soever they be" (8). Lane, like other grammarians, urged students to learn English in order to transfer the elements common to English and another language to that other language. Thus, grammarians continued to be locked into the concept that universal grammar validates English. Later, in the eighteenth century, Lane would be accused of abusing the practice of universal grammar by distorting English to fit whatever Latin model he wanted to use. In *Grammar of the English Tongue* (1712) Charles Gildon describes Lane as a competent grammarian, but one who "extended and tortur'd our Tongue to confess to the Latin" (2).

The author[8] of *Royal Grammar Reformed* (1695) takes the position that to learn Latin, one must learn English grammar first. He writes his text in English: "If this method were adopted in our Schools; if children were first taught the common principles of Grammar by some short and clear System of English Grammar, which happily by its simplicity and facility is perhaps of all others the fittest for such a purpose, they would have some notion of what they were going about, when they should enter into the Latin Grammar" (xii). The author argues that if there were better methods of teaching grammar, children "would hardly be engaged so many years, as they now are, in that most irksome and difficult part of literature, with so much labour of the memory, and with so little assistance of the understanding" (xii–xiii). Finally, he states one must know his mother tongue over anything else: "From the learned Languages we derive that Art and Skill which enables men for the highest Employments; for which reason the study of them will be necessary, as long as good Sense is esteemed in the world" (20).

In the early eighteenth century, Lane continued to use English models to illustrate Latin grammar, but he tried to give more credibility to grammar by insisting that it is a science of exact rules that governs decisions. In *A Key to the Art of Letters* (1700), Lane looks to the English model as the best way to explain Latin and other foreign languages, finding in it the "exactest rules." In the phrase "exactest rules," Lane implies that English is a formed, perfect language. He even goes so far as to say that grammar is "indispensable" and of "far greater importance to Mankind, than of any other Art or Science whatever: for Grammar, or the Art of Letters, is universally necessary" (vii). He calls it the "the Golden Key to unlock all other Liberal Arts and Sciences, and the gate that gives an easy entrance into all Forein Languages" (viii). It is the "hardest of all others to be attain'd to ... because it is every where misunderstood, and consequently misapply'd, ever since the Latin Tongue ceas'd to be a living language" (viii). Lane asks if "any thing be imagined more absurd and ridiculous, than to put Children to learn Latin and Grammar at once? To learn an unknown Tongue by an unknown Art, must needs be a Barbarous and Gothic Custom" (xi-xii). He claims that a boy can transfer his knowledge of English grammar to Latin grammar and uses the following example, *Pater amat filium* to illustrate what a student can do within a year if he learns English grammar:

> *Pater* is a Noun Substantive of the Nominative Case, of the Masculine Gender, and of the Singular Number; that *amat* is a Verb Active Transitive of the third Person Singular of the Present Tense, and of the Indicative Mood; that *filium* is the Accusative of the Object after the Verb *amat*, and so of any other plain Sentence: and all this in less than quarter of an hour, which many cannot do in the common Methods, after they have been a whole year at the Latin School (xii–xiii).

Lane's argument of applying the rules of one language to another was further proof that grammar could be approached as a science.

Lane also noted problems with idioms when students used English as a way to get to Latin. Lane recognizes the problem in *A Key to the Art of Letters* (1700): "That some will be ready to object, That the many Idioms, and burdensom Exceptions that are in the Latin Tongue, will stop the Youth's Career, and be a clog" (xiii). He answers, "first, That all Languages have their Idioms, and anomalous words no less than the Latin Tongue only, more than to English or any other Language." Second, he states, "That the only way they can be a hindrance to him is (by stopping his progress in reading Authors) to put him to get by heart as a particular Task, unconnected and loose Words, or Terminations, which like Ropes of Sand, are no sooner done but undone" (xiii). The solution to learning idioms is to look at context, a concept rarely mentioned in grammar texts: "But if no words, whether Analogous or Anomalous, be minded any where but in the contexture of good Sense; they will of course insinuate themselves into the Memory by frequent reading, as they do in the Mother-Tongue by frequent conversation" (xiii–xiv). When children learn idioms in their mother tongue, Lane says, they do it without knowing it, yet they understand them (xiv).

Richard Johnson points out another problem of using English to get to Latin: teachers do not know Latin. In *Grammatical Commentaries* (1706) he complains that there are "Learned Men" who have "a great deal of Learning without a great deal of Latin" and that there are not many good Latinists (B1v). He blames their inadequacies on the "small Number of Latin Books that have been written among us in so many Years" (B1v). He argues that if learned men had been competent in Latin, some of the treatises on divinity and morality would have been in Latin, and perhaps some Catholics would have been converted to Protestantism (B2r). It is interesting, though, that Johnson echoes what other grammarians are saying: learn the rules of grammar in one's own language first (B2r). Johnson also looks to the exactness of language, and he suggests that grammar should improve reasoning and speaking. He then proposes the kind of grammar school text that he feels would make learning grammar more efficient (B2v), using authors that are approved by learned grammarians and who would "prevent Innovation and Confusion in a Universal Language, which requires the utmost Exactness to preserve it" (B4v). He argues that grammarians commit an "unpardonable Fault in our common Method, to teach a Novice Latin by Latin Rules, who if ever he comes to understand it, but do it by the English of the Latin, and then surely much sooner by the English alone" (C1r). Unlike other grammarians, Johnson takes the unusual step of explaining what he does when the English and Latin rules are different: "I have follow'd that of the Grammar, as often as the English and Latin agreed, and when they did not, I have taken that which I thought the most natural" (C1v). He lists several rules in English and Latin that do not agree. For example, he states, "The Superlative exceedeth the Positive in the highest degree." Johnson explains that "The Rule gives a better account of this matter, saying *Superlativus qui supra positivum cum valdè, vel maxime significant, &c.* but this English Rule is always first taught, and most times only taught, and in that there's a Notorious Mistake. For the Superlative does not always exceed the Positive in the highest Degree, but sometimes speaks only of a considerable, and extra-ordinary, but not of the highest Excess" (226).

In *An Essay Upon the Education of Youth* (1736) John Clarke continues to find fault with the way grammar is taught, especially with a "Latin one so ill contrived as Lily's" (6). He argues that too much Latin grammar is taught too soon, that a child needs only declensions and conjugations (7). He claims that "It is not very practicable ... to bring a Boy to understand Grammar ... by making him read the Grammar only over and over again" and that "The going through the Rules of the Syntax, just in the same Order they lie in Lily, will never make them understand it" (7). Clarke states that "The only proper Method for that Purpose, is, to furnish Boys with Variety of proper English Examples to their Rules, for them to translate into Latin, beginning with the easiest first, and advancing by degrees to what is more Difficult" (7). Regardless of what schoolmasters do, whipping, he says, is not the way to motivate children (8). And, he poses a frequently asked question of his period: If schoolmasters must begin with grammar, why must the grammar be in Latin? He asks, "What can be more ridiculous than to deliver Rules for the Learning of any Thing, in a Language the Learner understands not?" (9). It is a "palpable Piece of Absurdity" (9). Clarke asks yet again: "If Boys must begin with Grammar, in the Name of Wisdom, what is the Meaning of putting Rules upon them in a Language they are going to learn, and consequently as yet know nothing of?" (9). He states they should be in a language they are acquainted with. It would be the same as trying to learn the Hebrew tongue with a grammar in Hebrew (9).

The concept of universal grammar shared by eighteenth-century grammarians also factored in their decision to use English models as a logical means of teaching Latin grammar. Grammarians came to believe that languages shared common linguistic principles, and that the elements of one language could be found in another one. Thus the models of universal language implied reciprocity – English to Latin, and conversely, Latin to English – and factors other than linguistic theory would declare which direction was favored. It might be efficient for example, to describe direct objects in the mother tongue and then show the corresponding form in another. The advantage, they argued, would be that students would learn their mother tongue, learn a foreign language, and appreciate the universal elements of language. In *Treatise on Education* (1743) James Barclay advises that students learn English first because resemblances run throughout all languages. In suggesting that Latin wait until a foundation of English grammar be acquired, he worries too much, perhaps, at this late stage, about the anger of fellow grammarians: "To speak against Latin grammar, is to fly in the face of antiquity, to pretend to more experience than teachers of an unblemished character, and is reckoned a kind of reflection against the first rate scholars of former generations, who all acquired the elements of language in the Latin tongue" (88). But Barclay suggests that once a student understands his own language, he can transfer the principles to Latin; then he can apply his knowledge of Latin to English grammar, thus reinforcing his understanding of the grammar of both languages (65). His argument, then, is a universalist's argument, that a student can transfer the linguistic knowledge from English to Latin back to English. Barclay forcefully states his position on learning the mother tongue before attempting Latin: "Any boy will advance with more success that he is first taught the grammar of his mother-tongue, what it is, and how to point out the different parts of speech. As these are much the same in all languages, this must be of great use when he comes to distinguish them in Latin" (64). Barclay then explains how to apply the rules of English to Latin by examining parts of speech and conjugating. For example, he states: "I would, in conjugating verbs, have him particularly notice the helping verbs, *do, did, have, had, shall*, &c. as they are the signs of the several Latin tenses" (65). He continues by illustrating rules in English: "Under the article of English grammar, we should also explain the nature of cases, genders, voices, tenses, and other accidents of nouns and verbs. The beginner will find this easier, than if we were to illustrate every thing by Latin examples. The explication however, once understood in English, may be applied to Latin, without any great change; the nature of these accidents being much the same in both languages" (65). He states throughout the text that "there are still more advantages from a Latin grammar in English" (85).

Bishop Robert Lowth argues in *A Short Introduction to English Grammar* (1762) that students must be fully acquainted with their native tongue before they can master a foreign language such as Latin. He instructs, "When [a learner] has a competent knowledge of the main principles of Grammar in general, exemplified in his own Language, he then will apply himself with great advantage to the study of any other" (xi). He states adamantly that "a competent grammatical knowledge of our own Language is the true foundation, upon which all Literature, properly so called, ought to be raised" (xii). Regarding the learning of a foreign language, Lowth states, "if children were first taught the common principles of Grammar, by some short and clear System of English Grammar … they would have some notion of what they were going about, when they should enter into the Latin Grammar" (xii).

English for its Own Merit

Many grammarians thought that English could stand on its own merit. Schoolmasters often debated the question of how much Latin should be in the curriculum. Many grammarians and pedagogues argued that the common man needed to know only what would be beneficial to him in his apprenticed trade. There was also the issue of specifying who would learn English and who would have advanced instruction that would include Latin. With their traditional access to instruction in classical languages and the trivium of grammar, logic, and rhetoric, the more privileged classes continued to maintain their distinction from and power over the lower classes. Overall, however, grammarians were building the strength and credibility of the vernacular, and they continued to make learning the native tongue a priority, especially when their national identity was being defined by the mother tongue. George Snell stresses the value of knowing English in *The Right Teaching of Useful Knowledg* (1649): "It shall bee esteemed, of all that understand, to bee a verie excellent and useful skil, in one that knoweth nothing but meer English, to bee able, out of his Grammar, for the English tongue, to give a warrantable rule and reason, for everie word and sentence which hee speaketh, and to justifie the same for sound and approved" (28). Therefore, he states, "Let the English youths bee taught to learn and approve their own language, by rules of Grammar, made fit for that purpose; and they may speak English as intelligently as ever the Romanes did speak Latine: and better then anie other people, since the Romances lost the perfection both of their Empire, and of their Eloquence" (30). Snell warns that "The neglect of this teaching of English by Grammar, is the nurs and cherisher of manie, and verie hurtful mischiefs" among common scholars as well as the more privileged ones (32). Grammarians did not want to make the teaching of English dependent on Latin.

In *English Grammar* (1654), Jeremiah Wharton claims that it is the responsibility of the schoolmaster to teach English as well as Latin: "it should bee the care of every Teacher, as well to accustom [students] to the exercise of good English, as of good Latine" (A4r). His reason is that "our mother-tongue is likely in the practice to bee most useful, and is as capable of any Scholar-like expressions, as any whatsoever" (A4r). Next, Wharton appeals to national pride: "Besides the puritie and Elegancie of our own Language is to bee esteemed a chief part of the honor of our Nation, which wee all ought to our utmost power, to advance" (A4r). Last, he reasons that a thorough knowledge of English will be more useful to students who will leave school early and use it in their professions. Vocational students who are not concentrating on a classical education should take an easier route by memorizing English models to learn Latin grammar, he states, "because for one that is trained up in the Grammar-Schools, to any perfection, fit for the Universitie, or any learned Profession, a hundred are taken away before; of whom the most, very shortly after, wholly in a manner, forget their Latine; so that if they bee not bettered in the knowledg of their Native Language, their labor and cost is to little or no purpose" (A4v). He questions whether such students might be better off to learn English models and forget about the Latin ones altogether.

In *School Pastime for Young Children: or the Rudiments of Grammar* (1669), John Newton expresses his concern about England lagging behind in international status. He talks about how ill prepared vocational students are when they are sent out to their apprenticeships. He argues for better instruction in schools so that England "would be once more raised up to a Height beyond the contempt of our neighbouring Nations" (The Epistle Dedicatory A2v). Better schools would also mean "All Manufacture would be so improved, that no Nation under Heaven should be able to outdoe us in any honourable Undertaking, or to compare with us in wealth and plenty" (A2v–A3r). He states that "English Orthography hath not such an absolute dependence on the Latin Tongue, as almost a general Tradition would make us believe: but that our Tongue hath in it self sufficient matter to work her own Artificial Directions for the right writing thereof" (A8r). He acknowledges that "every Speech and Language hath an Idiom proper to itself: or shall the English onely be denyed that Privilege or Prerogative? Or be constrained to learn from a Forreign Language that Idiom which is proper to our own?" (A8r). He concludes with the resolution that "It is sufficiently known, that a great part of the English Tongue hath no dependence at all upon the Latin" (A8r).

Newton is critical of schoolmasters who do not teach the mother tongue first so that students will have a foundation before beginning Latin. He may well have been familiar with educational practices that Czech educator and philosopher Johann Amos Comenius tried to change: rote memorization, inconsistency in rules, and physical abuse. Newton describes how this kind of education makes students hate school and prepares them poorly for their trades.

> Grammar-masters ... cheat the Parents of their money, and the children of their time, taking in the Children to be instructed in the rudiments of the Latin Tongue, before they can either write or read, and teaching them in a method quite contrary to what is prescribed in the Epistle [opening letter stating aims of grammar text] usually printed before the common Accidence [9]: if ever they will justifie themselves, they must either get that Epistle left out, or conform themselves to it. But all they care for is the Parents money, and as for the Children, let them learn or be whipt; and thus they make more Blockheads than ever God made, and ruine more Children with their severe Glister-pipes, than ever they made with their instructions. St. Paul tells us, that thrice he received forty stripes save one, but several of these Whipping-masters have exceeded that antient Roman cruelty (B3r).

The problem is aggravated when students are almost finished with schooling in grammar because "they are sent to a writing-master to learn to write in 3 months, which is impossible to do. They should have been learning to write all along." Then "without help of recovery, how unable they are to manage those Trades, by which not onely themselves and families must now live" (B3v). Newton argues that useless skills in Latin are given priority over useful skills in vocational training.

In *The English Grammar* (1693) Joseph Aickin goes even further and calls for codified rules: "The daily obstructions and difficulties, that occur in teaching and Learning our Mother Tongue, proceed from the want of an English Grammar, by Law establish'd, the Standard of education" (A2v). Aickin felt the teaching of the mother tongue should be the same as other languages, "Since then all other Tongues, and Languages are taught by Grammar, why ought not the English Tongue to be taught so too" (A2v). He claims that foreigners take too long to learn English because they do not learn grammar (A2v). And, in the same vein, Aickin states that "Children go to ten or eleven years or more to School, and yet do not attain the Perfection of the English Tongue: Nay some scarce learn to read and write well in that time: but are forced at length to go to Latin Schools to attain its perfection: and sooner become masters of the Latine, than their own Tongue" (A2v). Aickin cites the "want of such a Grammar, which ought to be the standard of the English Tongue" as the cause of the problem (A2v–A3r). Aickin blames schoolmasters for the poor teaching of grammar for "not having the advantages of knowing the best methods of teaching: and so following their own fancies, for want of an approved Method, make the business of teaching and learning an Herculean Labor" (A3r). If youth learn the mother tongue well, then they "might be serviceable in Church and State sooner ... [and] School master would be held in greater veneration, and their Livelyoods much augmented" (A3r). He states that people underestimate the richness of the English tongue because "in reality the English Tongue is far more copious than [Latin]" and can "express every thing and notion" (A3r). English can be "perfectly acquired, without being beholden to the Latine" (A3v). Aickin adds, although the idea might have been skeptical to some, that the English tongue is the "easiest tongue to be taught and learned in the world," he proceeds to argue his case with Latin and English examples (A3r–A3v). With a touch of national pride, Aickin describes the virtues of the English tongue as having "more kinds of verses, than any other Tongue, yet the mystery of versification is facile and almost at every Poets own discretion: our Poetry nevertheless is excellent and lofty and inferiour to none" (A3v). He adds that the purpose of his grammar text is to provide a basis for English grammar so that students will not have to waste precious time going to Latin schools (A4r). And the author of *Royal Grammar Reformed* (1695) also complains that children do not spend their time productively learning grammar, which in turn causes them to spend more time than necessary in grammar instruction. He argues that a knowledge of the mother tongue is necessary because "after all the Greek and Roman Authors are read, the main of all our business is perform'd in our own Language: in English we eat and drink, buy and sell; in English we live, and when all's done at last must die in English" (20).

In *Tutor to True English* (1699) Henry Care complains that "there is scarce One in Forty that writes Tolerable English" (A1r), and argues that "'tis a Vulgar

Error to think, that none can write true English, but such as have been taught Latine" (A1v). He decries the years that students waste in Latin schools to take little away to remember or to use in vocations: "Upon which false Notion, many ordinary People keep their Sons at Latine-Schools, two, three, perhaps four or five Years together, to their great Charge; and then being forced to take them off, and put them Apprentices to Mechanic Arts, Shop-keeping, and the like; all their petty Acquirements vanish through dis-use, and are quickly forgot" (A1v). During the years in the Latin school, they attain "little contemptible Smattering, which turns to no real account." Moreover, it is "rather apt to render them Idle, Superficial, and over-confident Pratlers, (the Bane both of Business and Reputation)" (A1v). Care argues that some of the time allotted to teaching students grammar should be "spent in Instructing them in the genuine Idioms and natural Dress of their Mother-Tongue, in Fair Writing, in (that Ground-work of Useful Arts) Arithmetick" and in the "neglected Study of Christian Ethic's, or Morality" (A1v). Care sees grammar as an important skill that will help in "rendring them both Better Men, and more Expert for the Negotiation and Conduct of their Affairs; Nay, more Accomplisht in this very respect of true English, than those other half-Codled Grammaticasters" (A1v–A2r). He knows students who "understand nothing of Latine or Greek, yet in several Sheets of their Writing, you shall scarce find one Word Mis-spelt, or any thing that may offend even the most Critical Eye" (A2r). He credits their having gained this "Perfection" through "Observation" (A2r). Care also addresses his text to foreigners "that desire to be Master of Our Language" and to the "Fair Sex" (A2r). Thus, in his argument for the mother tongue, Care has mentioned several controversies of grammarians: validating the vernacular, preparing for a vocation without Latin studies, preparing to be a good citizen, teaching foreigners the language, and allowing that females could learn grammar.

Some grammarians went so far as to say that any Latin was a waste of time for students who were not going to use it. In *Essay upon Study* (1731), for instance, John Clarke advises students who have no occasion to write in Latin in the professional world not take the trouble to learn Latin grammar because it would be useless to them (185–96). Clarke argues that students should invest their school years in the courses that will benefit them the most when they are in their vocations:

> It's certain a Man's Native Language, is of infinitely more Importance to him, than any other can be. In his own Country, he can have little or no Occasion, that can make it necessary, or reasonable, to spend so much Time, upon a dead or a foreign Language, as must be spent, for the attaining to speak it, with tolerable Readiness and Propriety; and he can have still less Occasion to write it, unless his Parts quality, and his Inclinations lead him, to write for the Instruction of the learned World in general: But Men so qualified and disposed, are, I think, not many; and therefore it is a good Rule for the Generality of Students, never to engage in any Attempt

of that Kind at all: It is sufficient for them, to be Masters in the writing, and speaking of their own Language, elegantly and handsomely, upon all Occasions (186–87).

Latin is too different, Clarke continues, and claims it will be a hindrance (187). He even goes so far as to say that Latin will affect the way students express themselves because it is so different from the

> English Tongue, that to spend Years together in the Pursuit of it, as they must do, if ever they mean to succeed in such a Design, will have no good Influence upon their English Style; but be apt to render it stiff and unfashionable: And for a Man to be able to speak, or write Latin, better than his own Language, may serve to make silly People admire him for a great Scholar, but can never . . . answer any useful Purpose of Life, or be at all for the Credit of his Discretion, among such as know how to set a due Estimate upon Things, and rate them according to their real Value (188).

Thus, Clarke laments the "Variety of Languages in the World" brought on by the "fall of Adam" (186). Man, he observes, invests much effort on languages, time that might be "profitably employed upon things themselves." And, he asks, "Did but Grammarians and Criticks duly reflect upon this, they would not be so generally guilty of over-rating their Professions as they do, nor imagine the Height of all Learning to consist in a critical Knowledge of Languages, and such too as have been dead for many Ages" (186).

Well into the eighteenth century grammarians spoke out against using Latin to teach English. The unknown author of *The Pleasing Instructor* (1756) claims that learning grammar is not popular because grammar texts are too dependent on Latin (vii). These grammars "appear only Translations of them [Latin texts], introducing many needless Perplexities; as superfluous Cases, Genders, Moods, Tenses, etc. Peculiarities which our Language is exempt from" (vii). Schoolmasters, he argues, "must proceed from Ignorance" or "pretend much Advantage" when they teach from these texts to "mere scholars" (viii). And because of "this Ignorance or unsuccessful Pretence," English Grammar is "so much neglected or so lightly esteemed" that even "Men of Learning" are deficient. No one can "speak or write properly who are ignorant of Grammar; therefore it becomes necessary that a Practical English Grammar (*See Fisher's English Grammar) should be consistent with itself, and independent of the Latin, except in such Articles as are common to both" (viii). His argument ends with the prescription of learning the native language for the language itself, not as a means to learn a foreign language: "None can ever display their Talents to much Advantage, either in Writing or Conversation, unless they have a Taste for the Beauty and Propriety of their Mother Tongue; and which they can never have, without learning it, so as to know the Nature and Kinds of Words with their Connections and Dependencies upon one another" (viii).

A different kind of dispute raged briefly in the early eighteenth century within the context of promoting English for its own merit. Some men of letters saw a need to guard against the corruption of the rapidly expanding vernacular. Grammarians were afraid that the English language would run amok so drastically that future generations would not recognize it. They had not yet censured specific errors or formulated rules for correctness, and they were still dealing with the problems of custom and usage. Daniel Defoe proposed an academy to regulate the English language like the Académie Française, a body of learned men who made decisions about variants and changes in the French language. In *An Essay upon Several Projects* (1702), he cites the French academy because it was able "to Refine and Correct their own Language," and he claims that the "English Tongue not only Equals but Excels its Neighbours" (228). The proposed English academy would "polish and refine the English Tongue, and advance the so much neglected Faculty of Correct Language, to establish Purity and Propriety of Stile" (228). It did not, however, gain much support.

Still, the uncertain state of the English language was a source of anxiety to scholars and other learned men. Jonathan Swift, for instance, argues in *Proposal for Correcting, Improving, and Ascertaining the English Tongue* (1712) that "fixing" the language would make it consistent and regular.[10] In his proposal sent to the Lord High Treasurer, Swift outlines the causes in religion, politics, history, and economics that have brought on the corruption and deterioration of the English language. In that context, he states, "our Language is extremely imperfect; that its daily Improvements are by no means in proportion to its daily Corruptions; that the Pretenders to polish and refine it, have chiefly multiplied Abuses and Absurdities; and, that in many Instances, it offends against every Part of Grammar" (8). Swift argues for consistency: "I see no absolute necessity why any language should be perpetually changing; for we find many examples to the contrary." Swift continues to hammer home his point: "But what I have most at heart, is, that some method should be thought on for ascertaining and fixing our language for ever, after such alterations are made in it as shall be thought requisite. For I am of opinion, it is better a language should not be wholly perfect, than that it should be perpetually changing" (31).

In answer to the *Proposal for Correcting, Improving, and Ascertaining the English Tongue*, John Oldmixon replies in *Reflections on Dr. Swift's Letter* [1712] that the author expressed "nothing worthy" of Swift's "Character" (Preface). He observes that Swift's *Proposal* may have been prompted by affairs in France: "Tis probable, our late Correspondence with France put such a Whim into some Folks Heads." He does not agree with Swift that just "because they have an Academy for the same Use at Paris, we forsooth must have one at London" (Preface). He humorously observes that the plans have not "come to any thing more yet than meeting over a Bottle once a Week, and being Merry: At which Times People mind talking much, more than talking well" (Preface). Oldmixon is skeptical of the mention in Swift's letter that "we are to be happier than we thought of, and to be surpriz'd with a Society that shall make us as Polite as that of Reformation has made us Godly" (Preface), and, he calls Swift's *Proposal* a "silly superficial Performance, and to be design'd only for an Opportunity to shew what a Nack he has at Panegyrick" (Preface). Swift, he argues, "meant to Bully us into his Methods for pinning down our Language, and making it as Criminal to admit Foreign Words as Foreign Trades, tho' our Tongue may be enrich'd by the one, as much as our Traffick by the other" (2). Oldmixon is aghast that Swift proposes language be "corrected, enlarg'd and ascertain'd" by turning it over to women because they are "softer mouth'd, and are more for Liquids than the Men" (2), and he chides Swift by asking how universities would give up linguistic control to women. He cannot resist adding that the plan reminds him of "Fontenelle's way of learning a language [that is,] having an Intrigue with some Fair Foreigner; and beginning with the Verb *I Love, You Love, &c.*" (3). He adds sarcastically that "It is well enough from Him, a Papist, or Layman, but for a Protestant Divine to erect an Academy of Women to improve our Stile" is unthinkable (3). Although Oldmixon's reply tends to ramble, he attempts throughout the piece to criticize Swift – his language, his religion, and his politics. He states that the "merriest part of the Project [Swift] has been hatching, for an English Academy to bring our Tongue to his pitch of Perfection, is that he has assign'd, that Task to the Tories. … If there has ever been Man among 'em who had a right Notion of Letters or Language, who any relish of Politeness, it had been something. But as there never was one, unless it were two or three Apostate Whigs who had been bred up by the Charity of those Friends they deserted" (6). Thus, Oldmixon continues through the reply in the same scathing vein.

In sum, grammarians were generally in agreement at the end of the seventeenth century that learning the mother tongue was a prerequisite to learning Latin because the rules of one could be applied to the other. English was also assuming a credible identity of its own and was recognized as a language of the educated. What remained for the English language was the last step of standardization.

Latin as a Way to "Fix" or Legitimize English

By 1650, centuries of tradition behind the use of Latin in education had bestowed upon it a certain prestige, and since Latin grammars had been available for centuries, it was natural for textbook authors to copy the grammatical categories of Latin grammarians and apply them to English grammar. They went to Latin to find answers to grammatical questions in English. Grammarians referred to Latin to bring some sort of consistency to the English language.

Therefore, although the Latin models of grammar do not always apply to English, it is perhaps not surprising that grammarians forced them to fit English anyway. What is perhaps more puzzling is that the illogical practice of forcing models of Latin rules of grammar onto the non-latinate grammar of English has persisted into the twentieth century. A reasonable explanation for this logical and illogical use of models may lie in how rigorously they were applied to language. Grammarians in the seventeenth century, for instance, may have applied English models to Latin only when they fit. They were not enslaved to forcing rules of English grammar onto Latin because Latin was already a codified language, and English models were merely a teaching aid to explain Latin grammar. It did not matter that the English language had not been codified and standardized. For example, George Snell argues in *The Right Teaching of Useful Knowledg* (1649) that grammarians were responsible for getting language to a "fixed and immutable state," one that would not go "out of date and knowledge, but that posteritie may bee abel to read and understand, what was written by the Elders, that lived five hundred years before" (40). Snell advises that Latin proves useful if it reinforces his English grammar:

> It seems little better then a brutish and reasonless Reason, for a man to bee able to saie no more for the defens and justification of the speech which hee useth, then this, I speak so and so, becaus I hear and see that all others do speak, as I speak, and do write as I write: and for a truth, this idiotish reason is all the reason that anie man can geve, for anie things that hee writeth, unless by help of a wit more then ordinarie, hee can applie the Ruels of His Latine Grammar, to maintain the rights of his English speech (30).

Along with the increasing prevalence of English instruction, eighteenth-century grammarians used Latin models to address this lack of codification and standardization.

The new generation of grammarians in the early eighteenth century still felt a bond with Latin, but in a more distanced way than their predecessors. Latin was no longer required to do business, and grammarians were rethinking their pedagogy for teaching both English and Latin grammar in the public schools. Latin instruction did not necessarily mean classical studies, and subjects formerly required – like imitation and translation – might not be offered at all. English grammar was taught for the purpose of learning the vernacular. As Latin was taught less and less, Latin models were used to settle disputes over matters of usage. These models provided structures for teaching grammar and for explaining difficult rules. Even though the application of Latin models to English was often illogical, and even though the models forced a Germanic language into a Latin framework, pedagogues accepted the Latin models of grammar more readily than they did the English models.[11] In *The New Spelling Book* (1700), George Fisher inventories latinate forms in an attempt to codify orthography. He canvassed literary books for forms because he claimed that "A careful Observation of good authors ... will make [a person] a perfect English writer" (56). Fisher was characteristic of the grammarians who thought that if they could standardize spelling, they could fix the English language and its rules. However, he discovered that no one could control the many variations of spelling in spite of using the most polished of Latin models to arrive at the correct forms.¹²

Richard Brown in *English School Reformed* (1701) depends on the use of Latin models to organize a spelling book enlarged by the addition of an "Accidence adapted to Our Native Tongue." Brown even uses Latin to structure his format of questions and answers, freely admitting that he is dependent upon Latin. He admits his use of a Latin precedent: "Note, that I divided the Parts thus, on the account of the Method we use in teaching Latin" (xx). In *English Scholar Compleat* (1706), the anonymous author states something similar to Brown: "In English, as in Latin, there are Eight Parts of Speech" (1).¹³

Even though the practice was illogical and did not always work with the concept of universal grammar, grammarians like Richard Johnson rigorously applied the models of Latin whether they fit English or not. In *Grammatical Commentaries* (1706) he promotes Latin as a universal language, rather than an unfamiliar, dead language. Because Latin is not actively spoken, he claims, people naturally have a difficult time with it. But if a system to learn a simplified Latin grammar in school could be devised and if a student spoke the language everyday, then Latin could easily be retained as the dominant language for communication. Moreover, if Latin were the dominant language, it would be easily available to help with English grammar. Citing the "insufficiency of common grammar," Johnson argues that schools should make Latin a requirement so that students speak it like a mother tongue and apply the rules of grammar to all other languages they might learn. Johnson argues that Latin should be used and the grammar stressed: "A Language gotten by Use, wou'd be lost again for want of Use, there being no conversation to be had in that Language sufficient to retain it: And then what Help to recover it but by a Grammar?" (A4r) He cites the inadequacies of English grammar:

> Now our common Grammar is intolerable in all these several Particulars: The Rules it gives do not contain one half of what is necessary to be known in the Latin Tongue. They are beside that in many things directly false, and contrary to the Use of Authors. They are in many things obscure; and though wanting in Necessaires, yet abounding in Unnecessaries, as often giving two Rules where one wou'd serve or a long and tedious one, where a short one wou'd do the Business better, as is sufficiently shewn in these Animadversions (B1r).

Johnson claims that the current method of learning the mother tongue and the Latin grammar is discouraging and burdensome to students (B1r).

In *The English Accidence* (1733), the anonymous author sets up tables for pronouns and adjectives according to nominative, genitive, dative, accusative, vocative, and ablative.¹⁴ Other examples of applying Latin rules were plentiful. *It's me*, which was considered correct for centuries, was now considered incorrect since the Latin construction *ego sum* made use of the subject form of the pronoun *ego* rather than the object form *me*. If one were to follow this reasoning, one would have to say in English, *It's I*.[15] This question of usage is still hotly debated in university grammar classes and newspaper columns today. Dick Leith describes another practice of following Latin, that of "a presupposed knowledge of etymology, the origin of words" (52). He uses the term "etymological fallacy" to demonstrate the false association between what might have once been the meaning but is not necessarily now (52). Grammarians did not like change, and when they could cite a model from old forms of Latin, they did. In *A Social History of English* Leith provides the following examples:

> *Different from* was preferable to *different to*, or *different than*, because the *di* part of the word originally indicated "division" or "separateness"; and therefore *from* suits the etymological argument better. Similarly, the constructions *averse to* and *under the circumstances* were considered incorrect, since the meanings of the *a* in *averse* and the *circum* in *circumstance* are respectively 'from' and 'around,' and these meanings were not felt to be congruent with those of *to* and *under*. The grammarians failed to see that the use of such prepositions as *to* and *from* is in any language highly idiomatic. (52)

Another example of following Latin forms appears in Thomas Dilworth's *A New Guide to the English Tongue* (1751). As if he were teaching Latin, he first defines declension as the "Variation of a Word by Cases" (100). Here is one of several examples of nouns he declines:

Singular

Nom. A Book.
Gen. Of a Book.
Dat. To a Book.
Acc. The Book.
Voc. O Book!
Abl. From a Book.

Plural

Nom. Books.
Gen. Of Books.
Dat. To Books.
Acc. The Books.
Voc. O Books!
Abl. From Books.

Next Dilworth declines adjectives (101).

Singular

Nom. A good Boy.
Gen. Of a Good Boy.
Dat. To a good Boy.
Acc. A good Boy.
Voc. Good Boy!
Abl. From a good Boy.

Plural

Nom. The good Boys.
Gen. Of good Boys.
Dat. To good Boys.
Acc. The good Boys.
Voc. Good Boys!
Abl. From good Boys.

Dilworth continues the same format for pronouns (103).

Singular	*Plural*
Nom. I.	Nom. We.
Gen. Of me.	Gen. Of us.
Dat. To me.	Dat. To us.
Acc. Me.	Acc. Us.
Voc. Is wanting.	Voc. Are wanting.
Abl. From me.	Abl. From us.

A quick browse through eighteenth-century grammar texts will attest to the fact that Dilworth's text is not an anomaly.

Resistance to Prescriptivism: Descriptivism

By the second half of the eighteenth century, Latin models were supporting prescriptive English grammar.[16] We do not have to search too far to find examples of the way Latin distorted English grammar. For instance, the centuries-old double negative "I don't want nothing" became stigmatized because it did not conform to the Latin pattern which would translate "I don't want anything."[17] Grammarians declared the double negative incorrect and illiterate. Another example of forcing Latin onto English can be see with the Anglo-Saxon word *sceal* (shall), a modal verb meaning "be obliged."[18] Latin had a verbal inflexion to mark future tense, but Anglo-Saxon did not, and when scholars had to find a way of translating Latin future tenses into English, they used "shall." Problems arose when grammarians forced rules from Latin to fit whatever rule in English they were teaching. For example, "will," a modal verb in English, does not carry tense in English as it does in Latin. Grammarians in favor of applying Latin rules to English grammar reasoned that Latin forms were inherently better than the corresponding ones in English.

Bishop Robert Lowth was a prescriptive grammarian who did not like change or variation because he thought language would be corrupted. In *A Short Introduction to English Grammar* (1762), he goes back to ancient Latin rules in an attempt to fix the English language. He cites the rule using a *to be* verb: "The Verb to Be has always a Nominative Case after it; as, it was I" (111).[19] Lowth also applies the Latin to gerunds: "The Participle with a Preposition before it, and still retaining its Government, answers to what is called in Latin the Gerund: as, 'Happiness is to be attained, by avoiding evil, and by doing good; by seeking peace, and by pursuing it'" (111). Lowth also rules on ending a sentence with a preposition: "Prepositions, so called because they are commonly put before the words to which they are applied, serve to connect words with one another, and to shew the relation between them" (91). He observes that a preposition is "often separated from the Relative which it governs, and joined to the Verb at the end of the Sentence, or of some member of it: as, 'Horace is an author, whom I am much delighted with'" (91). He condemns this idiom that is prevalent "in common conversation, and suits very well with the familiar style in writing" (127), and he argues that "placing of the Preposition before the Relative is more graceful, as well as more perspicuous; and agrees much better with the solemn and elevated Style" (128). Thus, Lowth was a prescriptivist who wanted to use antiquity to codify and enforce rules of grammar, and who did not want language to be subjected to changes and variants. He complains in *A Short Introduction to English Grammar* (1762), "In last two hundred years English language bounds greater and more polished and refined, but it has made no advance in grammatical accuracy" (iii).

Latin grammar was attractive to eighteenth-century grammarians because it was no longer spoken but only encountered in written form; it was a fixed, codified language safe to transfer to English (i.e., it was not going to do anything surprising). Consequently, they subjected grammatical variants in English to their static equivalents in Latin. Grammarians found comfort in the traditional Latin models because they were a means of codifying the English language and establishing linguistic authority. By the eighteenth century, students were accustomed to seeing Latin only in textbooks, therefore giving it unquestionable authority over grammar usage. Tradition sometimes led well-meaning scholars astray, and unusual and sometimes even incorrect forms in the "good" English grammar of today reflect the illogical use of Latin models in the eighteenth century.

Grammarians found that using Latin models to standardize the English language accomplished what Swift suggested: "to fix" the language, even if the transference of Latin to English was not always logical. Not everyone, however, agreed that they should be trying to fix language. Benjamin Martin in *Lingua Britannica Reformata* (1749) is sympathetic to Swift's views on the problems of a fluctuating language but does not see how the problem can be solved. He states: "I know of nothing that can be done; for as to the pretence of fixing a standard to the purity and perfection of any language, while the state of the people remains unchanged and unmix'd with others...because no language as depending on arbitrary use and custom, can ever be permanently the same, but will always be in a mutable and fluctuating state; and what is deem'd polite and elegant in one age, may be accounted uncouth and barbarous in another" (111).

Joseph Priestley, a descriptivist, believed that language cannot be fixed. In *Rudiments of English Grammar* (1761) he writes that the English language will "come in for some share of improvement, and acquire a more fixed and established character than it can boast at present" (xvi). He states that the "best forms of speech will, in time, establish themselves by their own superior excellence; and, in all controversies, it is better to wait the decisions of Time, which are slow and sure, than to take those of synods, which are often hasty and injudicious" (vii). He argues in *The Rudiments of Grammar* that literature will provide models so that "custom can take priority" (60). He surveys examples from contemporary writers (i.e., Pope, Swift, Addison), claiming that "when good authors vary and when standard is the custom one authority may be of as much weight as another" (60). According to Priestly, the "conjectures" of such writers as Pope and Swift that "the language of their time would, at length, become obsolete in this nation, are absolutely groundless" (60). Furthermore, he claims that the "schemes of some still more modern writers, to add something considerable to the perfection of the English language, in order to contribute to the permanency of it, cannot, according to the course of nature, produce any effect" (60). With a resounding note, he states that "If the English language hath not already attained to its maturity, we may safely pronounce that it never will: and if it be not now in a condition to perpetuate itself, and stand the attacks of time, no method that we can at this day take will rescue it from oblivion" (60). Furthermore, he argues, "It is *writing* that fixes, and gives stability to a language: for hardly any of the causes that contribute to the revolutions of *vocal* language do at all affect that which is *written*. And when a language is so much read, written, and diffused in books through the bulk of the nation that speaks it as the English, in its present state, it would be absolutely miraculous were it to receive any considerable alteration" (60–61).

Unlike Lowth, who wanted to find a rule from the distant past to make a rule for the present, Priestley followed a more liberal practice of rules and custom. He used models of grammar both from old Latin books and from the best authors in classical and contemporary literature. Priestley argues in *A Course of Lectures: On the Theory of Language, and Universal Grammar* (1762) language was invented by men who had to "conform to established vicious practices" or appear "ridiculous" (116). He states that the "analogy of language is the only thing to which we can have recourse, to adjust these differences" (xviii–xix). And he, too, agrees that a public academy was "unsuitable to the genius of a free nation [and] in itself ill calculated to reform and fix a language." He warns against grammarians' incorrect method of fixing language, and counsels that language can

> never be effected by the arbitrary rules of any man, or body of men whatever; because these suppose the language actually fixed already, contrary to the real state of it: whereas a language can never be properly fixed, till all the varieties with which it is used, have been held forth to publish view, and the general preference of certain forms have been declared, by the general practice afterwards (xvii–xviii).

Priestley comes to the conclusion, as did Jonathan Swift and Samuel Johnson, that language moves of its own volition, but unlike them, he was not alarmed by it.

Many controversies accompanied the vernacular as it replaced Latin as the language of the educated in the seventeenth and eighteenth centuries. The power lay with those who claimed the privilege of deciding what language would be taught, how it would be taught, and who would learn it. And the two groups, prescriptivists and descriptivists, would vie for power in deciding how to codify and fix the English language. Since the elite made the rules and the lower classes did not expect much upward mobility, the middle class was the most anxious to have rules that would not change so that they would have linguistic security.

II. Inversion of Linguistic Authority

During the seventeenth century in England, grammar books often included lexicons, while dictionaries consisted of crude lists of words with synonyms. These simple, incomplete lists of words also served as dictionaries for translating Latin and, sometimes, French, Spanish, and Italian. Hard-word lists were often made up of polysyllabic, Latinate words that were difficult to understand because they were not yet assimilated into the mainstream of usage.[20] Hard-word lists were a challenge for grammarians. These lists were supposed to include only those words which a normal reader did not know, but determining exactly which words were little known was not an easy task for those early grammarians who also worked as lexicographers. The other kind of dictionary, the bilingual (e.g., French-English and Latin-English), was common, but was more of an aid to translation than a source of definitions. By contrast, in the eighteenth century Samuel Johnson was to write an entirely different kind of dictionary, *A Dictionary of the English Language* (1755), one that would list the range of meanings, list quotations for examples, and contribute to the study of the history of language and its grammar.[21]

By the eighteenth century, dictionaries began to include grammar, while grammar books started reducing the amount of lexicographical material. It is possible to explain this change as a simple development in the emerging field of lexicography: from within the large and loosely defined group of grammarians there slowly emerged a smaller group of increasingly well-defined lexicographers.[22] But simply to state that lexicographers emerged from grammarians makes an assumption that grammarians were lexicographers by another name. In the context of early modern England, however, the enterprises of these two groups were distinct, and the developments in the relations between grammar and lexicography do not constitute a progression so much as they do an inversion: in the beginning, grammar embraced lexicography, but later, lexicography embraced grammar. We can trace this inversion through three successive stages.

Primacy of Grammar In the first stage, grammar embraced lexicography. Early grammar books were in Latin, with some explanation in the vernacular, and they covered a wide range of language-related material. "Grammar" texts might include such varied components as hard-word lists, spelling, pronunciation, synonyms, homonyms, etymology, Latin-English dictionaries, poetry, logic, rhetoric, and Scripture lessons. Grammar texts were not considered reliable linguistic referees. Also, because of Latin's traditional authority, grammarians looked to Latinists to arbitrate grammatical questions. William Lily's *Introduction of Grammar*, for example, not only held the rights to a nationally approved grammar to be used in the schools, it also held a position of authority and prestige. Eventually other grammarians like Charles Hoole translated Lily and included word lists in their grammar books, thus making the texts lexicographical references.

Lexicography in seventeenth-century grammar books is especially interesting because authors use a variety of methods to teach grammar and vocabulary. As early as 1649 George Snell argued that a dictionary separate from a grammar book was needed. In *The Right Teaching of Useful Knowledg*, Snell calls for a "second medium to make the English tongue a settled, certain and corrected language, would bee to caus a Lexicon to bee composed, wherein a full measure of all sorts of words, as in a common store-hous, may bee laid up" (35). He lists eight requirements to be included in the dictionary: (1) words which are fair and pleasing words to the ear; (2) "origination" (i.e., etymology); (3) a brief description of every noun and verb; (4) words used frequently; (5) words with different levels of meaning; (6) words that are Anglicized; (7) standardized lexicon and grammar; and (8) rules that come from a designated authority (36). This list is surprisingly well defined for the middle of the seventeenth century. Snell claims that if these instructions are followed, "language and the writing of it, and the Signification of it will bee alwaies undoubted and certain, without variation and change; and held to an immutabilitie; as the Latine now is, by the power of the Grammar and Dictionarie for Latine" (40).

In *Orbis sensualium pictus* (1659), also considered to be an early foreign language dictionary, Comenius defines words by using pictures to connect the names of objects with their referents. He advises that "words should not be learned apart from the objects to which they refer; since the objects do not exist separately and cannot be apprehended without words, but both exist and perform their functions together."[23] A tool for teaching vocabulary to young children, the book consists of a series of drawings in which each picture has numbers affixed to things for the students to name. Below the drawing the numbers are listed with vocabulary to correspond to the picture. Comenius adds an extra touch by incorporating emotions, feelings, and other abstract concepts. The picture becomes not only a vocabulary lesson, but a visible means of teaching all subjects: grammar, science, biology, mathematics, history, religion, and literature. In this sense, *Orbis sensualium pictus* functions as an early dictionary, although Comenius would not have called it that.

Elisha Coles uses a lexicographical format in *Nolens Volens: or you shall make Latin whether you will or no* (1675) to explain rules in English with Latin examples, a method unusual for grammar texts in the seventeenth century. He places an English word by a small drawing of an object, then uses the word in a quote from the Bible, first on the left side in English, then on the right side in Latin.

Educational reformers like Comenius experimented with pictures and words to teach visible language, but the attempt did not change the format of other grammar books. And although Coles's method was an efficient one for teaching grammar, vocabulary, pronunciation, spelling, etymology, and religion, teachers found it easier to stay with known, traditional ways of teaching grammar. But in the eighteenth century, lexicographers continued the practice of using pictures in dictionaries because it was a more efficient method of defining words. The pedagogy of connecting words with pictures is still used today, especially with young children and in foreign language classes.

In the seventeenth century, grammar books satisfied both Latin and English vocabulary needs, while dictionaries were usually in one language. Grammar books had an advantage because they listed Latin-English and English-Latin word lists, while dictionaries specialized in difficult English words. Until the end of the century grammar books were still all Latin, even when written in English, even when they were called "English grammar" in their titles. Latin grammar books, therefore, were not always practical for someone who wanted to find an English word and its synonym, spelling, or pronunciation. Dictionaries, by contrast, could focus on short definitions and could include more information about the word. For example, in *A Table Alphabeticall* (1604) Robert Cawdrey lists "hard usuall English Wordes" that the reader may come across in Scriptures, sermons, or other places. With *The English Dictionarie* (1623), Henry Cockeram's goal was to interpret hard words so that the reader could gain competence in the vernacular when he or she was reading, speaking, and writing. Cockeram claimed to be publishing thousands of words never published before. Grammar books could not make that claim because of space limitations; they were increasingly concerned with explaining Latin grammar rules in the English vernacular. This bilingual format meant that definitions had to be listed twice.

Grammar embraced lexicography in the early seventeenth century, when grammarians still held the same authority to make language decisions they had held since antiquity, and lexicographers had not yet emerged as a distinct group. This imbalance of power began to shift in the second stage as the vernacular lexicon moved into the world of the educated.

Emergence of Lexicography The early eighteenth-century publication of English grammar books created a greater demand for vocabulary in the vernacular. This demand increased even more as the vernacular lexicon began to stabilize and the dictionary-type material outgrew the parameters of grammar books. Dictionaries, however, were still elementary, with only a short definition, synonym, or commentary for each word; grammar books included the more analytic information: pronunciation, meaning, parts-of-speech classification, etymology, spelling, and usage. At this stage, grammarians continued to make decisions about language usage.

Nevertheless, grammarians had been experiencing conflicts within their own ranks for some time, conflicts over whether to teach grammar with Latin or English models, whether to continue the practice of translation and imitation, and whether to learn grammar first in Latin or in the native tongue. Grammar books were being called upon to play a stronger and larger pedagogical role. With the increase in availability of public education, children of the lower and middle classes were filling classrooms, and schools needed grammar texts to make them literate.[24] In addition, the increased need for skills in the commercial world forced authors of grammar books to include practical instruction such as in familiarizing students with the formats of the business letter and the receipt. Thus, while grammarians were battling over teaching methods and grammatical theory, and at the same time producing texts for an increasing curriculum and student body, lexicographers focused on setting standards. The time was ripe for lexicographers to make a bid for linguistic authority.

Grammarians had argued over custom and usage versus authority without reaching a decision. Lexicographers, however, had a stronger base from which to impose "correctness" on the vernacular: research. Eighteenth-century lexicographers inventoried definitions, pronunciation, and various forms of spelling. John Kersey (*A New English Dictionary*, 1702), Edward Cocker (*Cocker's English Dictionary*, 1704), and Nathan Bailey (*An Universal Etymological English Dictionary*, 1721) helped establish the methodology of lexicography and position the dictionary as a source of authority.[25] Lexicographers envisioned themselves not as authors of grammar texts, but as protectors of the language.

Time, moreover, seemed to be running out. England had no academy like the one established in France (Académie Française 1635) to legislate linguistic matters, and the consensus seemed to lean toward not establishing one.[26] Most grammarians wanted language to develop naturally and not be bound by an academy that would dictate language decisions. However, some learned men were afraid that the English language would become corrupted, and some even expressed the concern that what was being written at that time would be unrecognizable to future generations. One such man was Samuel Johnson, who represented himself as both a scholar and a grammarian. Afraid the English language would change beyond recognition, he set about to do what the creators of grammar texts had not yet accomplished: codify and standardize the English language. With the help of books written by scholars and men of letters, Johnson assumed the role of a lexicographer, asserting that he had the authority to legislate rules of language, an assertion that dictionary editors retain to this day. According to Johnson, it was the responsibility of lexicographers to record anomalies so that undesirable language habits were not perpetuated and reinforced. As he states in the preface of his dictionary, "every language has likewise its improprieties and absurdities, which it is the duty of the lexicographer to correct or proscribe" (1747 Plan).

In the early eighteenth century, as the lexicon stabilized, as the vernacular became the language of the educated, and as grammarians assumed a stronger pedagogical role in teaching English to larger groups of students of the rising classes, lexicographers assumed the task of improving dictionaries. In the seventeenth century, their entries had been unreliable, but now they were documenting inventoried lists with an increasing degree of necessary accuracy. The dictionaries, however, were still at times misleading, because they were incomplete documents of the language with inadequate histories of words and word families, unrepresentative examples of earlier words, and unclear definitions.

Primacy of Lexicographers The last stage in the inversion of linguistic authority, that in which lexicographers embraced grammar, is more difficult for us to see because we are still in it. The forces described in stage two finally culminated in the publication of Thomas Dyche and William Pardon's landmark *New General English Dictionary* (1735), the first dictionary to have a compendium of grammar.[27] Dyche, also a grammarian, saw the necessity of such an inclusion. He claimed that his work was for those who wanted to write "correctly and elegantly," and he covered difficult words, technical terms, spelling, accents, and pronunciation.

The publication of Dyche and Pardon's dictionary meant that grammarians lost a battle they were unaware they were fighting. Lexicographers were working with historical and empirical data and keeping abreast of linguistic changes. Grammarians, on the other hand, were pedagogues, teaching students how to use language, publishing and republishing little-changed textbooks. The decline in the status of the grammarian was evident by the middle of the eighteenth century. In *A New General English Dictionary* (1744) Dyche and Pardon denigrate the grammarian as a person who spends too much time on insignificant niceties (Introduction), and perhaps they could claim to know since they were themselves both grammarians-turned-lexicographers. With Dyche and Pardon, the responsibility for protecting the standards of English usage from corruption and deterioration moved from grammarians to lexicographers, a transfer that is still in force today though perhaps not fully recognized. Grammarians who had in ancient times been pre-eminent were now criticized and questioned for their pedagogy and theories, while lexicographers were looked upon as authorities.

Lexicography was also able to embrace grammar because it had the advantage of clarity. A good example of this advantage is *A Vocabulary or Pocket Dictionary* (1765), which more clearly identifies usage errors and more coherently and consistently lists preferred usage than did grammar books (C1–C8).[28] This dictionary combines functions that were once separate. The author claims that his text "contains only those more difficult words which occur in sensible genteel company," yet he launches into the first chapter with a general, but detailed, view of English grammar (Preface). He describes what he calls the inflected parts of speech (nouns, adjectives, verbs, pronouns) and the non-inflected parts of speech (adverbs, conjunctions, prepositions, interjections). In the following section, "Of the Signification and Use of Certain Words," he describes how to make decisions on usage by referring to custom and to the best writers. The third section of this chapter cites examples of incorrect word order and preferred order. A second chapter on grammar, "An Account of the Most Usual Mistakes in English

Grammar," clarifies structural and grammatical problems. A structural mistake, for example, would be "I had the same thought as you," whereas the preferred usage is "I had the same thought that you had" (C3). This particular dictionary also has such information as the part of speech each word belonged to, shades of its meaning, and its etymology. It even included a history of the English language. Although the anonymous author assumes that custom and usage should determine rules, he acknowledges that the grammarian should share in the responsibility of fixing the meaning and use of words. Otherwise, the grammarian has no further powers. He "has nothing left him belonging to the Language, but the Inflections, which are extremely few; and the Order in which Words are placed in a Sentence" (B5r–B5v).

Other lexicographers continued to go beyond the limited scope of the dictionary to cover both grammar and lexicon in even more detail. In *A New Dictionary of the English Language* (1773) William Kenrick includes, for each entry, information on orthography, etymology, and idiomatic use in writing, all of which had appeared in the grammar books of the seventeenth century. He cites the correct pronunciation according to the "present practice of polished speakers in the Metropolis," further proof of the increased focus on communication at that time. He also includes what he calls a "rhetorical" grammar to help people with contemporary speech and communication. Two other publications aimed at the lower and middle classes are James Barclay's *A Complete and Universal English Dictionary on a New Plan* (1774) and John Ash's *The New and Complete Dictionary of the English Language* (1775). Both lexicographers include discussions of grammar and communication skills. Barclay also adds an outline of ancient and modern history, and Ash includes some essays on linguistic matters.

Lexicographers were also more alert than grammarians to issues of conforming to rules and standards, especially to the way people used language in social situations. John Entick, for example, promises in *The New Spelling Dictionary* (1765) to help the reader "write and pronounce the English tongue with ease and propriety" (Preface). In the introduction, he reinforces his aim for people "to speak and to write correctly and properly, to be instructed in the rules for right pronunciation, and in the art of true spelling; and or how to write every word with proper letters" (ix). He wishes "to assist young People, Artificers, Tradesmen and Foreigners, desirous to understand what they speak, read and write" (Title page). He offers help in "accenting" for correct pronunciation and in distinguishing the parts of speech, all in the convenient format of a pocket reference. Entick claims that his grammatical introduction will facilitate the user's proficiency in English and help him gain necessary social and linguistic competence.

When lexicographers included grammar, they were unaware that they were gaining an authority over grammarians as to standardizing the language. While grammarians served as pedagogues, concentrating on classroom exercises and fighting battles over teaching methodologies, lexicographers quietly inventoried and researched usage. In sum, lexicographers became the guardians of language. The transfer of linguistic authority from grammar books to dictionaries was complete by the latter part of the eighteenth century. Dictionaries now held linguistic authority, while grammar texts served a purely pedagogical function.

As one might expect, the transfer of linguistic authority brought with it the propensity for controversy.[29] The battles were not just about word change, but about who controls language, what social classes are included, and what groups are excluded. Previously, such grammar books as Lily's had the power to decide those issues. As dictionaries became more powerful and were able to reach more people, they began to dominate the linguistic sphere. They could encode values and reflect current language usage. Language is power, and dictionaries could wield that power by standardizing language.

Thus, in seventeenth- and eighteenth-century England, some significant issues in the development of the English language played themselves out. The shift from Latin as the learned language to the vernacular as the official language brought to light many issues other than grammar. It played upon questions of which class would control language. The use of Latin to codify and standardize English prompted many a heated argument among grammarians and linguists. The argument to learn the mother tongue first played on issues of national pride (socializing foreigners to British ways), vocational objectives, religion conversions (converting Catholics), and scientific communication. Eventually English would reach maturity and English grammar texts would teach English grammar. The controversy over the need to codify, refine, and fix the English language placed many prescriptivists, who looked to ancient rules for authority, and descriptivists, who used custom and habit to make language decisions, on a battlefield, each fighting to preserve the native tongue. The inversion of linguistic authority from grammarians to lexicographers instituted another source of who would decide issues of grammar and usage. Whoever controls language holds power. The search to codify, standardize, and fix language was absurd at times, but the middle classes wanted linguistic security.

Notes

1 Leith (1983:87).
2 Leith lists these misconceptions (1983:89–90).
3 Per Michael (1987:317), "Almost without exception our seventeenth- and eighteenth-century predecessors believed that linguistic control, in English, was achieved through the study of grammar."
4 For a lengthy discussion on the teaching of English and Latin, see Jones, 1953:272–323.
5 As translated by Tucker (1961:36).

6 For a discussion on the dominance of Latin, see Michael (1970:492–507) and Jones (1953:310–23).
7 Michael (1970:214–40).
8 The author is uncertain; ESTC lists him as "[Wheeler?]."
9 Michael (1970:108) defines *accident* as a "blanket term to cover all those features of words which have not been used in determining the parts of speech."
10 Two replies were made to Swift's *Proposal*: John Oldmixon's *Reflections on Dr. Swift's Letter* (1712) and Arthur Maynwarning's *The British Academy* (1712).
11 Lane (1695) was already making this argument (preface).
12 Several earlier grammarians had tried spelling reform as a way to standardize the vernacular: Bullokar (1586); Hume (16th century, published 1865); Gill (1619); Butler (1633).
13 Entick (1728:1) makes the same kind of statement in his question/answer format: "Master: How many Parts of Speech ... are there in English?" "Scholar: Eight, just as many as in the Latin." For a full discussion on the history of the parts of speech, see Michael (1970:201–80).
14 This practice was not a new one. Jonson (1640) tried to force the English tongue into a Latin system of conjugations and declensions.
15 Leith (1983:52).
16 See Milroy and Milroy (1985:1–28, 70–89).
17 See Baugh and Cable (1994:278) who make this the rule of Bishop Lowth (1762).
18 Leith (1983:111).
19 Leith includes another example of interest, the double negative: "Perhaps the most notorious example concerns the pattern of negation in English. In common with many languages today, English had since Anglo-Saxon times signalled negation by the cumulative use of negative particles. Hence, *I don't know nothing* was a traditional English pattern. By the end of the eighteenth century this had been condemned as illogical, by applying the principle that 'two negatives make a positive.' That great writers like Shakespeare used the traditional construction was a source of some embarrassment to the grammarians" (1983:52–3).
20 Leith (1983:50).
21 Horgan (1994:85–94, 210–211, n. 51); DeMaria (1986:34–57).
22 For an historical background on lexicography, see Burchfield (1986); Hayashi (1978); Starnes and Noyes (1946); Riddell (1974, 1979).
23 Hoole (1658).
24 Watson (1909:121–34).
25 Hayashi (1978:57–89).
26 For a discussion on language change and academies, see Leith (1983:31–57).
27 The section on grammar is titled *Youth's Guide to the Latin Tongue* (1735).
28 *A Vocabulary or Pocket Dictionary* (1765); a similar book was *A Pocket Dictionary or Complete English Expositor* (1753).
29 For accounts of battles fought over dictionaries, particularly *Websters Third New International Dictionary* (1961), see Sledd and Ebbitt (1962).

Chapter Two
"Reformation of Schooles": Hartlib, Comenius, Milton

Pedagogues and grammarians in the seventeenth and eighteenth centuries agreed that reform was needed in education, but they could not agree on how to execute those changes. Grammarians and linguists argued for a newly devised universal language, while others favored an existing tongue (i.e., Latin, Hebrew, Chinese). A newly developing mercantile economy called for increased literacy, and school curriculums were adjusting to necessary vocational training. The shifting of pedagogic focus from Latin as the language of the educated to the vernacular as the language of primary use forced teachers to rethink their methods of teaching language. Education for females and foreigners was beginning to receive more serious attention because of their potential roles as productive members of the commonwealth. Also, many grammarians included religious doctrine and moral training in school texts as a way of shaping the character of children. However, practices such as brutal whippings in school and inconsistencies among school curricula were fixtures of education and would not disappear easily.

I. Architectural Metaphors

During the seventeenth century people from all professions wrote innovative texts suggesting ways of learning language, and ideas from this period have endured for more than three centuries. The debates about Descartes's innatism and Locke's blank slate have sparked debates in language acquisition ever since, just as the schemes of universal language devised at this time have continued to influence modern linguistics and are a major topic in linguistic journals today. We can also see that grammarians used the familiar comparison with architecture to argue that reforms should include stronger pedagogical theories, better language instruction, and a new universal language. Grammarians used the concept of building a foundation to impose a needed structure on the teaching of grammar at a time when there was little consistency in rules and procedures. They were also able to extend the building images beyond the confines of grammar to other issues, such as religion, good citizenship, vocational skills, and patriotism. Pedagogues may have found that building was an effective image to use with the rising classes because people still did their own construction of houses, barns, and shops, and they understood the analogy. To describe the process of one skill (learning a language) in terms of another one (building) reinforces a person's understanding of the process. In building and modifying existing educational

"REFORMATION OF SCHOOLES": HARTLIB, COMENIUS, MILTON   47

structures, some pedagogues argued to repair the old foundation, while others wanted to raze the foundation and build a new one.

Contexts for Architectural Metaphors   To argue for reform in schools, educators developed a model of pedagogy that they explained in metaphors drawn from architecture. They argued that grammatical competency was achieved in increments, just as buildings rise in stages, beginning with the foundation, then the

Figure 2.1   Tower of Knowledge, *Margarita Philosophica* (1504). Stages in Medieval Education, Courtesy of the Library of Congress.

frame, then the walls, and so forth. Pedagogues, philosophers, and scholars have argued aspects of the relationship between grammar and architecture since antiquity, and the relationships may even predate the metaphor itself. In the fifth century BC, for example, Protagoras was reputed not only to have made advances in grammar, but actually to have invented the bricklayer's hod.[1] What varies over the centuries is the emphasis that different authors place on different aspects of the metaphor. Quintilian in the first century AD stresses the foundation of a child's education;[2] Vinsauf in the thirteenth century, the art of building writing;[3] Gregorovius de Reisch in *Margarita Philosophica* in the early Renaissance, the metaphorical Tower of Knowledge (see Figure 2.1).[4]

In *The Art of Memory* (1966), Francis Yates discusses the Renaissance use of architectural structures as mnemonic devices (119–20). One of Yates' examples, Johann Romberch, describes memory schemes in *Congestorium Artificiose Memorie* (1533), which features a drawing of old Grammatica, the first of the liberal arts, with her emblematic scalpel and ladder, tools that can be used for building the memory (see Figure 2.2).

Yates points out that old Grammatica is "not only the well-known personification of the liberal art of Grammar, but a memory image being used to remember material about grammar" (120). Romberch's Grammar is important to the student of artificial memory, she says, because personifications of familiar figures become memory images. Many educators and grammarians, such as Johann Amos Comenius and Elisha Coles in the seventeenth and eighteenth centuries, were following these same principles by using a familiar figure or other drawings to produce visual learning.

Architectural metaphor and knowledge Architectural terms make it possible to look at grammar texts in ways we have not done previously in this book. Key terms that would have had meaning to a seventeenth-century audience are *foundation, models, remodeling, structure, grounded, temple, gate, door, wall, roof, frame, materials, spaces, rooms, inner recesses, plans, establishment, house, building, habitation, erect, tower,* and *settlement.* These terms provided a method for framing or organizing language activities.

The metaphor was applied to grammar texts as early as the sixteenth century. In a *Shorte Introduction to Grammar* (1567) John Colet and William Lily write that "[A pupil's education is like a] Buyldynge, [which cannot] bee perfect, when as the foundacion and grounde worke is readye to fall, and unable to uphold the burthen of the frame" (1). They go on to argue that it is parents' responsibility to make sure their children receive a proper education. In *The School of Skill* (1581) Abraham Fleming advises parents to start with a good foundation with their children: "For he that determineth to erect and build a dwelling-house, beginneth not at the roof, but at the foundation, otherwise, as it were a preposterous kind of attempt, so all the world would judge it fond and ridiculous" (21). The association between education and parental responsibility is based on the idea of building a strong foundation for learning. What children learn in the formative years, the argument goes, will be a blueprint for the rest of their lives.

People in the seventeenth century were familiar with the architectural metaphors used in the Bible to illustrate the principles of laying a solid foundation in religion.[5] For example, Christ employs the metaphors of the house built upon rock and the house built upon sand at the end of the Sermon on the Mount (Matt. 7.24–27). St. Paul says that the Christian religion is built upon the foundation of

Figure 2.2 Johann Romberch, *Congestorium Artificiose Memorie*, Venice (1533). Grammar as memory Image. Courtesy of Princeton University Library.

the apostles and prophets with Jesus Christ himself as the cornerstone (Eph. 2:19–22). Preachers often used architectural metaphors as vivid sermon illustrations.[6] Edward Leigh (1639) offers this architectural metaphor in his theological observations:

> The Scripture is named a Canon, by a metaphor taken from architecture: for as Architects which build houses, do try them by the rule and square, that all the parts may cohere amongst themselves by a just symmetric and proportion; so those that teach and build the Church of God, must measure and examine all things by this rule, that a certain and perpetual tenour of doctrine may be observed (291).

One of the many Biblical verses that Comenius cites reinforces his idea of training children from the moment of birth: the righteous will "build the old waste places" and "raise up the foundations of many generations" (Isaiah 58). Because people recognized the biblical passages, the building metaphors were especially persuasive illustrations.

Grammarians also argued that students should reinforce a foundation for studying other languages. Randle Cotgrave describes in his *French-English Dictionary* (1650) that learning grammar first makes a strong basis for mastering any language:

> What Foundations are to material fabriques, the same is Grammar to a language. If the Foundation be not well layed, t'will be but a poor tottring superstructure; If grammaticall grounds go not before, there is no language can be had in any perfection. ... Now, for a Dictionary, which contains the whole bulk of a Language, to go before the Grammar, is to make the Building precede the Basis (3).

Christopher Wase refers to the building process in *Methodi practicae specimen* (1660). In illustrating his image of reinforcing learning, he states that teachers need to hammer knowledge into a child's head: "Some wits are of a more yielding, others of a more sturdy matter. Now each single instance propounded to be wrought, is as a knock of a Hammer, to rivet into the understanding and memory, that rule, upon which it depends in the working: And the several heads of sense serve the more to clench it down" (A3).

John Wilkins, who argues for a universal language in *Essay Towards a Real Character and a Philosophical Language* (1668), uses an architectural metaphor at the beginning of his sermon manual:

> An immethodical discourse (though the materials of it may be precious) is but as a heap, full of confusion and deformity, the other, as a Fabrick or building, much more excellent both for beauty and use.[7]

In this architectural metaphor, he names the parts of a building to correspond to the parts of a clergyman's sermon.

> He [the clergyman] represents the whole body of Divinity under the notion of an edifice or building, wherein there are two things considerable ... the Frontispiece or Porch [and] the Fabrick or Pile ... In the Frontispiece he proposeth foure generall heads, which are premised as the praecognita to this series... In the first story is contained the chiefe principles to be knowne or believed, Either more Generally, Particularly in each of these 12 heads. In the second story, things for practice, Duties, Helpes, in each 12 particular heads.[8]

Many grammarians were active in church-related professions, thus making it natural for them to view both grammar instruction and religious training in terms of building a foundation.

Within *Some Improvements to the Art of Teaching* (1669), William Walker expresses gratitude in "The Epistle Dedicatory" to William, Lord Bishop of Lincoln for setting up a school "for the Grounding of young Scholars" (A5). Walker thanks his lordship for being "a right Wise Master builder and so the fitter to be ordained a repairer to the ruines of this decayed Church: for to see that the Churches foundation be rightly laid, is the way to have its Superstructures long to hold; and the School is the properest place for the laying of the first stones of the Churches foundation in" (A4). Walker even suggests how he can be of humble service to the Lord Bishop: "If I may but fetch, though I cannot fit materialls for the work, or if I may but hew stones, and temper mortar; though I be not able yet to lay a stone in the building; it will be a very great satisfaction, and no less a contentment to me" (6). In the Preface to the Reader, he claims that he wants to "improve the Art of Teaching" in what is most neglected, "the very First Grounding of the Schollar, and laying the Foundation of all his future attainments." If a proper foundation is laid, a teacher "shall follow his Teaching with delight," and the student will "proceed in his Learning with comfort, and both come off from their several employments with reputation and credit."

Several grammarians used the foundation metaphor to encourage schoolmasters to lay a strong foundation in the teaching of grammar. In *School Pastime for Young Children: or the rudiments of grammar* (1669) John Newton asks teachers to lay a strong foundation so that children can learn incrementally. "Notions received by the Ear, will be more and more confirmed unto them, and a good foundation laid not only for Reading and Writing the English Tongue, but also for the Learning of any other Language" (B2v). Eventually, Newton promises, children will learn to write well, with the "gathering of Phrases, and writing of Letters and Epistles" (B3v). Elisha Coles reminds the reader in *Syncrisis, Or The Most Natural and Easie Method of Learning Latin* (1677) of the necessary connection in learning: "There must be, (and always is) something common between the Learner and the Teacher, as a Foundation for both to build upon" (A1r). And, he continues, the teacher must know both English and Latin language well so that he can proceed from one step to the next "to have laid a good Foundation of the first." Problems occur when grammar rules are "commonly learnt by Rote," and "the Foundation is not good enough, until they have learnt at least the General Grammar of it also, which must lead them to the Grammatical Learning of the other" (A1r). The same principle applies to the writing process: incremental steps must be taken to establish composition skills. In *The Writing Scholar's Companion* (1695), the anonymous author describes the building of writing skills:

> The First Part, furnisheth you with Materials for a Foundation.
> The Second, gives you the whole Body of the English Tongue, for a Superstructure.
> And the Last Part, Embellisheth it with the Necessary Ornaments of Pointing and Accent.

This process takes on a traditional rhetoric cast in that one begins with invention and builds through delivery.

In the eighteenth century the metaphor of architecture continued to hold its strength in illustrating a point. In *Right Spelling Very Much Improved* (1704), the anonymous author calls for laying a "solid Foundation upon the Grounds and Reasons of the English Tongue, that if duely attended will in short time, make a perfect English Scholar" (2). He continues, "you must settle in your mind, as the Ground and Foundation of all, Fifteen distinct Sounds, made out of the Five vowels" (2). Robert Lowth has prescriptive precepts in mind when he calls for building a foundation. He states in *English Grammar* (1763) that a "good foundation in the General Principles of Grammar is in the first place necessary for all those who are initiated in a learned education" (xiv). And, he states, children need to learn their mother tongue: "For these plain reasons a competent Grammatical knowledge of our own Language is the true foundation up which all Literature, properly so called, ought to be raised" (xvi). Lowth thought schools should adopt this method so that children of lower and middle classes would learn the foundation of grammar in English.

The architectural metaphor still holds its value because people understand each facet of it and can then reapply it to abstract situations. The idea of laying a foundation and building a structure has universal meaning. The image has the advantage of clearly projecting the goals one wishes to reach, such as laying a foundation of grammar rules in the mother tongue and then of building a structure of learning other languages.

II. Comenius and Hartlib

The architectural metaphor was especially appropriate for Comenius because he was arguing for the building of a "Universall Temple of Wisdome" dedicated to knowledge much as religious temples are dedicated to God. Comenius's architectural vision for constructing such a program was more complex. A temple of wisdom, more so than a house, is a structure that provides a large central location for building a knowledge of pansophy. In *Reformation of Schooles* (1642), Comenius describes the significance of choosing the word "temple" for a building (71–72). The "Ancients chose higher places, as hills, and risings of the ground" because these were pleasant places to worship their Gods and erect altars (72). The worshipers found it advantageous to build walls around their sacred area and call their building a temple.

Not only did Comenius propose to build a temple to house knowledge, but also at the perimeter of his ideal structure to build a gate that would be the gateway to universal language. Comenius also visualized it as a gateway to all knowledge under heaven that would lead to a spiritual wisdom united with nature. In *Janua linguarum reserata* (1652), he writes of wanting to build a gate on the perimeter of his temple of wisdom so that people might move into the "whole universality ... for a true discovery of the grounds of all things" (50). Many people at once would be permitted to pass through the gate to a universal language and universal knowledge. It would be a gate of wisdom "open for Christian Youth, that they may come to behold the rich treasure" (58). Through a door one person may enter, but "whole troupes through a Gate. A Dore is shut as every one is entered in: but Gates in peaceable Cities, stand always open" (59–60). A door leads into the holy Scriptures, but universal knowledge is a gateway to both the world and to God (49).

In *Reformation of Schooles* (1642) Comenius claims that a newly erected temple of wisdom, built on Christian models, can provide a locus of knowledge. Education, he says, can be improved with a "Universall Temple of Wisdome, truly glorious, and refulgent with the ornaments of Harmony, and the light of Truth."[9] Comenius cites Lucretius, saying that a temple of wisdom can help a student on "learnings solidnesse." He adds that unless a "Palace of true Wisdome be attempted by the followers of Wisdome, they will be like a slothfull builder, who is always doing something about his building, but never drawing it towards an end" (74). In the absence of such a palace "learning it selfe will at length fall with its owne weight" (74). Comenius maintained that the mind does not have the architectural skill to build a palace, but only "Wisdome her self, can build an house fit for self to dwel in" (75).

Comenius claimed that the key to opening all doors and all gates could be found in universal knowledge. The builder of the temple of wisdom would use "solid judgement" with the "design" and would have "survayed [all things] from the beginning to the end."[10] People would progress through the temple of wisdom and through the gate to a universal language free from ambiguity. They would know the real character of language and of the world of God. Comenius argued that wisdom can only be found in God, and that the process must begin with youth in school. He writes, "The minds of Children ... are most fit to draw in these new, and purer conceptions of things: and by this meanes will be accustomed, not to superficiall, and opinionative knowledge ... but [to build a] more reall, solid, and well grounded Wisdome" (58).

The architectural metaphor was a favorite of the entire "Hartlib circle," a group consisting of educational reformers like Samuel Hartlib, John Dury, and Comenius.[11] Its members were arguing not only for a reorganization of the educational system, from the poor school to the university, but also for the complete integration of their model into society.[12] Their goals embodied their philosophy of producing good commonwealth men by replacing the fancies of scholastic learning with the ideals of public service. They also wanted to introduce religious doctrine in the classroom and to emphasize vocational skills. The aptness of their metaphor was contested in three areas of reform: focusing on vocational skills rather on classical learning, making divine knowledge part of the language instruction, and teaching grammar in innovative ways.

Repairing the Old Foundation or Building a New One In *True and Readie Way to Learne the Latine Tongue* (1654), Hartlib compares the intellectual process of reforming the educational and linguistic practices of his time to the physical process of demolishing and an old foundation and building a new one with a new building.[13] This graphic image illustrates his belief in the necessity for educators to integrate new models of grammar, religion, civic duties, vocational training, and science into a child's education. In the "Dedicatory," Hartlib complains that educators cling to old practices and continue to ignore the new models of education: "in the Wayes of Education, and the Reformation of Schools (the deepest foundation of all other good Settlement both in church and Common-wealth) it hathe not been followed hitherto" (A3).

The plan for reforming schools was an ambitious project that called for support in England in order for the changes to take place. Hartlib tells educational reformers that they must raze the old building, dig out the old foundation, and put in a new foundation and building. They must start completely anew "because it is not possible to build a new House where an old one is standing, till the old one be pulled down" (A2–A3). Hartlib and his circle were prepared to rebuild pedagogical principles by laying solid foundations to "introduce a Better, Easier, Readier Way of Teaching" (A5). However, to prevent the mere "Overthrow and Deformation of former Establishments," he insisted a "New Modell" be "prepared before the old one be removed."[14] To make good his promise, Hartlib and his friends worked diligently in developing models to reorganize the curriculum and to include textbooks with some sort of psychological foundation.

An Innovator and Reformer Some of the educational practices Hartlib and his circle objected to were rooted in political, religious, and social issues. To help them fight for badly needed reform, they invited well-known Czech philosopher and educator Comenius to bring his innovative teaching ideas to England in hopes of getting government support for him. A minister in Unity of Brethren in Moravia (Kingdom of Bohemia), Comenius had been a target of political and religious conflicts during the Thirty Years War. Armed with a vision of world unity and his religious convictions, he believed that through education youth would come to know God and be enlightened. Education would also help them relate their acquired verbal knowledge to their sensory experiences for a greater understanding of the world. His religious beliefs made it necessary for him to go into hiding from 1621 to 1627, at which time he wrote *Labyrinth of the World* and *Paradise of the Heart*. *Labyrinth*, an allegory, was pivotal in moving him toward educational reform because he saw the cause of corruption of man as stemming from problems in the way children learned. In *Paradise of the Heart*, Comenius recognizes the Christian faith as being the foundation to learning, and his purpose was to reconcile faith and reason.

Comenius's strongest educational writings for reform came in *The Great Didactic*, later published as *Opera Didactica Omnia* (1657). These arguments had not been so explicitly presented in England before, and some of the radical thinking was not accepted. In *The Great Didactic*, he claims to describe how children could attain a foundation in academic subjects and at the same time acquire the moral and virtuous traits that would make them one with God in this world and in the next. He flew in the face of tradition and rejected popular practices like rote memory, which contributed little to an understanding of the material. More than anyone else in England, except perhaps Francis Bacon, Comenius based his educational reform policies on how children's minds develop. He used sensory perception as a foundation on which to build on complex, abstract concepts. The teacher had the responsibility of ordering knowledge into linguistic categories so that as a child progressed through developmental stages, he could use language to speak and write what he learned. All of these stages would move him toward combined knowledge and sensory experience in which he would come to know God.

Comenius's plan for education placed much greater responsibility on schools for the training of all youth than had been previously known in England. His empirical and anti-grammatical approach to teaching language was in contrast to the rote memorization methods schoolmasters used. Comenius's motto was "All things flow spontaneously in the absence of violence,"[15] and he searched for a method that would accomplish that end. He introduced the idea of pansophia as a key to the "encyclopedic and spiritual understanding of nature" (22).[16] In *The Way of Light* (1668), Comenius defines pansophia as a "single and comprehensive system of Human Omni-Science" (188). Pansophism was of particular interest to intellectuals of the time because it was represented as a universal science, and as a tool for advancing not only school reform, but also a reform of civilization by overcoming evil. Pansophism rejected artificial divisions and classifications in favor of the precept that every element of life, physical and spiritual, was interrelated to make a unified whole. It was a system of knowing all things under heaven. Comenius also believed that if one could find an order to reality, to the world, one would be able to apply that knowledge to language and find truth as well as knowledge (187). He argued that the idea of a language should be "adapted to the exact and perfect representation of things" (191).[17]

Grammar and Divine Knowledge Both Hartlib and Comenius wanted groundwork laid for instilling religious faith young children. They believed that schoolmasters needed new models not only for teaching language, but also for instilling moral principles that would support the commonwealth and religion. Hartlib argued that education could and should be the foundation for religious harmony and social reconstruction. With reconstruction the "breaches of old are repaired," he writes in *True and Readie Way*. And, he continues, "Instead of confusion, the foundations are laid for many Generations to build upon, and in stead of feare, a great doore is opened to us, that we shall be firmly and fully settled in all abundance of peace and truth" (2).

To help illustrate his point on religious teachings, Hartlib included in *True and Readie Way* a major section by the German Eilhardus Lubinus (1565–1621).[18] For youth, Lubinus prepared a special New Edition of the New Testament "from whence Children might learn Latine, and straightaway being striplings, the Greek Tongue" (44). His intent was to "provide for Children that they might be brought sooner and more maturely then hitherto to those studies of wisdome, and principally, to that true and eternal wisdome Christ Jesus, who bids Children come unto him, and faith expressly, That theirs is the Kingdome of Heaven" (43–44). Religious teaching, Lubinus argued, is part of the foundation of learning, and the new models of education included it in the curriculum.

Comenius attempted to bring together faith and reason:

> a twofold clear inward light – the light of reason and the light of faith – and both are guided by the Holy Ghost. For he who enters [on the Christian road] must put away and renounce his reason, yet the Holy Ghost returns it to him, purified and refined … . Then the light of faith gleams on him so brightly that he can already see and know, not only that which I before him, but also everything that is absent and invisible (218–19).

Comenius's dilemma was defending his foundation of faith in an ever-increasing world of reason. Comenius also claimed that the way to knowledge was through God, and he promoted a Christian education because "the true fountain of knowledge is the Holy Writ, and the Holy Ghost our teacher, and the purpose of all true knowledge is Christ" (248–49). True knowledge, Comenius argued, was gained by knowing God and his wisdom, and man reached that knowledge only through a Christian education.

Comenius emphasized incorporating morals and virtues with other academic subjects as an important element of educational reform. In *School of Infancy* (1630), he outlines the precepts for educating a younger child. A mother, he claims, is a child's first teacher of morals and virtue. Also, parents should help the child learn the names of objects and their purpose in his environment. Comenius continued to be committed to the idea that an encyclopedic approach produced the best results. He also remained constant to the idea that a child should develop the senses, then use his sensory knowledge to make a connection between language and experience.

Comenius argued for schools to make learning relevant to the duties students would perform in life. Perhaps Comenius's own childhood memories made him argue staunchly for changes in pedagogical practices: he was forced to learn a grammar he did not understand, to memorize lists of rules by rote, and to translate Latin without a suitable dictionary.[19] According to Comenius in *The Reformation of Schools* (1642), the materials for reform in education were "brought together into various heapes, which yet lie severed, and not united" (23). The educator had to "use a skilfull hand in bringing these heapes of materials into their due forme and order" (23). To mention specific problems in curriculum, he complains about "that inveterate custome, or rather disease of Schooles, whereby all the time of youth is spent in Grammaticall, Rhetoricall, and Logicall toyes" at the expense of "those things which are reall, and fit to enlighten mens minds, and to prepare them for action" (20). The solution for Comenius is "to propound all things seasonably unto youth, and to make serious exercises the preparatives of serious employments" (20).

In *Reformed School* (1649) fellow educational reformer and member of the Hartlib circle John Dury concurs: "Nothing is to bee taught but that which is usefull in it self to the Society of mankind, therin fitting them for employments" (19). As a reminder to the Hartlib circle, George Snell in the *Right Teaching of Useful Knowledg* (1649) claims that "English youths may no longer bee taught to bee emptie Nominalists and verbalists" but should "know the verie things and matters themselvs, and yet onely such matters as may best further a man for the sufficient doing of all duties and works pertaining to his own profession and person" (A6). Snell again reinforces both Comenius's and Dury's argument for relevant education: "All learning in the School was but to prepare a Scholar to bee abel to do and execute the duties of a vocation and trade of living" (162).

Language instruction In their writings, both Hartlib and Comenius attempted to build upon new models of language instruction and then integrate them into the foundation of school curriculum. They argued that schoolmasters would be more efficient if they were consistent in teaching rules of grammar, used the vernacular to teach Latin, and avoided rote memorization. Moreover, students would be more successful if they learned Comenius's method of visible language, that is, seeing words together with their corresponding pictures. Hartlib claimed that the foundation of language instruction was weak because teachers were not consistent in teaching the rules of grammar. Eilhardus Lubinus states in his own essay (included in Hartlib's *True and Readie Way*) that the grounds of learning are destroyed when "the precepts of Grammar are so many times in a manner increased, so oft changed, as often as a new Moderatour is put in authority for the School" (7). The problem, then, occurs as often "as a youth goes away from one school to Another, so often is his old Grammar to be unlearned, and a new one to be learned." Lubinus argues that "tender mindes of the younger sort are not onely hindered and troubled, but also that Golden age is both worn out and tormented" (8). Hartlib was also troubled by the inconsistency among schools. His idea was to set the foundation of grammar rules so that each builder (teacher) could use the same remodeling plan, so that whatever school the student entered, he would learn the same material. However, this consistency was not the norm in the seventeenth century because language itself was full of experimentation, and pedagogy was embedded with individual philosophies on how language should be taught.

Comenius's method of teaching visible language, or the pictorial method, was an important part of Hartlib's reformation of school curriculum. According to Lubinus, "the eyes of children" see the thing or the image, whether it be painted or engraved, then they will learn it by heart. Therefore, "this knowledge ... is certain and solid, by which a certain and solid foundation of the Latine Tongue is laid [at the] beginning or entrance being made from Things falling under the sense of the eyes" (25). Later in the essay Lubinus states that "a boy [will] learn to speak Latine far sooner ... after he hath in some sort perceived the Latine words joyned together with their Things" (28).

Comenius used the visible learning of language to connect objects with the world. In *Reformation of Schooles* (1642), he claimed that "words should not be learned apart from the objects to which they refer; since the objects do not exist separately and cannot be apprehended without words, but both exist and perform their functions together" (207). Comenius believed that a child learns a new word most efficiently by seeing its picture at the same time: "For by once looking upon an elephant, or at least, upon his picture, a man shall more easily, and firmly apprehend his forme, than if it had beene told him ten times over" (14).

Comenius demonstrates his technique of the visible learning of language by writing the popular *Orbis sensualium pictus* (1658), a text that resulted from his forty years of thinking and writing about education.[20] Although children's texts had been illustrated for several centuries, *Orbis* is the first notable illustrated text designated for school use. Charles Hoole, translator of the English edition of *Orbis sensualium pictus* (1658), claims that Comenius "descended to the very Bottom of what is to be taught, and proceeded (as nature it self doth) in an orderly way" (A7r). Comenius's method, Hoole explains, is "first to exercise the Senses well, by presenting their objects to them, and then to fasten upon the Intellect by impressing the first notions of things upon it, and linking them one to another by a rational discourse" (A7r). Hoole argues that the present method of instruction is to train children to be "Parrats, to speak they know not what" and "do puzzle their imaginations with abstractive terms and secondary intentions, which, till they be somewhat acquainted with things, and the words belonging to them, in the language which they learn, they cannot apprehend what they mean" (A7r). For these reasons, he explains, parents do not send their children to school until they are eleven or twelve years old, an age when they have already an understanding of words.

This delay amounted to years of lost educational opportunities. Hoole suggests that when a child can read English, he should use his accidence with *Orbis* each day, and he outlines a procedure for using the text (A7v–A8r). It consists of a series of drawings in which each picture has numbers affixed to things he wants the student to name.[21] Below the drawing, numbers are listed with corresponding vocabulary. Although several grammarians like John Wilkins, Francis Lodwick, and Cave Beck had written books of this type, Comenius added another cognitive level by incorporating emotions, feelings, and other abstract concepts. The picture becomes not only a vocabulary lesson, but a visible means of teaching all subjects: grammar, science, biology, mathematics, history, religion, and literature. The example in Figure 2.3 is, among other things, a science lesson. The drawing has the key word *air* and shows faces blowing different kinds of winds, such as a tornado, by which air is personified with a face blowing trees into a house. Drawings like this understandably proved to be attractive to a child learning grammar and vocabulary.

The example in Figure 2.4 is a drawing of children playing several different kinds of *games*. The picture offers a variety of vocabulary words that children would enjoy learning and using in sentences. It also reaffirms Comenius's commitment to teaching relevant material.

Language instruction was undergoing many changes in the seventeenth and early eighteenth centuries, and Comenius's visible language represents one example of these innovations. Although the system was practical, efficient, and easy, it was not widely accepted among more traditional pedagogues. In order for the method to become part of the curriculum, schoolmasters would have to leave traditional ways of teaching behind and adapt to news ways of teaching. It also meant rethinking how students learned language: by rules and practice or by pictures and words. The jump was too great for traditional pedagogues to make, and the results from a new method were not certain.

One of Comenius's central goals was to ensure that all schools had consistent rules of grammar, spelling, and pronunciation. His idea was to begin by tearing down the "sinful," arrogant structure of languages and constructing a tower of a universal character.[22] Building a new tower of a common language was especially attractive to Hartlib, Comenius, and Lubinus, and their fellow supporters Joseph Webbe and John Dury. These men were also active in religious reform, and they wanted to use universal language as a way for men of all countries to read the Bible and understand God. At the same time, the new universal models could be used in educational and pedagogical reform. Universal language was a way of recording models of reform for education, agriculture, and science.[23] Latin was no longer the

VI.

Aër.

A cool Air 1. breatheth gently.	*Aura* 1. spirat leniter.
The Wind 2. bloweth strongly.	*Ventus* 2. flat validé.
A Storm 3. throweth down Trees.	*Procella* 3. sternit Arbores.
A Whirl-wind 4. turneth it self in a round compass.	*Turbo* 4. se agit in gyrum.
A wind under ground 5. causeth an Earthquake,	*Ventus subterraneus* 5. excitat *Terræ-motum*;
An Earthquake, causeth gapings of the Earth, (and falls of Houses.) 6.	*Terræ-motus* facit *Labes* (ruinas.) 6.

Figure 2.3 Johann Amos Comenius, *Orbis sensualium pictus*, (1658). Drawing and corresponding vocabulary words for air. Courtesy of William Andrews Clark Memorial Library, University of California, Los Angeles.

The Air.

"REFORMATION OF SCHOOLES": HARTLIB, COMENIUS, MILTON 61

(276)

CXXXVI.

Ludi Pueriles.

(277)

Boyes
use to play either with
Bowling-stones; 1.
or throwing
a Bowl 2.
at Nine-pins; 3.
or striking a Ball
thorow a Ring, 5.
with a Bandy; 4.
or scourging a Top 6.
with a Whip; 7.
or Shooting with
a Trunck, 8.
and a Bow; 9.
or going upon
Stilts; 10.
or tossing
and swinging
themselves upon
a Merry-totter, 11.

Pueri
ludere solent,
vel *globis fiĉtilibus*; 1.
vel jaĉtantes
Globum 2.
ad *Conos*; 3.
vel *Sphærulam*
Clavâ 4. mittentes
per *Annulum*; 5.
vel *Turbinem* 6.
Flagello 7.
versantes;
vel *Sclope*, 8.
& *Arcu* 9.
jaculantes;
vel *Grallis* 10.
incedentes;
vel super *Petaurum* 11.
se agitantes
& oscillantes.

T 3   *Regnum*

Boyes-Sport

Figure 2.4 Johann Amos Comenius, *Orbis sensualium pictus*, (1658). Drawing and corresponding vocabulary words for games. Courtesy of William Andrews Clark Memorial Library, University of California, Los Angeles.

international language, and European scholars were now in contact with other scholars in the Far West and East who spoke non-European languages.

Hartlib worked closely with his "honoured Friend" Comenius, and "other Fellow-labourers and Correspondents" in trying to come up with a universal character that would be adopted by all countries. Hartlib describes in *True and Readie Way to Learne the Latine Tongue* (1654) how they visualized a language that could be "studied to make as little Alteration as could be, seeking onely the best Advantages which upon the Ordinary Foundation of School-teaching could be introduced" (A3–A4). Hartlib wanted to introduce a new international language that could be taught by using Comenius's visible language method, but he knew the difficulty he faced, admitting that "in this Endeavour for a great many years we have Continued, and many wayes attempts have been made to facilitate the Course of Universall Learning, and especially the teaching of Learned Tongues" (A4).

To build a new character, or universal language, Hartlib and his circle spent much time making plans to put the new models into practice. In *True and Readie Way*, Hartlib writes that he has to "abridge the time which is spent, and to ease the toil after long experience," and that he knows it will be "impossible to raise a Firme And Commodious Building upon the Old Foundation; for which Cause [he] must ... shew now the weaknesse and defaults thereof" (A4). Even more important than Hartlib's own work in educational reform, perhaps, was his ability to disseminate information. He put his own work aside to concentrate on getting support for Comenius and John Dury and their programs in education, theology, and philosophy. Their work in universal language was especially important to Hartlib's plans for educational reform. Hartlib and his circle hoped to gain financial support for their language and educational reform, but knew that "it is no small difficultie and hazard to venture upon the contradicting of a Custome so Universally received, as is the Grammatical Tyranny of teaching Tongues" (A4). Hartlib was right in his assessment that his plan for universal language reform would not receive support from his government, and Comenius would leave England without support for his educational reform.

III. Reception of Comenius's Ideas

Comenius might well be considered the father of modern education because many twentieth-century schools and universities worldwide have incorporated his philosophies and methods of teaching. However, this homage to Comenius has not always been the case. In the seventeenth century, many scholars, politicians, and government officials disagreed with his radical ideas of combining religion and education, of favoring vocational rather than classical education, and of teaching an encyclopedic knowledge in a non-grammatical approach. Many dismissed him as having impractical ideas and as being a religious fanatic. He wandered from country to country during the Thirty Years war, often destitute. Hartlib's circle was one of the few groups that celebrated his ideas for reform. His contemporary educators and philosophers in Germany had much to say and appreciate about Comenius, while educators beyond the Hartlib circle in England had very little. A few progressive scholars in England, however, took note and left commentary about their reception of his ideas.

Clergyman John Eachard treated Comenius's precepts of educational reformation with studied attention. Eachard complains about him in *The Grounds & Occasions of the Contempt of the Clergy and Religion* (1671). Eachard, master of Catharine Hall, Cambridge and twice vice-chancellor of the university, was concerned about how students training for the clergy received a poor education because of a "wrong method" (8). In this treatise, he explains that clergy are generally regarded with contempt partly because of the inferior education, often because of poverty, that makes them appear incompetent and untrained for their work. Eachard cites Comenius's advice to "instill language at beginning" but does not agree completely with the Czech educator (8). Eachard suggests instead that students training for the clergy should read philosophy and other authors rather "than *Janua Linguarum*'s crabbed Poems, and cross-grain'd Prose" (10).[24] He disagrees with how some schoolmasters use Comenius's text: "it is the fashion of some Schools, to prescribe to a Lad for his Evening refreshment, out of Comenius, all the terms of Art belonging to Anatomy, Mathematicks, or some such piece of Learning" (10). However, he states, it is unlikely "that a Lad should take most absolute delight in conquering such a pleasant Task, where, perhaps, he has two or three hundred words to keep in mind, with a very small proportion of sense thereunto belonging" (11). He then claims that it is not "likely to be very savoury, and of comfortable use, to one, that can scarce distinguish between Vertue and Vice, to be tasked with high and morall Poems" (11). Even the reading of Homer, he claims, is good but of questionable value to young, untrained students: "But the committing of such high, and brave sens'd Poems to a Schoolboy, whose main businesse is to search out cunningly the Antecedent and the Relative, to lie at Catch for a spruce Phrase, a Proverb, or a quaint and pithy sentence" serves "little purpose" (11). Eachard complains that schoolboys "having gargl'd only those elegant Books at School," do not read them at a later time and furthermore have no desire looked at them again (11). The result, he laments, is "that all that improvement, whatsoever it be, that may be reap'd out of the best and choicest Poets, is for the most part utterly lost; in that a time is usually chosen of reading them when discretion is much wanting to gain thence any true advantage" (11–12). Thus, one of the works that suffers is the "admirable and highly useful Morality, *Tulli's Offices*." He continues, "because it is a Book commonly construed at School, [it] is generally afterwards so contemn'd by Academicks, that [it] is a long hours work to convince them, that it is worthy of being look'd into again, because they reckon it as a Book read over at School, and no question notably digested" (13). He warns that "the ill methods of Schooling does not onely occasion a great loss of time there, but also does beget in Lads a very old opinion and apprehension of Learning, and must disposes them to be idle, when got a little free from the usuall severities" (14). The universities need to improve, he argues, for the good of the Church, and the only way to do it is with better "management of Schools that the Clergy be not so much obstructed in their first attempts and preparations to Learning" (13–14).

In contrast to Eachard, Charles Hoole in *New Discovery of the Art of Teaching* (1660) describes the value of Comenius's method. A child's understanding, Hoole stresses, occurs when "the inward senses of the Childe are instructed by the outward, and the more help one hath of the outward, the surer and firmer the instruction is within" (6). Comenius's *Orbis pictus* is a "most rare device for Teaching of a Childe at once to know things and words by pictures" (6). Moreover, he states that the "words and things by pictures" "may also serve for the more perfect and pleasant reading of the English and Latine Tongues, and entering a childe upon his Accidents" (6). In reference to the cost of *Orbis pictus*, he wishes that the "dearnesse of the book (by reason of the brasse cuts in it) did not make it too hard to come by" (6). The book, however, may be easily obtained, he states, "as who would not bestow four or five shillings more then ordinary to profit and please a Son?" (6–7). Hoole recommends that a child bring it with him to grammar school and "be employed in it together with his Accidents, till he can write a good legible hand" (7). Next, a schoolmaster may "ground him well in Orthography, and Etymologie, by using that Book according to the directions already given in the Preface before it, and causing him every day to write a Chapter of it in English and Latine" (7). Although Comenius did not receive government support in England, many pedagogues and grammarians like Hoole later argued the educational validity of his method of teaching. Although Hoole praised John Brinsley for a "perfect method" that was not well received or used in his time, and Thomas Farnaby and John Clerke for their teaching methods, it is Comenius that "hath lately contrived a shorter course of teaching, which many of late endeavour to follow" (305).

In *School Pastime for Young Children: or the Rudiments of Grammar* (1669), grammarian John Newton praises Comenius's method of teaching reading. Newton includes much of Comenius's Epistle to the Reader from *Orbis sensualium pictus* and states that his book "will afford a device for learning to read, without using any ordinary tedious spelling, the most troublesome torture of wits" (A6r). For his reader, Newton paraphrases Comenius's directions of how to use *Orbis* to learn to read. Comenius's method sounds a bit idealistic for a child, looking at a table of syllables, studying the pictures, and then learning the titles to the pictures, all this without any formal training: "having looked over, saith he [Comenius], a Table of the chief Syllables, let the Child proceed to view the Pictures, and Inscriptions set over them; where saith he, the very looking upon the thing pictured, suggesting the name of the thing, will tell him how the Title of the Pictures is to be read" (A6r–v). Newton continues his paraphrase of how students learn to read and acquire a habit of reading by studying the pictures and titles in *Orbis*: "And thus the whole Book being gone over, by the Titles of the Pictures, reading cannot but be learned: and when they are thus acquainted with the Titles, the often reading over the Book it self, or those larger descriptions of things set over the Pictures, will be able perfectly to beget a habit of reading" (A6v). Next, Newton restates Comenius's directions on how to use the text:

I. Let this Book be given to Children, to delight themselves withal as they please, with the sight of pictures.
II. Then let them be examined ever and anon ... so that they may see nothing which they know not how to name, and that they can name nothing which they cannot shew.
III. Let the things named them be shewed, not onely in the Picture ...
IV. Let them also be suffered to imitate the Picture by Hand ... (A6v)

To support his argument for Comenius's method, Newton then cites Mr. Hezekiah Woodward's *Gate to Sciences*, Chap 2: "The use of Images or Representations is great, if we should make our Words as legible to Children as Pictures are, their information there from would be quickened and surer" (A7r). He continues his case for teaching with pictures: "And if we had Books wherein were the Pictures of all Creatures, *Herbs, Beasts, Fish, Fowl*, and such like, they would stand us in much stead: for Pictures are the most intelligible Books that Children can look upon. They come closest to Nature; nay, saith Scaliger, Art exceeds her" (A7r). Taking Comenius's method of word and thing to the next level, he suggests: "if we had Pictures, not onely of these things, but of all Utensils in a house, or elsewhere, with their Names in Greek, Latin, and English, the looking over such Books, would very much further a Child in his Reading, Writing, and Drawing, and be no small furtherance in his learning of the Latin and Greek Tongues also" (A7r). Thus, Newton not only embraces Comenius's innovative way of teaching, but he suggests making the method part of all daily living.

Bathsua Makin presents a female perspective on Comenius's work. In *An Essay to Revive the Antient Education of Gentlewomen* (1673), Makin recommends his method for learning Latin. She argues that Comenius's *Janua linguarum* works in offering vocabulary and sentence patterns for learning a language, because it "consists of a thousand Sentences; ten of which may be learnt in one day, fifty in a week, the thousand in twenty-six weeks" (37). She describes how this system could easily be applied to learning French (37). Also, a teacher wants students to learn "things" according to their categories, such as "Names and Natures of Herbs, Shrubs, Trees, Mineral Juyces, Metals, and Precious Stones" (34). She praises *Orbis sensualium pictus* because it "contains all the Primitive Latine words, and the representation of most things capable of being set out of

Pictures" as Comenius had arranged them (37). What appeals to Makin is the way Comenius has divided his subject matter into categories and then illustrated each subject with people, things, and activities that are relevant to it. She states,

> Words are the marks of things, and they are learnt better together than asunder. As a man shall sooner remember Names, if he sees the persons, so a Girl shall much easier fasten in her memory the names of Herbs ... as also the names of Birds, Beasts, Fishes ... if she see the things themselves in specie.... if there be any such thing as a concatenation of Notions, as doubtless there is ... the thing being perceived, Words freely flow.

Makin pinpointed and used the most efficient parts of Comenius's method.

In *The English Grammar* (1693) Joseph Aickin credits Comenius for his own use of pictures to illustrate language. He claims, "Pictures are the most intelligible Book, that Children can look upon" (66). Echoing Comenius's own commentary, Aickin states "The ingenious part of the world have much desired such a work, wherein the Pictures of all creatures, beasts, Fishes Fowls, trades and occupations, and whatsoever is visible to the Eye might be evidently presented, to the Senses: which would make such a powerfull impression on the understanding that Children could never forget what they once learned" (66). Aickin concerns himself with the same issues of the ability of the senses "being the conveyers of all things to our understanding," and therefore, the schoolmaster should "give the senses a true representation of all objects" (66). He mentions that he would like to have done an adaptation of Comenius's profitable *Orbis sensualium pictus* in the English tongue, but the problems in printing forced him to change his plan.

IV. Less Grammar, More Reading and Writing

There were two approaches to grammar in the seventeenth and eighteenth centuries which went in very different directions, one toward the larger level of *text*, the other toward the smaller level of isolated *word*. One tried to enhance the visibility of grammar in its systematic aspects; the other tried to make those same systematic aspects invisible. Both of these approaches share the same Latin context (rather than the vernacular context of most of this chapter) and each is related to the other. But each approach takes its different direction as an immediate consequence of having a different purpose in mind for grammar. The cases of John Milton and Johann Amos Comenius demonstrate (albeit from the Latin world) how a single context can permit very different purposes and hence very different executions.

Comenius and Milton were contemporaries, both connected intimately with Hartlib and his circle, yet there is no record that they ever met. Even so, they both were involved in education reformation and language instruction. Milton would have agreed with Comenius that children spent too much time learning grammar and that language is a means to other study, not an end. However, they would disagree on several issues. Milton's interest was humane, while Comenius' was vocational. Milton wanted a shorter time with grammar so that students could begin their study of literature, which Comenius was willing to eliminate. Milton wanted to teach language as a key to other studies, but did not support Comenius's scheme for universal language as a way of reversing Babel. Milton's attitude comes across in *Accedence Commenc't Grammar* (1669) as he proposes a text for correctness and stylistic precision, while Comenius promotes a common man's study of Latin.

Milton dedicated *Of Education* (1644) to Samuel Hartlib with whom he shared a goal of educational reform. Milton concurs with Comenius on the idea that education should include divine learning: "The end then of Learning is to repair the ruines of our first Parents by regaining to know God aright, and out of that knowledge to love him, to imitate him, to be like him" (366–67). The way to know God, Milton claims, is through learning: "Because our understanding cannot in this body found itself but on sensible things, nor arrive so clearly to the knowledge of God and things invisible, as by orderly conning over the visible and inferior creature, the same method is necessarily to be follow'd in all discreet teaching" (367).

In *Accedence Commenc't Grammar* (1669) John Milton separated the teaching of grammar from the teaching of composition. His distilled approach is as pedagogically effective as the more innovative methods of his contemporaries, yet it did not receive much attention in its time.[25] He did not intend for his grammar book to meet the needs of the more vocational students who were beginning to fill the schools, and he did not enter into the controversies over grammar in linguistics, pedagogy, standardization, and social mobility. Perhaps the biggest reason that Milton's grammar has been overlooked, however, is that it was not published until a time when rapid pedagogical and linguistic changes had rendered it obsolete, changes such as the increasing use of the vernacular.

Milton spoke to several issues of his time. He believed children should spend fewer years learning grammar and more time learning to read great authors and composing. He writes in *Of Education* (1644) that little is accomplished by subjecting a child to many years of grammar instruction: "Hence appear the many mistakes which have made learning generally so unpleasing and so unsuccessfull; first we do amisse to spend seven or eight years merely in scraping together so much miserable Latin, and Greek, as might be learnt otherwise easily and delightfully in one yeer" (370). The problem, he claimed, is that children are expected to be simultaneously proficient in grammar, composition, and literature, an impossible task that makes them lag behind in proficiency of both their native language and a foreign tongue. He also argued that students lose too much time in "idel vacancies given both to schools and Universities, partly in a preposterous exaction, forcing the empty wits of children to compose Theams, Verses, and Orations, which are the acts of ripest judgement and the finall work of a head fill'd by long reading, and observing, with elegant maxims, and copious invention" (371–72). Milton recommends one year on Latin grammar taught in English before moving on to more complex language tasks.

Milton rejected novelties of teaching grammar that would interfere with competency in the native tongue and fluency in second language acquisition. To prepare for reading and writing in any language, he argued, a student must have a strong foundation in grammar, and novelties do not build that foundation. Unlike the long, dry grammatical treatises written by his contemporaries, Milton's grammar is a clear, succinct text. He did not labor over definitions or examples, but instead, treated his grammar as a means to get into literature as quickly as possible. He states in *Of Education* that he would not include contemporaries such as William Bathe or Comenius in his teaching of grammar: "To tell you therefore what I have benefited herein among old renowned Authors, I shall spare; and to search what many modern *Janua's* and *Didactics* more then [sic] ever I shall read, have projected, my inclination leads me not" (364).[26]

Even though his name is sometimes linked with Comenius, Hartlib, and Dury, Milton departed from them in his pedagogy for teaching Latin. Milton attempted merely to clarify and simplify the traditional divisions of accidents and syntax, and thus remediate the pedagogical system. Comenius, in contrast, advocated a concentration on vocabulary alone without any study of accidents and syntax. He presented an encyclopedic collection of technical terms and rules, resulting in long lists of unconnected words without a scheme to link them all together.[27] In an attempt at cohesion he divided common words by subjects such as weather, trades, school, the body, hunting, and religion. He asserted that by acquiring a vocabulary and reading the language a student would learn grammar. What Comenius was really teaching, however, is a conversational grammar, lacking in humanistic and literary value. Comenius's Latin is a utilitarian one, not a preparation for reading classical authors and composing themes. Milton resisted the new methods of Hartlib and Comenius, trying instead to restore grammar, as it were, to its primitive purity. Milton did agree with Comenius and Hartlib that the traditional programs of learning Latin grammar were slow and tedious, but Comenius and Milton had different goals. To Milton, grammar was a step in the progression toward literature and composition, while for Comenius and Hartlib's circle, literature itself was far less important than what they called universal knowledge, or a gateway leading to a spiritual wisdom linked with nature.

Milton was not fond of grammarians; he claimed that they focused on details and theory without moving on to the real task at hand. Grammarians, he claimed, made their discipline all-important instead of seeing it as part of the whole educational process. When Milton wrote his grammar, he was not writing it as a grammarian, but as a pedagogue who knew what he wanted a student to learn in a framework and in a sequence of steps. His purpose was to correct other faulty Latin grammar texts. Milton did not labor over definitions or examples, because grammar was a means to an end for him, not the final product, as it was for other grammarians. The value of Milton's grammar, then, is that he concentrates on language at the coherent stage of *text* rather than on the atomized stage of *word*. Unfortunately, the rare simplicity of Milton's concise text pronounced its downfall. His grammar was lost in the midst of grammar texts promising "more for the money." It did not meet the needs of the rising classes, an economic factor that is still important to textbook publishing today.

Eighteenth-century grammarians thought they could improve on Milton's work by altering the grammar. Grammarians dictated a single word order for all writing situations, but rhetoricians discriminated among composing tasks and discussed a variety of syntactical patterns in prose and poetry. Grammarians clung to rules with an overly atomistic focus and wanted literature to conform to those precepts at all costs. Milton was the most frequent victim of their zeal to straighten what they saw as unnatural word order in poetry, probably because in the eighteenth century Milton was considered to be England's best poet. The opening of *Paradise Lost* was the repeated target of this correction:

> Of Man's first disobedience, and the fruit
> Of that forbidden tree, whose mortal taste
> Brought death into the world and all our woe
> With loss of Eden. Till one greater man
> Restore us, and regain blissful seat,
> Sing, Heavenly Muse.

Eighteenth-century grammarians objected to the long prepositional phrase in the opening five lines, yet this phrase was actually the English equivalent of what had once been a familiar Latin construction, in which the preposition *de* ("of") was followed by the topic to be discussed. Such phrases often occurred in Latin books at the beginnings of chapters or discussions, or even served as titles, as in Cicero's *De Oratore*, or Boethius's *De consolatione philosophiae*, or in the Renaissance, Eramus's *De copia verborum ac rerum*.

Grammarians, unable to sort out Milton's rhetorical techniques in his poetry, set about inflicting on school children exercises to straighten out what they called Milton's mistakes. Supposedly, students would learn grammar and writing from these assignments. In *Practical English Grammar* (1750), Ann Fisher presents exercises of transposition, the "process by which words were put out of their proper order. Fisher defines it as, "the placing of Words in a Sentence ... out of their natural Order, to render their Sound more harmonious and agreeable to the Ear" (122). She claims that "The clearest and best writers in Prose have the fewest Transpositions in their Discourses, and in Poetry they are never used but when the Nature and Harmony of the Verse require it; as, of Man's first Disobedience. ...The Order is thus: Heavenly Muse, sing of Man's first

Disobedience" (122). Fisher does not understand the rhetorical imperative of emphasis in presentation and tries to impose a grammatical imperative.

In *The First Six Books of Paradise Lost rendered into Grammatical Construction* (1773), James Buchanan proposes a similar technique to improve writing style. It is called resolution, or the "the unfolding of a Sentence, and placing all the Parts of it, whether expressed or understood, in their proper and natural Order, that the true meaning of it may appear" (217). But Buchanan never defines his terms "proper" and "natural." He adds elliptical, or missing understood words, and transposes other words to a position he considers a more natural word order. Buchanan presents the following transposition exercise:

> Original: Do you, Father, take in your Hand the sacred Symbols, and the Gods of our Country: For me just come from War, so fierce and recent Bloodshed, to touch them would be a Profanation, till I have purified myself in the living Stream.
>
> Transposed: Father, do you take in your Hand the sacred Symbols, and Father, do you take in your Hand the Gods, of our Country: For it would be a Profanation for me to touch them, who am just come from War, and who am just come from so fierce and from so recent a Bloodshed, till I have purified myself in the living Stream (217–18).

The problem with this exercise is that students could have been misled into thinking that a sentence must include every word that could be expressed and that every word must be in a "natural order." The exercise requires students to have a degree of sophistication in stylistics in order to understand why they are changing syntax. These exercises could have a negative effect if students thought the aim was simply to fill in missing words and force a sentence into a formulaic order that did not convey the intent of the author. The exercises also encouraged an artificial kind of writing that was bland and vacuous.

Milton was thus blamed for artificial writing and grammatical inexactitudes. Critics seemed to overlook that he wore both hats: he wrote a grammar text and he wrote rhetorical prose and poetry. When grammarians attacked him, they failed to see the transcendent pedagogical aims of his rhetorical structures. But not all eighteenth-century grammarians put Milton in the wrong. John Clarke recognizes that in ordinary speech:

> *Paradise Lost* would begin with an imperative, as "Sing, Heavenly Muse, of Man's first Disobedience," and so forth. Clarke mentions the context of the speaking situation: "the Nature of the Poem, the Harmony of the Numbers, and Turn of the Versification, seem to require the Transposition; it is in this Pace therefore properly used" (205–07).

Still, grammarians continued to find Milton guilty of unnatural word order.

Thus, in the seventeenth and eighteenth centuries, grammarians used the architectural metaphor to argue for reform in education. A strong foundation for learning, they claimed, must be part of curricula. For Comenius, learning was a gate through which one could reach divine knowledge and know God. In an innovative approach, he emphasized vocational skills and other relevant life experiences. He introduced a controversial method of teaching grammar in which a student learned by visible language, which some critics claimed was fragmented. Milton may have agreed with Comenius's argument that students should spend less time on learning grammar, but he differed in his emphasis on a humane education. Comenius de-emphasized literature while Milton placed importance on reading classical authors and learning Latin. Both men have influenced educational practices, but in ways that appealed to social and intellectual classes.

Notes

1 George A. Kennedy (1963:32).
2 Quintilian, books I and II.
3 Geoffrey of Vinsauf, trans. Kopp (1971:31–108).
4 Donatus, trans. Chase (1926), title page.
5 I am indebted to Professor Jameela Lares (University of Southern Mississippi) for these biblical references.
6 For architectural metaphors in sermons, see e.g. Allestree (1675:58); Hyperius, trans. Ludham (1577:110–11; Rodriguez (1697:I.208).
7 Wilkins (1646:4).
8 Wilkins (1668:62).
9 All quotes in this paragraph are from Comenius (1642:23).
10 Comenius (1633:56).
11 Dury said that he, Hartlib, and Comenius were part of a brotherhood: "though our taskes be different, yet we are all three in a knot sharers of one anothers labours, and can hardly bee without one anothers helpe and assistance" (1642:41–2), as cited in Webster (1974:107).
12 Turnbull (1947:185–90) notes Hartlib's and Comenius's discussions on the "building" of education. Turnbull was given the Hartlib papers by an office worker who did not want to store them any longer. Upon Turnbull's death his widow donated the Hartlib material to the University of Sheffield, and the Hartlib Papers Project was established to provide scholarly access.
13 Hartlib was so well known for his educational reform that his peers dedicated works to him (e.g., Milton [1644]). Snell (1649) praised Hartlib and Dury as "men notedly known for their earnest endeavours to promote the welfare of more profitabel learning, in English Schools."
14 Hartlib (1654:A3).
15 "*Omnia sponte fluant absit violentia rebus.*"
16 Webster, (1970:22).

17 Comenius saw language as a potential roadblock to educational progress. Latin, the language of the scholarly world, was often too difficult for the uneducated. He thought that a new universal language was the ideal answer, but he also recognized the difficulty of teaching an entire world a new language; he reconciled himself to Latin.
18 Webster (1970) provides the following helpful information: "The major section of the *True and Readie Way* is a translation of the 'didactic' of Eilhard Lubinus (1565–1621), which formed the preface of the 1617 edition of his trilingual New Edition (1–44). This is followed by a short essay, possibly written specifically for Hartlib, by Richard Carew of Anthony, Cornwall, who died in 1643 (45–49). Finally, there is a short extract from essay 25 of Montaigne's *Essays*, Book I (49–52). The texts by Lubinus and Montaigne had been discussed in chapters 7 and 8 of Comenius's *Linguarum methodus novissima* (1649). This discussion possibly determined Hartlib's choice of texts for the *True and Readie Way*" (192).
19 Keating (1898, 1910, repr. 1967:1–101) presents a lengthy biographical introduction to his translation of Comenius's *The Great Didactic*.
20 In 1658 *Orbis sensualium* pictus appeared for the first time as a Latin-German edition in Nuremberg and subsequently went through many editions in several countries over the next two hundred years. Per Bowen's introduction to his edition (1967:1), the *Orbis*, "was unique in its day both in conception and appearance. Many of its features, such as the numerous illustrations, the encyclopedic organization of content and the use of the vernacular language alongside Latin, were radical innovations that departed markedly from the traditional form in which Latin grammars were presented."
21 Bowen (1967:1) claims that Comenius was influenced by the bilingual texts of Irish Priest William Bateus of Salamanca, by the *Janua Linguarum* (*Gateway of Tongues*); by Eilhard Lubinus (1565–1621), a professor at the university in Rostock who sought a more meaningful approach to teaching language; and by Wolfgang Ratke (1571–1635), a disciple of Bacon and another scholar who wanted better language pedagogy (10–11). Comenius's own work on language pedagogy, *Janua Linguarum Reserata* (*The Gate of Tongues Unlocked*) (1631), consisted of ninety-eight topics divided into one hundred sections with one thousand sentences in different languages.
22 Per De Mott (1955), Bacon was the first Englishman to mention "real characters" and the first to insist on a precise meaning of words. See also Knowlson (1975) for an excellent discussion of Wilkins and Comenius; further useful discussions in Kroll (1990), and particularly Salmon (1979:129–56).
23 The University of Sheffield has placed on CD the correspondence of Joseph Webbe and John Dury to other members of the Hartlib circle. For biographical details on Joseph Webbe, see Salmon (1961). For those on John Dury, see Webster (1970) and Turnbull (1947).
24 Bathe (1615), *Janua Linguarum*.
25 Modern linguistic historians have ignored Milton's separation of grammar from writing and have paid almost no attention to his grammar book. The text has similarly received little attention from Milton scholars. The sole studies that consider it are J. Milton French (1961), Campbell (1976), and David P. French (1953–82).
26 Milton is referring to William Bathe's *Janua Linguarum* and Comenius's *The Great Didactic* (1632) and *Janua linguarum reserata* (1652).
27 For an extended discussion, see Corcoran (1911:44–49).

Chapter Three
The Battle: Good Grammar or Good Writing

School grammar texts of the seventeenth and eighteenth centuries do not look like the systematic grammar texts of our own period. The differences are often so great that we are apt to mistake earlier grammar texts for works in other genres. The writers of these texts did, in fact, work in other fields like agriculture while providing contexts and proposing practical applications for their grammars. As a result, a subtle shift of emphasis (either as intended by the author or as perceived by the reader – contemporary or modern) may be the only thing that distinguishes a text in grammar from one in rhetoric, in general education, or in popular self-help. To demonstrate what happens when grammarians attempted to put their grammars to work, we will explore a number of these border-incursions.

Grammarians responded to the needs of their middle-class audience in the seventeenth and eighteenth centuries by including material relevant to everyday lives and vocations. Their task was to provide a practical text that would help students function independently once they left the classroom. Many grammarians hoped that students who learned the lessons of a grammar text would, as a result, be competent in their jobs, productive in society, and effective in domestic relations. Curriculum was supposed to offer students the skills for ordering merchandise or writing letters of complaint to a landlord or delinquent customer.

Writing was an important survival skill. Grammarians, however, approached the teaching of writing from different perspectives. Some authors emphasized rhetorical approaches, such as plain versus eloquent styles in letter writing.[1] Others provided utilitarian manuals with step-by-step instruction for shop owners. Academic writing instruction leaned heavily on either literary forms or on classical rhetoric formulas. By the eighteenth century, rhetoric became a heavy influence on the teaching of writing in grammar texts, and grammar books also moved toward correctness in grammar as a standard upon which to measure the effectiveness of writing.

I. Putting Grammar to Work

Pedagogues of the seventeenth and eighteenth centuries argued that training students to do real-life tasks would be more beneficial than making them grind out academic exercises. This followed the general educational trend toward vocational relevance championed by educators like Comenius and Hartlib. Two types of writing skills were in demand in the English mercantile culture: writing letters, both for business and for personal correspondence, and writing commercial documents like receipts, contracts, and purchase orders. Letter-writing exercises appeared in traditional rhetoric texts as well as in school grammar texts. Instruction for commercial applications of writing were covered in what can perhaps be most accurately called self-help manuals, grammar texts that offered advice in a wide variety of life skills.

Business and personal correspondence Letter writing had been an important rhetorical form for centuries, and was one of the most common means of teaching writing in the seventeenth century.[2] Even John Locke recommends that schoolmasters dictate model letters for students to imitate and memorize.[3] Students who practiced letter writing had the same considerations as students of any good writing: audience, purpose, content, organization, and tone. The letter was a vehicle for teaching grammar, punctuation, vocabulary, and syntax. Instruction in letter writing also had a decided advantage over other kinds of writing because students knew exactly who would be reading and responding to their correspondence, whereas they had little sense of audience when they wrote a theme or composition. Despite the long tradition behind the pedagogical use of letter writing, however, in the seventeenth century there was an inherent conflict along class lines. Texts aimed at the upper class stressed elements different from those in texts aimed at the middle and lower classes.

Models of letters included in rhetoric books differ in context and purpose from those in grammar texts because the former were aimed at the more privileged classes with a wider circle of correspondence and more time on their hands. For business, social, or personal correspondence, rhetoric texts favored the eloquent prose of the aristocratic tradition, a prose that had flourish and style. Grammar books, on the other hand, promoted functional writing that would serve the most basic of purposes. As the middle classes rose in status, wealth, and education, they created a demand for instruction in a more utilitarian kind of letter writing. Grammarians taught letter writing with the barest attention to decorum and social requirements; rhetoricians assumed a higher level of letter-writing ability in their students and were, therefore, more concerned with social amenities and decorum.

Thomas Blount's *The Academy of Eloquence* (1654) contains a good example of letter-writing instruction aimed at the privileged class, the "youth of both Sexes," who are asked "to make the perusal of it their subservient Recreation for vacant houres" (Epistle Dedicatory). He assures them that his text "will not only facilitate your discourse into the moding language of these times, but adapt your pens too with a quaint & fluent stile." After his opening section containing "a more exact English Rhetorique," Blount provides a pair of sections on letter-writing formulas to be imitated. The first of these sections, "Formulae Majores, or, Common Places" has an alphabetical listing of topics likely to be encountered in correspondence, with "eloquent" examples of how one might write about them. For the first topic, "Absence," Blount provides the following formula: "As thou art the food of my thoughts, the relief of my wishes, and the onely life and repast of all my desires: So is thy love to me a continual hunger, and thine absence an extream famine" (49). Under the heading "Man commended," Blount offers: "He is the Orpheus, who with his looks onely, without setting his hand to the Lyre, enchants and ravishes the most savage of our Wilderness" (85).

A shorter section called "Formulae Minores, or, Little Forms," contains an assortment of what Blount describes as "Portals and postern dores of stile and speech, and of no smal use" (Preface). Examples of these short bits of fancy meant to liven up a young person's correspondence are "To Seal the Deed of my purchased favor, is the *Gordian* know I most wish to unloose" (119); "About the time that Candles begin to inherit the Suns office" (124); and "Whetting his tender wit upon the sandy stone of her edging importunity" (133). The text also includes a section with seventy-seven examples of letters for a variety of occasions, plus a section of superscriptions. *Academy of Eloquence* does its best to live up to Blount's promise: "Here shall you be furnisht with all necessary materialls and helps in order to the acquiring so great a treasure; such helps as have bin advised and often wisht for, but never before published" (Preface).

Another rhetoric text that illustrates the aristocratic approach to letter-writing instruction is *Wit and Eloquence* (1697), in which the anonymous author concentrates on decorum and style.[4] He claims that the book "answers on various subjects and Matters, as they relate to Love, Business, Friendship, Visit, Commendation, Consolation, and Familiar Letters, in a curious Stile" (1). Although he states on the first page that his manual has "Plain Directions for Inditing Letters on sundry Occasions," this letter-writing text is not designed for a middle-class clerk composing letters at the office or a housewife writing to her sister in the next village, but rather for the privileged person with a different level of social decorum: "I Present you with a Royal Posie, made up of the choicest Flowers of Wit and Eloquence, so fram'd and order'd, that it must consequently be pleasing to all Degrees and Capacities" (A2r). He goes on to announce, in fact, that the text will not be in plain style at all, "but so mix'd and interwoven with Variety of whatever is delightful, that, even intrenching somewhat on the strict Rules of Modesty, I am constrain'd to say, it exceeds all of this kind" (A2r). The book talks of fancy: "By it, either Sex may abundantly benefit their Understandings, and enlarge their Fancies to an immense Degree, in finding what they never hit on before in all their tedious Search or Reading" (A2r).

Letter writing for the upper class was expected to proceed at a leisurely pace with a refined style and purpose, and also with a certain degree of pretentiousness. *Wit and Eloquence* features letters such as "The Slighted Lover, to his Scornful Mistress" (12) and "A Letter from a passionate Lover, to his Mistress, upon receiving a Letter from her" (30). The titles of the chapters also reflect the concerns of an upper-class audience. One chapter purports to focus on the "Choice Rules To Write Letters of various Kinds, Dialogues, and the Art of Pointing, in Writing. Instructions for Gentiel and Courtly Breeding. With Art and Mystery of Making Love" (87). The author has instructed on how to "indict Letters"; now he will "lay down some brief Rules and Directions, that may be very useful" (87). Another chapter title reads, "Curious, Witty, and Quaint Dialogues, Relating to Love, Business, Intrigue, And many other Things, very pleasant and diverting to either Sex. Never before made Publick" (87). Both *Academy of Eloquence* and *Wit and Eloquence* appealed to an audience that associated itself with the courtly traditions of aristocratic Europe and England.

Wit and Eloquence would have shocked the middle class because by religious standards, it would have been immoral for them to think about letters directed to the mysteries of love and projected intrigues. If they were able to mull over the leisurely directions in the book to consider genteel and courtly breeding in letter writing, it would have been a sign that they had too much time on their hands. Moreover, for the middle and lower classes, instruction in letter writing was not directed to "either sex," but instead to a predominately male audience. A number of texts addressed the needs of rising classes.

George Snell describes a plain style of writing letters in *Right Teaching of Useful Knowledg* (1649). He recommends, "regent masters of the rural Schools should often dictate to their Scholars models, and forms of well penn'd letters to everie degree of persons ... that upon anie sudden occasion offer'd ... may bee abel to dispatch a well-composed letter, to anie person, of anie rank and qualitie" (104). Also, "Teaching Masters," he advises, "should caus the learners to inure themselves to the most useful phrases and forms of speech, for an Epistolarie stile: for there may beee a wittie choice made of words and expressions, which will give much grace and life to Epistolarie writing" (104–05). Snell simplifies the process for the letter writer by listing five rules that focus on audience awareness. The first rule states, when a writer uses "phrases of inchoation," he should be aware of whom he is addressing and assume the appropriate greeting. The writer "may give notice that hee is sensitive of the dignitie of the person to whom his Pen speaketh, and that hee is apprehensive of his own inferiortie" (105). The second rule urges the letter writer to be aware of tone. The writer should know some "Interlocutorie forms of speech to bee used now and then in the bodie of letters, importing duteous respect, unwillingness to bee troubelsom, desire to have his petition granted, his serious intent to bee thankful, his instant and urgent necessitie, the great benefit, that the favor prai'd may do him" (105). The third rule tells the writer to choose an appropriate closing to the letter. One must be careful to "conclude letters not insultly and abruptly, but with words leading to a mature cessation; and, as the manner now is, with a close and wittie phrase of transition leading to the Subscription" (106). In the fourth rule Snell advises the writer about the length and attitude of a letter. It should "not bee long, yet that the Subscription bee filled with verie affectuous, and vigorous words, expressing all fulness of thanks, of dutie, of honor, of service, and of all other omnimodous observance" (106). The fifth rule calls for perspicuity: "That the indorsment and direction bee made, with such cautions, titels, and additions, that nothing bee redundant, nothing deficient" (106–07). These five rules were fairly comprehensive in teaching basic writing instruction.

Snell also insists that the skill of letter writing can make people more successful in business matters. He claims, he who can "attein abilitie to express neatly and cautiously all sorts of affairs in missive letters, is in a readie waie to bee assumed to anie imploiment of highest importance" (107). Snell implies that people associate written articulation with social behavior. To be well regarded, one had to be able to express one's thoughts in such a way that business connections, family members, and distant friends could understand. Themes and compositions were schoolroom exercises that carried little relevance beyond the assignment, but letters were taken seriously because they served a social need. Snell says, "Good dexteritie in the skill of a letter-writer makes a Scholar so qualified, verie readie and abel to use curious language, and verie courteous speech, in his common talk" (107). Snell's manual was especially important to a student who expected to work as a scrivener. His instructions include directions for the completion of model letters and a "book of dictates for missive letters" (107). The manual focuses on preparing a student to perform tasks in his vocation and in his daily life: "A scholar well experienced in the art of a good Secretarie, shall bee well prepared for a laudabel doing of all civil duties" (108).

Ralph Johnson's *The Scholars Guide* (1665), a village grammar, also covers letter writing. One might note, however, that the instructions hardly seem like practical information for young students because of the erudite way he puts them in terms of traditional rhetoric.[5] First, Johnson defines an epistle as a "Discourse wherein we talk with an absent friend, as if we were with him." Next, he explains that epistles have four accidents or parts: "superscription," "compellation," "subscription," and "a date." But the style they are to be written in, according to Johnson, seems suited to the middle class: "low, short, and pithy" without "affectation, periphrase or garrulity." He advises that all epistles "shun Tautologies, by varying the phrase, when the same sence is repeated." Unlike other grammarians, Johnson divides letter writing into demonstrative, deliberative, or judicial categories. Although Johnson defines each type and gives numerous examples, he does not supply any models, apparently assuming that the writer will get them from his instructor.

In *The Young Secretary's Guide or, a Speedy Help to Learning* (1680), a manual that would go through many editions in England and America, J. Hill also models and explains various types of correspondence. His aim is to demonstrate to students the true "Method of Writing Letters upon any Subject." Hill suggests that it is "highly necessary, not only to give Instructions to those who are not fully qualified in this kind," but to help them understand various "measures taken in Inditing Letters, according to the Terms properly given them by the Learned" (105). He offers as models a "Hundred useful Letters written on sundry and various Occasions, adapted to the Affairs, Capacities, and whatsoever of the kind relates to either Sex, smooth and easie to be understood" (105). Hill, like his fellow grammarians, does not overlook the importance of good language in letters.

He advertises his manual as illustrating "Style and Dialect most New, and Modish, in a most accomplished manner, with the most Accurate Spelling, and Elegant Phrases, Distances, Familiarities" (105). Moreover, he discusses such issues of epistolary decorum as "Condescensions or Humiliations, according as the Letter refers to Superiors, Equals, or Inferiors, with Titles, Superscriptive and Subscriptive, relating to the same end and purpose" (105). He offers suggestions on style, which he calls "Fancy, or Imagination and form, that may add Lustre to things of this nature" (105). Hill's purpose is to prepare the middle-class student to handle any type of letter-writing situation and to know the form, the decorum, the grammar and punctuation, and the tone for each. His book is a compilation of every kind of letter one would want to write.

In addition to the business-letter formats, grammar books and manuals also included personal correspondence, often the only means of communication. In *The Compleat English Scholar* (1680), grammarian E. Young presents models of persuasive letters for students to copy. Such model letters include a father's advice to his son, a son's excuses to his father, and a dying lady's letter of inspiration. Other grammar books and manuals like Nathaniel Strong's *England's Perfect School Master* (1697) contained many of the same models.

Some grammarians used gimmicks to keep their students interested in letter-writing exercises. These techniques included models featuring everything from humor to morals. In *English examples to be turned into Latin* (1685) Edward Leedes has a section on letter-writing in which he uses devices like colorful names, witty narratives, and didactic lessons in examples of correspondence. He writes in the preface that he has "ventured to put odd and unusual names upon those that write, as well as those that are wrote to, alluding for the most part somewhat to the matter discoursed of between them." His intent is to "please and allure the young men, that they might with more cheerfulness address themselves to their businesses." He dismisses what readers may think of his innovation and states: "I am very well pleased, although I be thought to have play'd the fool." He captures a student's attention with his names: "William Walk-abroad to Simon;" "Shut-up sendeth greeting;" "Francis Forward to Leonard Loth-to't sendeth greeting;" "Giles Choose-well to Henry Hug-all sendeth greeting;" and "Thomas Tell-troth to Christopher, Come-late sendeth greetings" (99).

Another important element, Leedes explains, rests on the point of view of the person receiving the correspondence. "An Epistle," he states, is "a writing that contains the talk or discourse of persons absent" (101). He advises a student to think of the receiver as someone in the room with whom a conversation is being carried out. Leedes explains several types of epistles: "Narratory, where we tell of any thing done. Petitory, where we ask some thing. Commendatory, where we recommend any person." For the purposes of his text Leedes takes a practical approach: "But in the Examples which we shall set down, we shall content our selves with such confused and trifling matter, as boyes use to talk among themselves; for they are the persons to whom we must accommodate all we write here"

(101). The author reminds the reader that the "Ancient Latins used to set the names both of him that rote, and him that was wrote to, at the beginning of their Epistles; and are followed by the most admired men of the latter Age; as, Erasmus, Budaeus, Thomas More, Scaliger, Vives" (101).

Leedes reinforces the idea of correctness both in grammar and in writing instruction. He warns the reader that the model letters he will use to imitate the Latin ones will seem a "little uncouth, and not fitted to the present way of writing in England, for though we write in English words, yet we do it with a design, that boys may thereby learn how to indite their Latin Letters." He directs the correspondent to write letters in a simple, plain style. Leedes anticipates an audience of schoolboys who would rather be outside playing ball, and he hopes to keep their attention by asking them to write letters as if they were talking among themselves. Instead of performing a boring academic exercise, the boys chat in letters about matters that interest them, yet learn the decorum required of them in vocational tasks. His first "uncouth" model letter is from John Seaman who "Sendeth greeting" to William Smith:

> Tis now a year well nigh (dear Will) since I saw you, and with what trouble of mind I have born the want of you, you may perhaps guess, if ever you were separated from any one so long that you loved so much. 'Twas the fear of the Pox I know that drove you away from us, and now the spreading of that disease is ceased, why should we still be kept a sunder? I hope that day will come ere long when we shall see one another, (and which was ever a great pleasure to me) play together. Given at Bury the fifteenth of the Kallends of March, in the year of our Lord (101–02).

The models in Leedes's text illustrate his points cleverly.

Leedes experiments with a technique not seen in other grammar books: glossing. In his model letters he numbers various elements, then provides corresponding words of explanation. The method is pedagogically sound in that students learn several skills simultaneously: syntax, tone, spelling, vocabulary, and composition. The following letter from Thomas Talk-well to Henry Do-little illustrates the number system:

> Tis very unpleasant news, which I heard lately (my dear Harry) that you are about to leave us and the School, and for no other Reason, but that you begin to perceive that if you be 2) a Scholar, you must take pains; it were fine 3) indeed, if when the Master readith and you open your mouth instead of your ears, it should presently be filled with all kind of Eloquence, and you should speak Orations as learned as those of Tully or Demonsthenes. But, my dear Harry, that can't 4) be; the way 5) up the two headed hill is not so easie, thou mayest if thou pleasest go home, and whilst thy Father is abroad, 6) bear thy Mother company; but with a short while thy Age will alter thy judgment, and 7) thou wilt be ashamed of thy employment, and 8) repent of thy laziness and folly as long as thou livest. Farewel, and if thou canst in time be wise (103).

[*Corresponding Key*]
1. res ingrata
2. learned
3. pulchrum
4. i.e. be done
5. which leadeth up
6. i.e. fit with thy Mother
7. it will shame thee
8. it will repent thee

From the model, students observed that a message could be phrased in several ways. Leedes hoped that glossing would help students improve their writing style in letters.

A few grammar texts, such as Charles Gildon's *Grammar of the English Tongue* (1723), combined both grammar and rhetoric in letter-writing instruction for the middle classes. Consistently aware of audience, Gildon guides the reader through "an easie and genteel way of conveying our Mind in the shortest and most expressive Terms" (193). With a focus on how a listener receives the message, Gildon advises, "Business requires no Ornaments, and a plain and succinct Information is all that is requir'd." In the text Gildon argues, "Letters of Complement must have Gaiety, but no Affectations. Easiness must shine thro' all, and a clean Expression; here is no room for the Luxuriance of Fancy, or the embellishments of longer discourses." The same may be said, according to him, of condolence, and even of persuasion. Gildon insists on plain arguments without embellishment and wordiness. Of argument, the "most poignant and coercive Reasons must be us'd, and those that by want of Native Force require Help of Art to recommend them laid aside" (194).

Another text that included grammar and rhetoric aimed at the middle-class is Anne Fisher's *A New Grammar* (1757). Fisher, one of the few women to publish a grammar text, provides directions for writing business letters and for addressing persons of quality. She begins by explaining that a "Tradesman's Letter should be plain, concise, and to the Purpose" (151–52). It should be "free from stiff, or studied Expressions; always pertinent, and writ in such Words, or Terms, as carry a distinct Meaning with them." The person receiving the letter should not have the "least Hesitation or Doubt about the Meaning of any Words, Part, or Order, contained therein." Fisher also requires that all "Orders, Commissions, and material Circumstances of Trade" must be stated clearly and exactly. More importantly, "nothing should be presumed, understood, or implied in obscure or ambiguous Terms," and the writer should also take care to answer all the questions addressed to him in the letter he has received. As for style, letters should be "neat, significant, and as concise as the Nature of the Subject will admit." Fisher says to "write to your Correspondent as you would talk to him, and without any formal uncommon Phrases." In letter writing one must also be "frank and affable without

Impertinence, obliging and complaisant without Bombast or Flattery." She notes, "nothing is more rude and unmannerly than to praise People to themselves" (152).

Fisher not only outlines the kind of letter a tradesman is to write, she also describes the style he should have. She warns the writer never to "affect high or hard Terms," but to write to the intelligence of the specified audience. As for social restrictions, she advises the writer not to attempt to write letters of "Wit, Humour, or Railery... until you become Master of such good Sense" and "good Breeding." The writer needs to learn from "Reading" and "Experience" what is "Pure, Moral, or Polite" and what is "Gross, Immoral, or Impure." The writer does not want to use wit or satire on improper subjects and appear "surprisingly ridiculous" (152). Fisher says that one must address the correspondent correctly, and she includes a chart that starts with royalty and moves down the social scale to servants and children.

In the preface to *The British Grammar* (1761), James Buchanan discusses the importance of teaching style through letter writing. He complains about the insufficient instruction students receive for a difficult task: "We have often seen the Writing of Letters recommended, without ever a Word of first forming a young Gentleman's Style; notwithstanding epistolary Correspondence, requires the most concise and purest Vein of Language, and is acknowledged by all Judges to be the most difficult Form of Writing" (xxvii). For instruction, he states, authors have provided collections with models of letters, "most of which are wretched," for students to copy (xxvii). He sees value, however, in using models through which young scholars learn about the "ruling Passions and distinguishing Characters of Men," the "Consequences of Actions," "Duties belonging to human Life," the "Rules of private and public Conduct," and the "Corruptions of Mankind, and the Snares and Temptations of the World." These model letters, Buchanan agrees, would introduce students "to the Knowledge of Mankind, and prepare them for appearing on the Stage of public Life with Honour and Advantage" (xxviii). Buchanan proposes his own method of teaching the difficult task of letter writing, one in which the teacher and the student read the letter orally and ask for responses (xxviii–xxix). Buchanan argues that this method works particularly well in teaching writing because students of all ages like to be treated as "rational Creatures" (xxix). Not all authors recognized the rhetorical value of reading aloud a piece of writing.

Charles Johnson's *The Complete Art of Writing Letters* (1779) is "Adapted to All Classes and Conditions of Life." As the rest of the title indicates, the text contains letters for all the duties one would expect to perform in life: "*Entertaining and Instructive Letters, as Examples for Improvement of Style; With an agreeable Variety of Original Letters on Education, Duty, Courtship, Marriage, Amusement, Business, Friendship, Compliment, Trade, and Modern Fashions.*" Besides including a "useful" grammar, Johnson also recognizes that correspondence is one of the most frequent writing tasks: "There is scarcely any Species of Composition deserves more to be cultivated, than the *Art of Writing Letters*, since none is of more various or frequent Use, through the whole Course of human Life" (A2r). As letters are "written on all Subjects" and "all States of Mind," he argues, "they cannot be properly reduced to settled Rules, or described by any single Characteristic" (A2r). A correspondent should be familiar with forms of letter writing, he advises, and he should observe qualities of epistolary style, such as "Ease and Simplicity, an even Flow of unlaboured Diction, and an Artless Arrangement of obvious Sentiments" (A2r). Letters, Johnson explains, are like "polite Conversation" that should be filled with "Affection; Ease, Elegance, Perspicuity, and Correctness" (21). The correspondent should be diligent in building a good foundation of "Purity of Language, and an easy, happy Style" that will produce a "glorious Superstructure" of "Sincerity of Thought, and Elegance of Expression" (21). The writer should write as if he is talking to a friend who is present, rather than "express far-fetched Conceptions" that require "stiff and formal Language, which is not more unpleasing to the Ear than disgustful to the Heart" (22). Johnson continues, "Graces of Writing and Conversation are of different Kinds; and though he who excels in one, might have been, with Opportunities and Application, equally successful in the other" (22).

Some letter-writing manuals included instruction in English grammar, such as George Brown's *The New English Letter-Writer* (1779). "Every letter," he states, "should convey some instructive precepts; and while we make use of pleasantry, we should never forget duty" (B1r). Brown recognizes that, for each writing situation, the writer should have "an accurate knowledge of the subject, and the circumstances of the person to whom we address ourselves" (B2r). Tone, he explains, is also important in writing: "In all letters let truth be the principal object in view; let no falsehood be inserted, and then there can be no inconsistency. If the letter is to contain an accusation of the conduct of a young person, let it be written in tenderness; for if otherwise, it will never be attended with any beneficial consequences" (B2r). For tradesmen, he recommends, "If on business in the mercantile world, let every thing be so clear, as not to admit of a doubt when you come to settle account. This will prevent many anxieties which often take place in families, and secure a part of the property which is often squandered away in suits of law" (B2r–B2v). And on a personal level, he observes, "In love and courtship, unless sincerity take place, no happiness can be expected: let a love-letter contain the language of the heart, and let that heart contain nothing but what is innocent" (B2v). Brown continues to reinforce the precept that sincerity in writing will make a letter "flow with elegance," and as the writer "improves his own rational faculties," he will "instruct and entertain his correspondents" (B2v). If the writer follows these rules, he will never "write with impropriety," and he need only keep careful watch over his grammar (B2v). So that all may acquire correct grammar, Brown has "Adapted [it] to the meanest Capacities" (B3r). In all writing,

"Grammar is the art of one human creature speaking to another, so as to be understood" (B3r).

Another manual worth noting for grammar and writing instruction is Thomas Cooke's *The Universal Letter-Writer* (1788). The manual, aimed at the middle class, includes instruction on how to write business letters with the "greatest perspicuity and brevity observed by the different correspondents" (18). Cooke states that these "rules may be applied to all other subjects, and conditions of life, viz. a comprehensive idea of the subject, and an unaffected simplicity, through modesty in expression" (18). Within a "few months," if the student takes the rules seriously, his time will not have been spent "in vain." If the writer pays "careful attendance to the plain and simple rules laid down in the preceding Grammar," he will be able "to write in the language of the present times; and if he carefully avoids affectation, his thoughts will be clear, his sentiments judicious, and his language plain, easy, sensible, elegant, and suited to the nature of the subject" (18). Cooke reminds the correspondent that letters are like conversations: "Just consider what you would say to your friend if he was present, and write down the very words you would speak, which will render your epistle unaffected, and intelligible" (18).

The Complete Letter-Writer (1797), a self-teaching manual for the middle and lower classes, provides extensive, yet simple directions. It forbids "quaint Expressions," "Book Phrases," "Flourishes," contractions, and abbreviations (50). Additionally, there are seven rules for writing letters: project a good attitude; do not show disrespect in letters; create an ethos; be clear; close a letter properly; write letters on fine post paper; seal the letter and address it properly (44–45). These practical rules for writing business letters were important for the tradesman. With them he established his professional ethos. By refraining from the use of contractions, he avoided a too familiar tone. By closing his letter with his name in larger print than that in the body of the letter, he prevented someone from adding text.

Self-Help Manuals Self-teaching manuals addressed a special need of the rising classes. Schoolmasters often would teach the skills of writing such documents as bill collections, bonds, acquitances, memorandums, covenants, indentures, and contracts. This kind of occupation-related writing made up the kind of schoolroom education for which reformers like Samuel Hartlib and Johann Amos Comenius had argued earlier in the seventeenth century, an education relevant to a student's life rather than one filled with useless information. In their adult lives, students of the middle-classes would not always have access to someone who could perform these tasks for them. However, if they did not get the instruction in a school setting, self-help manuals made up for the lack, outlining the process of drafting these documents.

Many popular texts like E. Young's *The Compleat English Scholar* (1680) offer examples of common writing tasks a student might be expected to perform. These models include bills of sale, agreements, merchandise ordering, and descriptions of services and products. J. Hill's *The Young Secretary's Guide or, a Speedy Help to Learning* (1680) went through numerous editions in England and America. Hill presents an "exact Collection of Acquitances, Bills, Bonds, etc." and clear instructions for legal writing that one could do at home (105). In an attempt to sell his text, he claims that if a person does not have an attorney or a scrivener handy, his manual will provide the models for writing legal documents, saving both time and money. He also argues that being able to write these documents may prove helpful to one's friends and neighbors when the work has to be done immediately.

Books that included both grammar and business English skills were published until the end of the seventeenth century. An unusual manual, William Mather's *Young Man's Companion* (1695) included not only business English instruction but also a wide range of diverse subjects. In this text Mather provides instructions for pruning fruit trees, treating breast cancer, experimenting with honey bees, making wines, and keeping teeth white. He suggests a method for treating "Burns or Scalds": "Immediately dip a four double Linen Cloth in the Juice of new Horse-dung, and apply it often to fetch out the Fire" (99). For "Bruises" he offers this treatment: "Apply fry'd Camomil, or Cows dung with Hogs Lard, or use the Red-lead Plaister" (99). For Bleeding at the Nose" he recommends, "Tye very hard the middle Bone of the little Finger, and hang a dead Toad in a Purse about the Neck, stuffing into the Nostrils the ashes of a burnt Hat, mixt with Rabbets Wool, and drink such things as increase but little Blood, and take heed of violent motion of Body" (100). To "preserve the Sight," he advises, "Wet your Eye-lids every Night with your own Urine" (105). He provides remedies for problems with vomiting, urine, worms, mouth sores, and rashes. And at "Sings of being Bewitched," Mather suggests, "Tye Quick silver in Parchment, and put it in the Feather Pillow (that the Parties lie on) two weeks after you will find the Featahers in Antick work" (115). Mather also interjects advice to husbands on how deal with women's pride.

Among these unusual remedies for illnesses and instructions for running a household and farm, Mather includes a grammar section and offers examples of writing tasks. He has models of letters from a scholar to his friends, an apprentice to his father, an excuse from a son to his father, and a letter of advice from a father to a son (66–69). The texts have generous instructions and models for business tasks. He offers the common man a list of terms used in law "Together with some necessary points in Law" to make Bonds, Bills, and the most necessary Precedents and Conveyances" (157–60). Mather supplies abundant models of legal and business writing tasks, such as memoranda for leasing a house or land, covenants in which the landlord agrees to free the tenant of tithes and taxes, indentures for servants, acquitances for money, bonds such as wills and marriage agreements, and deeds of sale (165–207). In the last section of the manual, Mather includes instruction for religious training and arithmetic and finally his own letter to children, entreating them to continue to love virtue and turn away from the learning of Latin and the classics. He advises them, "Do not corrupt the Knowledge which God has given you, (by learning at Latine Schools) lascivious Books, and Stage-Play-Books, too much in use in these days" (450). He advises pedagogues and students "not [to] imitate the vain Grammarian's Heathenish strain" (451). He hopes that the reading of classical authors of "such Heathenish Learning may be banished out of a Nation professing Christianity" (452).

While Mather offers a variety of utilitarian skills for the middle-class, by contrast, George Fisher's *New Spelling Book* (1700) focuses on spelling and related tasks such as accounting, receipts, and business records (77–86). In a section on "The Form of a Letter," George Fisher provides directions on "How to write to any Person of what quality soever, i.e. as to Title, Appellation, or as some term it, Internal or External Superscription" (80–81). He advises, "As to the Matter or Business of Writing, that's so various, and uncertain, that no Rule can be prescribed" (81). "Always observe," Fisher urges, "that Tautologies, or Repetitions are unpleasant; and be sure you rather give too much, than too little Honour, to the person you write to" (81). Fisher includes the usual example of a dutiful son writing to his father expressing respect and asking for "some Commands from you [his father], that by the performance thereof, I may manifest myself" (81). The author then lists three pages of titles of respect a correspondent may use to address someone in a letter (82–6).

A manual such as William Gordon's *The Young Man's Companion* (1765) was a no-nonsense instructional text on letter writing, as well as on measuring,[6] gardening, arithmetic, geometry and trigonometry (26). It is "adapted to the lowest capacity" in order to make it available to everyone, and Gordon urges the letter-writer to adopt a plain style.[7] People needed models of letters and other business correspondence to complete daily transactions. Besides providing the important business forms, the manuals also offered valuable writing instruction that a majority of users had never received in schools.

II. Rhetoric Subsumes Grammar: Grammar Texts as Rhetoric Handbooks

For centuries the trivium of grammar, logic, and rhetoric had been taught as three separate disciplines in three separate textbooks. For example, schoolmasters and tutors might choose two texts by the Port Royalists, *Grammaire générale et raisonnée* (1660) and *La Logique ou l'art de penser* (1662), and then Bernard Lamy's *La Rhétorique ou l'art de parler* (1676). By mid-seventeenth century, however, some grammar books began to include logic and rhetoric, causing grammarians to look at their discipline in a new way. They were forced to look at changes in classroom practice as rhetoric subsumed grammar and logic to form the basis of the rhetoric handbook that is still used for composition classes today.

Traditional grammar texts were more-or-less systematic in the modern sense of a grammar text: parts of speech, tenses, syntax, punctuation, spelling, and so on. The traditional text used in the latter part of the sixteenth century and into the seventeenth was William Lily's *Short Introduction to Grammar*, first published in 1527 and required in the classroom by royal edict in 1542. Grammarians could buy additional grammar books for their own reference, but they had to teach from Lily's text. To get around the royal edict, grammarians "corrected" and "improved" Lily's text.

In the early part of the seventeenth century, grammarians tried to phrase part of Lily's explanation of Latin grammar in the vernacular. By mid-century students favored vernacular explanations of Latin grammar. In an effort to resist the use of the vernacular to teach Latin, Thomas Farnaby wrote *Systema Grammaticum* (1641), an all-Latin text resembling Lily's. Farnaby made a conscious effort to recreate Lily's text because he believed a child should master Latin in order to read, translate, and memorize the classics. His text did not sell very well because teachers found their job easier when they used Latin textbooks partially written in English. Moreover, schoolmasters began realizing that an all-Latin text would not serve the vocational needs of some of the students. Farnaby's commercial failure suggests a pedagogical failure: an all-Latin text no longer worked. Another failure was Ralph Robinson's *An English Grammar or, a plain Exposition of Lilies Grammar in English* (1641). Robinson's grammar was one of the most competent adaptations of Lily in the seventeenth century, but his book was no more popular than Farnaby's because it, too, dealt with Latin grammar in great detail.

Charles Hoole tried to improve on Lily's text and still adhere to the royal edict. In *Latine Grammar* (1651) Hoole gets around the edict by saying that he is going to "translate" Lily's text and "correct" his mistakes. His changes are so numerous, however, that he is, in effect, writing his own new textbook of Latin grammar. He adds commentary, deletes parts of Lily's text, and rearranges rules and other material. His most significant change is a bilingual format, with the Latin text on the left-hand page and the English translation on the right-hand. His book was enormously popular, but it also sparked controversy because some traditional grammarians said the English translation would make schoolboys lazy.

John Milton's *Accedence Commenc't Grammar* (1669) is another traditional Latin text with much of the explanation in English. A comparison of Lily's grammar with that of Milton's shows that Milton's grammar is one of the best recensions of Lily, and it deserves far more credit than it has ever received. Other grammarians merely rephrased the wordy and repetitive Lily, but Milton summarized him succinctly. The difficulty of performing this task at all – let alone gracefully – is evidenced by the number of awkward and disjointed paraphrases of Lily that clutter the landscape of seventeenth-century pedagogy. In contrast, Milton omits or compresses many rules, explanations, and examples, and alters the presentation of other rules.[8] Lily, for example, lists fourteen figures of speech on six and one half pages, while Milton lists only six figures altogether. He finds a way to combine the "accidence," or study of individual words, with more global considerations such as syntax, even though in Milton's period accidence was usually dealt with in a separate treatise. In general, Milton targets what needs to be added, omitted, or altered in Lily's text and he does so clearly and concisely. He cuts some items such as prayers and long examples, but he leaves quotations in place to teach manners. Milton had a greater sense of how to improve the established school text than did the other grammarians in the seventeenth century.

Grammar Texts as Rhetoric Handbooks As educational opportunities for lower classes increased, the traditional school grammar was not always functional. A student would be fortunate to have one text for grammar, logic, and rhetoric, not three, and as grammar texts that included sections on logic and rhetoric began to appear, they marked a shift in the paradigm toward the association of grammar books with rhetoric texts, as they are associated today. Texts of this type have been overlooked in the history of language, possibly because they deviate from our own preconceptions as to what constitutes a seventeenth- or eighteenth-century grammar book or rhetoric text. These misconceptions are based on later canonical works, like the influential texts of Bishop Lowth (1762) and Lindley Murray (1795), and which lead us to expect from an early grammar text the same dry formulae.

The first handbook of this type, often overlooked by scholars, is most likely Ralph Johnson's *The Scholars Guide* (1665), a popular classroom text that went through nine editions. The first part of the book consists of traditional grammar, and the second instructs the student how to write colloquies, essays, fables, themes, epistles, declamations, translation, epitaphs, hymns, and orations. The textbook was unusual for that period because it combines the teaching of many skills in one book: grammar, rhetoric, logic, composition, elocution, poetry, reading skills, and letter writing. Another non-traditional item in his grammar book is a section on moving the passions, or engaging the emotions of an audience, from Book II of Aristotle's *Rhetoric*. His rules for making an essay are taken from Cicero's *Topics* and his instructions for declamations and orations come straight from Aristotle, Cicero, and Quintilian. Johnson's text has been overlooked in the history of language because it deviates from the paradigm of what a seventeenth century grammar book should look like. It might look superficial to a scholar who wants to research in depth any one of the three disciplines of grammar, logic, or rhetoric. An historian of logic would not be impressed by Johnson's formulae for invention. An historian of rhetoric would want to see more than a few classical phrases on the techniques of delivery. Furthermore, the instruction on writing and speaking would not look as comprehensive as Henry Felton's *Dissertation of Reading the Classics* (1713) or Thomas Wilson's *Many Advantages of a Good*

Language (1724). But these judgments lack an appreciation for how Johnson combines all these disciplines to form what we can call the first "modern" rhetoric handbook, one created specifically for the rising classes.

A Grammar of the English Tongue (1712) by Charles Gildon is another grammar text that resembles handbooks used in twentieth-century classrooms. The 1711 edition is strictly a grammar book. In the 1712 edition, however, grammar occupies only half this text; the remainder is filled with detailed, lengthy chapters on logic and rhetoric. Gildon also includes detailed, lengthy chapters on speaking, writing, and reading skills aimed at the rising classes. For teachers using the book, there is even a discussion on linguistic theory. The 1712 grammar edition is a remarkable text for its time because a variety of skills previously available only to the more privileged were finally accessible to the rising classes. Only a few grammarians like Ralph Johnson (1665) and Michael Maittaire (1712) attempted to include logic and rhetoric as a formal part of a grammar. Gildon states in the preface that he has written the best chapters in England on logic and rhetoric. The chapter on rhetoric is comprehensive, and the one on logic is so long it has to be divided into three sections. He argues that logic and rhetoric are crucial for study because they develop the student's mind and refine his style.

Another unusual facet of *A Grammar of the English Tongue* is that it also provides more directions for composition than any other grammar in the seventeenth and eighteenth centuries. For instance, the text includes instruction on various kinds of writing, such as oration, in which Gildon emphasizes not only a structured approach, but one reflecting social context as well. The writer is advised to be sensitive to time, place, and person in choosing the appropriate material for his audience. These instructions are standard in rhetoric, but they do not appear in other grammar texts contemporary with *A Grammar of the English Tongue*, beginning with the 1712 edition. In another section of the text, Gildon advises the writer of essays to be free, easy, and natural. In this context of writing essays, the writer is not limited to defined forms and audience restrictions, and he therefore can be more creative.

Michael Maittaire's *English Grammar* (1712) is not as extensive a treatment as that of Gildon's, but it still combines grammar, logic, and rhetoric. The author also explains punctuation rules that make smoother syntax, and he discusses grammar according to the four considerations of letters, syllables, words, and sentences. In an unusual move he includes a short section of grammatical and rhetorical tropes and figures, classified by what he calls the two kinds of "schemes of confirmation," that is, either clear illustration or convincing argument. The material on tropes and figures is shorter than it would be in a standard work of *elocutio*, but its inclusion is itself a deviation from the norm of grammar books of the time. His particular selections are not in and of themselves significant, but rather that he has selected from them at all. For instance, in the chapter on composition he discusses style, imitation, types of writing, and classical rhetoric. He even includes a detailed chapter on elocution, that is, voice and gesture, and his discussion of *pronuntiatio* includes how to deliver each of the various parts of an oration. Few other grammar books of the period include these items.

Looking at changing dictionary definitions, we may trace more theoretically how rhetoric subsumed grammar. In *World of Words*, (1658) Edward Phillips views the three disciplines as a correspondence between word and concrete referent. He defines grammar as the method of attaining a language by certain rules, logic as the art of correct disputation, and rhetoric as the art of speaking well and eloquently. His definition at this date shows little concern with either how the mind performs these activities or how society perceives them. Yet, in the 1696 edition of Phillips's *World of Words*, definitions begin to move toward a concern for the mental processes by which each discipline is practiced. Grammar is now the art of knowing how to "decline, conjugate, conster, and spell Nouns, Verbs, and other parts of Speech." Logic receives a great deal of attention in this edition. It is the "Art of disputing probably in any Argument. It is also the Art that teaches certain Rules to Define, Divide, Distinguish, and Argue. Furthermore, it is a Collection of Rules, by which the Mind of man is directed in its Operations to find out the Truth." All three disciplines – grammar, logic and rhetoric – are beginning to be described as acts of cognition.

But in the 1720 edition of Phillips's *World of Words*, the focus on mental processes that dominated the second edition has evolved into a focus on people and their acts of communication. Grammar is now defined as the "Art of Speaking and Writing truly, established by Custom, Reason and Authority." Phrases like "custom, reason, and authority" evidence a social aspect that was not a factor in earlier definitions. This is also true for Phillips's definition of logic, which begins by describing logic as the "art of Thinking, Reasoning, or making a right Use of the Rational Faculty," but then adds the socially significant phrase "which chiefly consists in shewing how to make proper Remarks on the Operations of the Mind." Finally, rhetoric is the art of "speaking well and eloquently; a Science that teaches to find out things most proper to persuade."[9] In this definition, we have a social requirement as well – a dictum that arguments must be socially appropriate – but then formal rhetoric has always included a consideration of time, place, and persons. Of the three definitions, rhetoric changes the least; it does not need to change. It already represents the direction in which all three disciplines are moving.

Texts like those of Johnson, Gildon, and Maittaire that combine the three disciplines of grammar, logic, and rhetoric are the links to the future development of twentieth-century composition texts. Although the three disciplines are all included under the heading of grammar, it is rhetoric that is already the most socially conscious discipline, and it is rhetoric into which the other two disciplines will eventually be subsumed for communication-type schoolbooks.

When we conflate the term "grammar" with "grammar text," we lose sight of the innovations and advances grammarians made in the teaching of language and the separation of independent subjects from grammar itself. We also do not take into account the social, political, and economic factors that influenced the content of those books. If we try to define grammar synonymously with grammar books, we overlook such things as the emergence and final separation of "rhetoric" from "grammar," not as these two terms had been defined for centuries, but as they were understood at the time in terms of theory and practice. We also lose sight of the important merger of communication skills with the discipline of grammar, a merger that becomes significant in the eighteenth century.

Authors of textbooks included logic and rhetoric in part because of how they understood the structure of language and the activities of people's minds. To them, logic was the discipline of thinking, grammar the discipline of memorization, and rhetoric the discipline of which brought together the first two. Rhetoric no longer meant elocution, and it became an umbrella for grammar and logic. We might say that when the three disciplines of grammar, logic, and rhetoric were combined, that rhetoric was the winner. Even though rhetoric always received the least amount of space among the three disciplines in grammar books, it was rhetoric nevertheless that subsumed grammar and logic and provided the principles around which the texts were organized. Perhaps because rhetoric received the least amount of attention in textbooks it could become the encompassing term for the other two disciplines. The English and American rhetoric and composition texts of the twentieth century appear to be direct descendants of the combined grammars from the early modern period.

III. Grammar Texts and Composition in the Schoolroom

In the seventeenth century, upper-class students followed the centuries-old practice of studying the trivium of grammar, logic, and rhetoric.[10] Tutors drew from sources like Aristotle's *Rhetoric* and the anonymous *Rhetorica ad Herennium* for instruction on how to develop an argument.[11] They also used Cicero to teach eloquence in writing, speaking, and reading with a special emphasis on analysis and illustration.[12] Writing exercises would be composed in Latin, translated into English, and then back to Latin. Students learned to write in the demonstrative, deliberative, and judicial modes. They studied the topics and causal relationships, and they analyzed the structure of an oration by breaking it into parts, such as preamble, narration, proof, and conclusion. A student of rhetoric followed this process in constructing an argument: learning one of the categories of analysis, memorizing some illustrations of that category, imitating one of the models using a familiar topic, writing a theme on an already-familiar topic, comparing that theme with that of an earlier author, and memorizing the earlier theme.

This process of constructing an argument worked well for elite students because of their training in logic and rhetoric. This curriculum, however, did not work well for middle-class children who had little or no background in Cicero or traditional rhetoric. As children entered large classrooms in the seventeenth century, schoolmasters were forced to streamline traditional rhetoric to satisfy the requirements of so many students. School children had little need to construct complicated classical arguments; instead, they required the kinds of communication skills that would help them function in their utilitarian world.

Relations with traditional rhetoric Grammar books that taught composition usually included discussions of traditional rhetoric – ranging from invention to figures of speech – not because grammarians were rhetoricians but because the rhetorical material seemed like a natural way to help students learn to organize their thoughts and put them on paper. The claim, such as that of Adam Smith at the end of this period, that rhetoric was a waste of time and not instructive should be viewed in the context of what grammarians were including in grammar books.[13] Although grammarians appear to have been rejecting traditional rhetoric, it was impossible to eliminate it. Traditional rhetoric is a means of collating thoughts into some kind of order and expressing them with perspicuity (at least, to an audience similarly trained), and grammarians did not have a better system to replace what had been practiced for centuries.

Indeed, grammarians were finding that they could, without too much difficulty, modify traditional rhetorical techniques to accommodate what schoolmasters needed to teach in village schoolrooms. Traditional rhetoric could be useful in teaching the less privileged a framework for thinking and writing as well as in forming an attractive association with what was taught to upper classes. With increased opportunities in education, the coming of the industrial age, and the rise of the middle class, parents held schools more accountable than ever before for the vocational training of their children. In *The Scholar's Guide* (1665) Ralph Johnson compiled a simple text that is succinct, clear, and relevant. He based the grammar on his earlier study entitled *Ancilla grammaticae* (1663), which in turn was taken from other grammatical treatises.[14] Johnson offers a wide range of skills in logic, rhetoric, poetry, and composition that are readily applicable to many situations in life.[15] With an eye on various ability levels, he does not go into abstruse, extended explanations, but rather offers succinct definitions and instructions. The lack of examples indicates that the schoolmaster had the only copy of the text and would use his own models as he explained the precepts.

Johnson's grammar is unusual for the period in that it includes the trivium. He takes rules from Aristotle's *Rhetoric* for moving the passions, that is, arousing emotions in the audience in order to persuade it. It is unusual for grammar texts in the seventeenth and eighteenth centuries to teach the passions, yet Johnson has a full list: fear, confidence, shame, joy, anger, lenity, love, hatred, indignation, envy, and pity (2.1–17).[16] Johnson discusses the composition of a "theme," which he describes as a "discourse amplifying a subject, by shewing the meaning and proving the truth thereof" in terms of its eight parts: *exordium, narratio, causa, contrarium, simile, exemplum, testimonium,* and *epilogus* (16). He defines oration as a "discourse wherein we praise, or dispraise; persuade, or dissuade; prove, or disprove" (19). Then he notes the three kinds of orations: demonstrative, deliberative, and judicial. He also includes a section on "declamations," for which he outlines the rules of each of the four kinds: "conjectural," "finitive," "qualitative," and "quantitative" (23). Johnson conflates Greek and Roman rhetoric, but at the same time makes it accessible to the middle class student.

In *Of Education* (1673), Obadiah Walker also uses some modified techniques of traditional rhetoric to teach writing. Walker recommends that students inventory their own ideas before searching for material in other books, an idea carried into writing instruction in grammar books (130–31). Walker encourages schoolmasters to get their students to take stock of their own ideas from their own backgrounds rather than depend on what they had (or had not) read in classical literature. Of invention, he says, "take heed of torturing your fancy too much at first" (10). According to Walker, students can use their imagination to find material, but they must be prepared to revise their papers to get rid of the "ordinary and common" and look at some other "new circumstance" (13). The use of invention was especially helpful to the village schoolmasters who were teaching writing to a diverse student body. Walker wisely recommends that students read their essays to themselves or their parents and listen for clarity and euphony: "read aloud your theme to try whether the words be well placed, and the numbers well fitted, and the phrase enough perspicuous" (113). Walker was ahead of his time when he warns that "an audible recitation" of written work should never be omitted in the last step.

In the first few decades of the eighteenth century, several grammarians demonstrated a similar interest in traditional rhetoric as a tool for the teaching communication skills. In *English Grammar* (1712) Michael Maittaire begins by using traditional rhetoric to teach composition. Once into the instruction, though, he reduces the use of rhetoric as means of writing instruction to the point that it is almost non-existent. He foreshadows the trend in eighteenth- and nineteenth-century composition toward the teaching of content rather than form. Maittaire does, however, divide discourse into proposition, exordium or prologue, confirmation, and conclusion or peroration, thus conflating Renaissance practice with a reading of Aristotle's *Rhetoric*.[17]

A significant contribution to writing instruction is made in *A Grammar of the English Tongue*.[18] Authors of formal rhetoric books emphasized traditional *elocutio*, but Gildon chose instead to focus on method, helping establish a paradigm that is still present in writing instruction handbooks today. Gildon complains in the preface of the 1721 edition that the "General Rhetorics of the Schools in

England meddle only with the Tropes and Figures of Words and Sentences, but neglect the cultivation of a young Invention" (A5v). He proposes to help students in composition by teaching them a "methodical invention."[19] This directive helped promote utilitarian writing skills that would stay with students once they reached their vocations. As part of the formula of teaching rhetoric, Gildon argues in the preface that following a process, or method, is the best way to learn and that "we have taken a particular Care in this Edition to observe all the Rules of Method" (A5r). What must have been comforting to many schoolmasters in teaching writing is that Gildon lays out the whole process in an orderly manner. He explains to them that "We begin with what is first to be learnt, that what follows may be understood and proceed thus Step by Step, till we come to the last and most difficult, and which depends on all that goes before it" (A5r).

For persuasive writing Gildon recommends the process or method of going through invention, disposition, eloquence, and delivery, as well as engaging the passions to enhance one's argument. He explains how "Rhetoric is the Faculty of discovering what every Subject affords of Use to Persuasion" (171). The first stage of invention cannot be omitted because "every Author must invent, or find out Arguments to make his Subject prevail" (171). Next, the writer must "dispose those Arguments, thus found out, into their proper Places, range them in their just Order" (171). After arranging the arguments, the writer then adds "those Embellishments and Beauties of Language which are proper to each Subject" (171). Gildon adds the last step for an author if he intends to deliver his discourse in public. He is to speak it "with that Decency, and Force, which may strike the Hearer." Gildon summarizes the process: "So this Art of Persuasion is generally divided into four parts, Invention, Disposition, Elocution or Language, and Delivery or Pronunciation" (171).

Gildon next continues with a detailed discussion on setting up an argument, even more unusual for a grammar text. He states that "Invention is the finding out such Motives, Reasons, or Arguments are adapted to persuade, or gain the Assent or Belief of the Hearer or Reader" (171). He divides these arguments into "artificial, and inartificial." "Artificial" is the "Invention of him who writes"; "inartificial" is when the "author or writer does not invent but borrows from abroad and applies and accommodates them to his Subject" (171). Gildon lists the three parts to "Artificial" arguments: "Reasons or Argumentations (inform the Hearer's Judgment), the Manners (ingratiate with him or win his Inclination or Favour), and the Passions (to move)" (171). Next, he directs the writer to sources for discovering arguments, reasoning, and proofs, and he breaks down each area according to the practices of traditional rhetoric (171). Of special interest to a writer wanting to improve his persuasive techniques is the section explaining how to use the passions effectively (177–79) and how to decide placement of sections for strength and coherence (184).

Some grammarians argued against the use of traditional rhetoric, saying that it imposed too many rules in the teaching of writing. In his *Essay upon Study* (1731), grammarian John Clarke claims that the use of rhetoric in the teaching of writing has little value and that students would not retain enough to carry over into their adult years. Clarke quotes Locke as saying that the rhetorician's rules "signify not very much ... they extend little further, than only to caution a Man against such gross Faults, as Persons of any extensive Knowledge, very conversant in good Authors, can hardly be guilty of, and consequently are of no very great Use" (75). Clarke's argument about the rules of rhetoric draws upon his experience as a schoolmaster, as does his support of the pedagogical principle that being able to express oneself is not dependent on grammatical strictures. He opposes the idea that invention is the mere application of rules, arguing instead that it is a natural talent that improves the more one writes: "A readiness of Invention, wherein the Talent of Eloquence chiefly lies, is a natural Gift, capable of Improvement indeed from Use and Exercise" (77). Clarke reinforces what Maittaire is saying, that the teaching of writing should be done in content, not in a series of rules about form.

Clarke makes other suggestions for writing with rhetorical techniques in *Essay upon Study*. First, after eliminating Latin, one should "write much, and in Imitation of the best Models; which, and which alone, should be read over and over again, for the Purpose" (192). He recommends reading the philosophical Language of Locke and the sermons of Arch-Bishop Tillotson and Dr. Clarke in which "The Politeness and Elegancy of Stile, are, I believe, inferiour to nothing in our English Tongue" (192). Works should be read "over and over again, and imitated in the constant daily Exercise of the Pen," which "may be enough, to bring any one to a ready, handsome, elegant use of the English Tongue" (193). Clarke continues to stress the importance of the correlation of reading and writing. One should read occasionally a "Sermon, Spectator, or Chapter in Locke, two or three Times very attentively over," and then the person should write on "same Subject" remembering as much of the "Thoughts and Language of the Author" as possible. If one follows this routine, it will eventually "work a Man in Time into a Way of thinking and writing, like that of the Models he proposes" (193). The writer will benefit because "invention will improve and he will not have to read to prepare himself to write" (194). In some final advice, Clarke suggests that a translation of a classic author will improve style (194).

Adam Smith took an even stronger position against rhetoric than did Clarke, saying that it has little value in teaching writing. In *Lectures on Rhetoric and Belles Lettres* (1762–63) he complains that grammarians gave too much credit to figures of speech. They "[un]wisely concluded that these figures gave the passage all its beauty; not considering that this beauty flowed from the sentiment and from the elegance of the expression, and that the use of figures was only a secondary mean" (23). Smith argues that it is from "these figures, and divisions and sub-divisions of them, that so many systems of rhetoric, both ancient and modern, have been formed." He even goes so far as to say, "Systems of rhetoric, both ancient and modern ... are generally a very silly set of books and not at all instructive." Grammar texts, Smith maintains, still included parts of traditional rhetoric and figures of speech partially because of the concise terms: "In the grammars, especially, the old rhetoric survived, sometimes dealing briefly with invention, arrangement, ornament and delivery, more often in a form reduced to the figures of speech, which kept their position because they were easy to teach and hard to learn" (30).

Grammarian Daniel Fenning makes a point of mentioning rhetoric in *A New Grammar of the English Language* (1771). "Rhetoric," he concedes, "is no part of Grammar, properly so called; and the latter teaching only plainness and propriety; the former paving the way to elegance and dignity" (v). In defense he states, "I imagined, that a short account of the principal *Tropes* and *Figures of Rhetoric* would be no unpleasing addition to my Grammar, as it would serve to free the reader from that languor which is usually occasioned by the dryness of grammatical disquisitions" (v). Fenning has taken his material from "*Dodsley's Preceptor,* who has copied it from *Blackwell's Introduction to the Classics,*" and he refers the reader who wants to be more "acquainted with the Rules of Rhetoric" to those sources (v).

Style in Composition As grammarians adapted traditional rhetoric to fit the teaching of writing, they also adjusted rhetorical techniques of style to fit the purposes of writing in the classroom. Schoolmasters, charged with preparing hordes of students to function in a working-class environment, knew that eloquent, fanciful styles would not be appropriate to vocational needs. Consequently, grammarians focused their instruction on practical writing assignments to teach students how to accomplish simple, practical writing tasks, assignments that required a plainer style appropriate for brief essays, themes, meditations, letters, bills of sale, business correspondence, and receipts. As one would expect, these utilitarian writing assignments did not leave much room for creativity.

Grammarians differed in their ideas of how much text space to devote to style. Ralph Johnson in the *Scholars Guide* (1665) devotes little space to style, that is, to the arrangement of words, phrases, and sentences. Although he is succinct and coherent in his categories of writing, he does not explain how to produce actual compositions. He defines the essay, but he does not say anything about how to write one: "An Essay is a short discourse about any vertue, vice, or other common-place" (16). Johnson adds three concise directions for style: review the parts of speech, use the flowers of rhetoric, and follow formulas for perspicuity (16). Form, according to Johnson, is the most important aspect of style. In *The English Grammar* (1688) Guy Miège states that a student should know the "Varieties of Styles, with Rules how to Speak or write well in any Style" (127–32). The three standard levels of style are plain, moderate, and lofty. Miège himself provides a model of style for students by stating his instructions with perspicuity and directness. He claims that writing should be determined according to the following criteria: placement of words, conciseness, decline of repetitions, pauses for the reader, and material appropriate for the style. He focuses on practical, functional writing that will be helpful to any student, but especially to one at the vocational level.

Like Ralph Johnson and Guy Miège, the anonymous author of *The Writing Scholar's Companion* (1695) describes the "Grounds" from which he will teach style. He, too, starts his text with the basics of teaching a student grammar and graduates to levels in the composing process: "The First Part, furnisheth you with Materials for a Foundation," that is, grammar; in the second, a student masters vocabulary and sentence structure to learn the "whole Body of the English Tongue, for a Superstructure" (xxii); and in the last part, a student learns to embellish his writing "with the Necessary Ornaments of Pointing and Accent," namely figures of speech or tropes. He disagrees with the idea that school boys are not "capable of so much reflection, as is necessary to treat any subject with propriety" (xxiii–xxiv), and suggests that it is very easy to "contrive a variety of exercises introductory to themes upon moral and scientific subjects; in many of which the whole attention may be employed upon language only." From that point, according to the author, "youth may be led on in a regular series of compositions, in which the transition from language to sentiment may be as gradual and easy as possible" (xxiv). This author argues for prewriting exercises to help a student figure out what he wants to write about.

Unlike other eighteenth-century grammarians, Michael Maittaire discusses the writing of compositions in terms of style instead of rhetorical or grammatical figures. In *English Grammar* (1712) he focuses on how a writer can write clearly and simply. He encourages the writer to look at how the sentences make a whole, and thus produce a coherent composition. The writer, according to Maittaire, must include a purpose in his composition and consider an audience that "disposes and puts together the sense of many Sentences into some sort of a Discourse; which is designed for Readers or Hearers" (228). Maittaire is also unique in that he emphasizes unity in a composition. He advises the writer to look at each sentence to make sure they all work to support the subject he is writing about. "The main business of the Composer," he says, "is to order every part thereof, that it may conduce to the Illustration and Confirmation of that one Subject." A good writer, Maittaire continues, will always "keep it in his view, never to go aside from it; but to keep close to it from the Beginning to the last Period of the Discourse" (228). Writing instruction in schoolrooms to this date had not included specific instructions on sticking to the subject and looking at the composition as a whole.

In choosing style, Maittaire states, a "plainer expression ought to be preferred" to something more elaborate (231). He points out that one should not be pretentious in his display of knowledge. Any reader should know that "he is not always most learned, who affects to shew most learning, but who can best communicate what he has, to others." Moreover, the person who "delivers his mind most clearly to the understanding of every body" best understands himself. Maittaire recommends: "no word must be ambiguous or idle, but every one conspire to clear and carry on the design of the whole." Every adjective, verb, and noun must further the quality of the writing. As for being laconic, he says it is better to run the risk of "being obscure. To write too flat is not a greater fault than to swell too much." Writing, according to Maittaire, must flow easily without any "rub, clashing, or harshness of sound by the concurrency of incoherent, uncouth and rugged letters, syllables and words." Moreover, the piece should not mix words of different languages. He suggests: a "correct writer ought to be the severest censor of his own work, and weigh every thing impartially, till he finds nothing that offends him" (231). His final advice is to lay the work aside and then go back to it at a later time.

Maittaire suggests that imitation in writing be used to choose the best pattern for the work at hand (230). Already, however, in the textbooks for the large classrooms of middle-class students, pedagogues are cautioning students against plagiarism. Maittaire warns that "a turn be put upon whatsoever is borrowed from another, that it may look as if it was one's own." In doing so, however, the writer must be careful to "lose as little as can be, but rather gain something by shifting its master." There are dangers in copying someone's work too closely, and if "some sense be transcribed out of some writer, let it be clothed in new words." But, he says, these words should be applied to a new sense. If not, "whatsoever makes bold with sense and words too, is to be accounted no other than a downright thief and plagiary" (231).

Charles Gildon recommends in *A Grammar of the English Tongue* (1712) that the writer consider the "entire Body of Composition when selecting subject, style, figures and tropes, and the passions" (191–94). He defines composition as the "apt and proper Order of the Parts, adhering to each other" and then lists instructions for a good piece of writing (186).[20] First, he says to choose a style that matches the subject: "Matter ought to direct us in the Choice of Style." If the style is inappropriate to the subject, the writer will lose credibility: "Noble Expressions render the Style lofty, and represent Things great, and noble; but if the Subject be low and mean, sonorous Words and pompous Expression is Bombast, and discovers Want of Judgment in the Writer." The writer must also choose his figures and tropes carefully because they "paint the Motions of the Heart." To make them "just, and truly ornamental, the Passion ought to be reasonable." The passions and matter, he says, are connected and should be considered together in choosing a style. He claims that there is "nothing more ridiculous than to be transported without Cause, to put one's self in a Heat for what ought to be argued coolly: "Whence 'tis plain, that Matter regulates the Style." For two other styles, he says, "When the Subject, or Matter, is great, the Style ought to be spritely, full of Motion, and enrich'd with Figures, and Tropes; if our Subject contains nothing extraordinary, and we can consider it without Emotion, the Style must be plain."

He explains that "Elegance, Purity of Language, and Perspicuity" are helpful to a writer's style (184). "Purity," he states, is for language to "be genuine," "free of our Tongue, not Foreign ... or not Obsolete, or quite out of Use ... give an uncouth and rough Cadence to your Sentences ... [and should] avoid vulgar and low Words" (184). "The Language of the Mob," he asserts "robs what you say of that Dignity" (184). He advises that the author not to have "too great Brevity on one side" and "not aspire to too great a Loftiness" because "both are enemies of perspicuity" (185). Therefore, a good composition has coherence, or the "apt and proper Order of the Parts adhering to each other" (186). It includes the use of tropes, sounds of words, and punctuation for smooth flow, but the writer should not use any of them excessively (187–88).

As do other grammarians, Gildon describes the three kinds of style: the "sublime," the "indifferent," and the "mean" (191–92). In discussing style, he aims to instruct students when to use each one. First, the sublime can still be lofty as long as it is not inflated and as long as it is "noble in subject, uniform in style." Second, the indifferent style requires that words be "proper and obvious with no meanness of expression." The writer must be careful to avoid "Mob Expressions" and "Vulgarisms" and to have a clean and natural style. Third, the mean or middle style consists of the "sublime on one side, and of the simplicity of the plain on the other." In addition to describing the three styles, Gildon lists the effects that student writers should aspire to achieve (192–93). First is "Easiness," that is, "when Things are deliver'd with that clearness and Perspicuity that the Mind without Trouble conceives them." Easiness is produced when the writer clearly understands his or her material. The writer must also be fluent and "avoid all Roughness of Cadence." Second is strength, or that which "strikes the Mind boldly." To make a style strong, the writer must use "short and nervous Expressions, of great and comprehensive Meaning, and such as excite many Ideas." Third is eloquence, because it "renders an [essay] pleasant and florid." Eloquence makes use of tropes and figures as the "Flowers of Style." Fourth is severity, which cuts everything not "absolutely necessary" because there is no "pleasure" as in using "Ornaments and Decorations" unnecessarily. In sum, Gildon says the most important act is for the writer to be natural, and for Essays to be "easie, free, and natural, and written just as you think, sometimes leaving the Subject, and then returning again, as the Thoughts arise in the Mind."

In *A Treatise on Education* (1743), James Barclay connects harmony and style in writing. His description differs from others in that he pays more attention to how sound affects the beauty of a piece of writing. He calls for "rules concerning the justness of expression, the remarkable proprieties of our own language, the force and harmony of certain phrases, the proper meaning of words, their connection one with another, and the necessary skill of placing them all in regular order" (66). A writer should avoid "vain" repetition of many synonyms for a word because he may be said to "harangue" when he writes this way. Instead, he should select words that are the "strongest and best," and he should avoid using too many verbs, empty expletives, and parentheses (68). Although Barclay appears to contradict himself, he does not when he recommends that the writer use "different phrases to express what we have occasion to say in a paragraph." He is using Erasmus's technique of copia, that is, not repeating empty synonyms but looking for a variety of fresh ways to say something: "English is a very copious language, and has a number of words to express one and the same thing. But we are so careless, that we chuse rather to repeat what was said before, than be at the pains to seek them." (70). Barclay asserts that the way to attain harmony in writing is to make "expressions run smoothly one after another, with an equal mixture of short and long words in a sentence" (71). The reasoning, he says, is that the pace moves quickly, "so that the expression and full sense strike the ear at the same moment. This is a particular beauty in English poetry, which the French could never yet attain. Their verses have generally a disagreeable stop in the middle" (71–72).

Barclay then makes a surprising observation that not all authors recognized: writers differ in style. And then, he recognizes that regardless of tutoring, "it is very hard either to speak or write properly in any language" (72). At this point, he offers suggestions for being a good writer. First, he states, "we must not only understand the harmonious arrangement of words, but feel within the things we resolve to communicate" (73). With a more human perspective than other authors, Barclay recognizes that "Language is designed to describe the passions we feel from the various events of life, and according as these are faint or strong, the expression rises or falls in proportion" (73). And he makes a statement about being creative and original in thought: "in spite of art, and best colours, we perceive no beauty in a performance, where the painter discovers no original fancy or genius" (73). After the analogy to art, Barclay compares good writing to music: "For language is a kind of vocal harmony, in which the mixture of long and short words resemble in some measure the short and long notes in any compositions of musick; as the tone and accent of the voice answers what we call the key, or cliff, in any instrument" (74). Like music, he states, "there is the same variety in describing the passions by words, as in painting them by colours, or breathing them by sounds. Each passion has its proper language to speak what we feel ... Love speaks in gentle strains, impatient anger storms" (74). Like the arts, the sciences have their own style, "formed from the different sensations we feel when we reflect upon them separately" (74). Those trained in those disciplines understand each other's "manner of expression" (76). He goes into great detail to explain how speaking or writing, "or the art of painting the passions in words, seems to be a thing of great labour, not to be acquired without an extensive view of nature, whence the colouring must be drawn" (76). He continues to emphasize that there are "different styles according to the passions" (76). A distinction, he reminds the reader, must be kept in mind between speaking and writing. One may "admire the person speaking and therefore like what he is saying." In writing, however, "we are deprived of all these advantages, and have nothing to support us but good sense, adorned to the best advantage with proper language. We must, in short, say something that is strong and striking, and write in such a peculiar way, that we may appear with all the charms of novelty and surprise" (77–78). Barclay is an interesting figure in the history of writing instruction because he spends more time connecting rhetorical reception to writing skills than do other grammarians of the eighteenth century.

One can hardly overlook the lengthy section, "Observations on Style," that Joseph Priestley includes in his *The Rudiments of English Grammar* (1761). He does something that will become increasingly common in the late eighteenth century: make a distinction between written (formal) and colloquial (spoken) English. Priestley states that the purpose in writing and speaking "is to express our thoughts with certainty and perspicuity" (45). He explains that since "*writing is a permanent thing*, it is requisite that *written* forms of speech have a greater degree of precision and perspicuity than is necessary in *colloquial* forms, or such as very well answer the purpose of common conversation" (45). His footnote then explains that conversation often requires a "relaxation of the severer laws of Grammar."[21] "Style," he explains, "which is the *manner of writing*, may be deemed perfect, when it adequately expresses the whole of what is intended" (46). He also makes a linguistic observation that when one thinks he does not need words, "he cannot so much as meditate or think without them" (46). He says that a writer who claims that he knows what he wants to say but cannot put it into words, probably does not know: "The ideas of words will accompany the ideas of things; and whenever a man's meaning cannot be expressed in words, he hath, in fact, only a confused apprehension of something or other, and no distinct meaning at all" (47). Priestley reminds the reader that vocabulary can be increased by reading books and by learning new ideas, and though they may not be completely new, the old ones will be "diversified" and "modified" (47). He argues that "Every thing ... that is maimed, distorted, or redundant, in a person's Style" is a result of some "imperfection in his ideas" (47–48).

Priestley verbalizes other rules about writing. He describes "Harmony of Style, or the agreeable musical sound of the words well pronounced" (49). A writer is to avoid "the too frequent recurrence of the same word, the same syllable, and the same manner of closing a sentence," but how much he avoids those things depends on the purpose of his writing (49–50). Priestley goes into great detail about techniques that achieve harmony, one of them being not to place *of* or *to* at the end of a sentence (50). Others are sounds that echo, that are smooth and soft, and that are rough and harsh (50–51). He covers the "principal grace and ornament of fine writing," or the "Figurative expressions," because they make a "composition resemble a beautiful landscape" (51). In the following pages, Priestley describes the merits and limitations of metaphors, the inclusion of foreign words in English, and the use of vulgar words and phrases (54–56). Critics, he argues, "seem not to have sufficiently attended to, and have, hence, been too hasty in establishing general laws of writing from particular instances of successful composition; and have defined and circumscribed the paths to literary excellence, in such a manner, that no writer, who pays a scrupulous regard to their rules, can ever arrive at it" (57). Priestley brings to a close his section on style by observing that "the chief use of written language must be to record, extend, and perpetuate, useful knowledge ... that we ought rather to aim at perspicuity and strength of expression, than exactness in the punctilios of composition" (61). In what sounds like a nod to Plato, he suggests writings of philosophers and historians are preferable to poetry, oratory, or romance "which are never read but merely for entertainment" and are "artificial canals" (61).

Composition and Correct Grammar Another emphasis in the eighteenth-century schoolroom was correct grammar in composition.[22] Writing instruction became a series of exercises in grammatical rules, creating battlegrounds where grammarians waged war over their preferences. The war was at the student's expense, however, because moving from one teacher or school to another meant encountering inconsistent practices. Students became the collateral damage in this war. Grammar became a focus of composition instruction in schools because teachers had an easier time concentrating on concrete rules than on more abstract writing concepts. Large, diverse classes forced teachers to rethink the way they taught writing, and they often found it easier to teach the correctness of the rules of grammar than to teach writing. This rigid adherence to the rules and precepts of grammar took away from the time that could be spent on writing.

In *The English Grammar* (1712), Michael Maittaire argues that learning grammar is only the first half of what is needed to be a good writer, the concrete application of grammar being the second half: "Having gone through the Rules of Grammar, which teach the true Reading, Spelling, Declining, Examining and Putting together of Words, Pointing and Distinguishing of Clauses and Sentences, together with such Ornaments as are by Figures given to all these, the work is yet but half done" (228). The writer must then put into practice what he has learned of grammar rules or it will be of little use to him: "if what has been so carefully prepared, is not applied to some Use, and reduced into Practice; those Materials will be to little purpose, unless brought together into Composition" (228). Grammar "teaches [one] to Speak as well as to Read"; it also makes one able to be "well uttered and Spoken, which is the business of Elocution" (228).

John Collyer illustrates in *The General Principles of Grammar* (1735) the connection between writing and grammar. He first provides some rules of grammar, but he is most interested in writing with elegance:

> Simplicity and clearness depend much on the natural order, and whatever interrupts that, so far perplexes our discourse; yet sometimes we are obliged to transgress, to avoid the concurrence of certain rough words,

which will not admit of conjunction, and another disposition frequently renders them harmonious (102).

Note that Collyer is not bound to the practice of transposition and resolution just to make a sentence work. He looks at the rhetorical aspects of a sentence for the ambiguities – an unusual practice for grammarians, even in 1735. He continues with other elements required of discourse that may not fit rules of grammar:

> Or when we have something to say in a Passion, or in a short, or other particular way of speaking it is frequently necessary: But this belongs to that Part of Syntax call Figurative (103–04).

Collyer then discusses the use of figures and their use in syntax, providing examples of each. He defines omission or suppression, also called ellipsis, as the "leaving out of certain words in a sentence for brevity, or smoothness, which yet are understood, and necessary to a full and grammatical Construction" (106). To demonstrate, he uses an example from Job i. 20:

> Original: Then Job arose, and – rent his Mantle, and – shaved his Head, and – fell down upon the ground, and – worshipped
>
> Rewritten: Then Job arose, and Job (or he) rent his Mantle, and he shaved his Head, and he fell down upon the Ground, and he worshipped: (107).

Just when we thought Collyer was breaking away from his fellow grammarians slavishly bound to rules of grammar, he follows with a construction in which he supplies the omitted words, filling in the missing pronouns, needlessly encumbering the original language.

In *A Treatise on Education* (1743), James Barclay focuses on the "Proper" time for boys to learn grammar and writing skills. He recommends waiting until "boys are somewhat advanced," have "a larger acquaintance with English books," and can write frequent compositions of their own" (65–66). But Barclay's complaint is that "English grammars give us but few directions. They abound with rules for pronunciation and declension, teaching us by proper definitions to distinguish the parts of speech. These however are rather [more] curious than useful" (66). Barclay asks grammarians for the following aids in teaching writing: "rules concerning the justness of expression, the remarkable proprieties of our own language, the force and harmony of certain phrases, the proper meaning of words, their connection one with another, and the necessary skill of placing them all in regular order" (66). These rules, he advises, "would discover the common errors in writing, and describe in what manner they were to be avoided" (66). Rules in this manner, he surmises, would bring about reform as the French had done with language, and England would become "as remarkable for elegance and propriety of speech, as she is already for thought and reflection" (66). He asks that grammarians teach boys not to use "harsh and rough expressions" and to avoid "vain repetition of a great many synonymous substantives" (68).

Barclay describes in detail how grammar affects the quality of writing. He rules out parts of speech for use as "mere expletives":

> This may be necessary for better sound sometimes, but is often useless and harsh. Is it not so in this sentence: *They esteem virtue for the advantages it never fails to procure them?* The pronoun *them* were better omitted, since *they* clearly expresses the sense. The frequent use of the helping verbs, *do, does, have, had, shall,* makes us also offend against this rule. I have read, *I shall now proceed to examine;* but were it not better to write directly, *I proceed to examine?* In prose, we do not so well perceive the harshness of *shall, will,* and the signs of the tenses; but in poetry they quite spoil the harmony of a line. The adverbs too, which are necessary to express some mode or circumstance of action, are frequently used in this expletive way; especially the adverbs, *really, indeed, surely, perhaps, at the same time,* and many more (69).

Next, he claims, "Too many verbs in a sentence make it run heavily, as it is impossible to use them without the helping verbs, and the persons or things of whom any thing is affirmed" (69). He suggests that the writer "change some of the verbs into substantive nouns, which are more agreeable to the ear, and the particular mark of an easy stile" (70) Barclay offers the following example: "instead of *They said that I had often promised, if it should happen at any time they required a favour of me, I would be ready to serve them,* let us rather write, *They made me remember how often I had promised them assistance if an occasion offered*" (70). He disapproves of the use of parentheses, "which are a sort of illustration to our thoughts." He argues that they add only "trifling additions." It would be better, he says, to write a new sentence and to include the information. The worst use of parentheses is to show "an affected kind of modesty of the writer; when he tells us frequently that he apprehends or perfumes a thing to be so or so; or, in the beginning of a sentence, when he humbly begs pardon of the reader, and says, (*if I may speak so*)" (71).

In the 1750 edition of *Practical English Grammar* Ann Fisher becomes more focused on writing instruction and its relationship to grammar. She states, "The Method of conveying, denoting, or expressing the Ideas of one Person to another, in Discourse or Writing, is universally called Language" (iii). And, she continues, a person who understands English grammatically "if he endeavors to learn any other Tongue, will, from this Analogy, find his Progress surprisingly facilitated" (iii–iv). She warns, however, that those who learn from rote or custom will not so easily be able to transfer the knowledge with "Propriety or Elegance" (iv). Learning by "Random" only will also be a detriment because the student will have trouble with solecisms and false concord. Moreover, he will show his "Ignorance upon the most trivial Occasions," and "being unacquainted with grammar," will be unable to express himself properly" (vi). To be "Stronger to the Beauties of Language, the Ease and Elegancy of Stile," he must know grammar" (iv–v).

In *The Rudiments of English Grammar* (1761), Joseph Priestley illustrates what is important to him in writing. Priestley includes examples of composition "from our most celebrated writers, for the exemplification both of the rules of Grammar, and of the Observations on Style" (65). He uses short sentences for "illustrating the fundamental rules of grammar," and long, complex sentences for showing "particularly those in which the natural construction hath been made to give place to the harmony of style" (65). Priestley also examines "the propriety and elegance of the several forms of *transition* from one sentence to another; a thing on which the beauty of composition very much depends" (65).

Exercises in which students corrected grammatical errors did little to enhance their writing. These exercises were supposed to be practice for students in writing correct English and composing model sentences. Instead students memorized lists of rules and applied them in isolation, a practice ultimately counter-productive to becoming a better writer. Since grammarians had long argued, though, that learning Latin grammar improved composition, a bond between writing and grammar was already assumed. Edward Leedes's *More English Examples Turned into Latin* (1726) is one of the first publications to include correction exercises in a grammar text. Part of his stated purpose was to correct the inappropriate social behavior of using bad grammar, seen as an indication of the corruptness of character. Another publication to follow the practice of bad exercises was Anne Fisher's *New Grammar* (1757). Correcting the following illogical examples could hardly have reinforced skills in grammar: "That no wimen can be handsom by the sorses of seaters alone, any more then she can be wittey Onley by the Help of speach" (131) and "The Ministers preaches, but Sinners hears" (121). Often histories of grammar credit Bishop Robert Lowth and his *A Short Introduction to English Grammar with Critical Notes* (1762) for having the first book of "bad exercises," when in fact Edward Leedes and Anne Fisher were some of the earlier grammarians to include those corrections exercises.

Daniel Fenning argues in *A New Grammar of the English Language* (1771) that he does not agree with the practice of using bad exercises to teach grammar and writing. "As to examples of *bad English*," he states:

> I not only think that they make a very awkward appearance, but I am even of opinion, that they may have a very bad effect. They are more likely to perplex a young Scholar, and to confirm an old one in error, than to direct the judgment of the one, or correct the bad habit of the other. The only plausible argument I ever heard urged for the use of these examples is, that are formed upon the same plan with *Clarke's* and *Turner's Latin Exercises.* But his argument, however specious, is founded upon a mistake. The words in *Clarke's* and *Turner's Exercises*, though put out of the order of construction, are still Latin words; whereas the words in some of the examples

of *bad English* which I have seen, are neither English, Irish, Welch, nor Scotch words, nor words of any other language (vi–vii).

Fenning claims to have the best method for finding examples of "bad English." The procedure, he says, is "for the master or some of the higher Scholars, to dictate occasionally a sentence or two from any book to the lower Scholars," because "in copying down the words, they will be guilty of many instances of false spelling." For "false Construction" he recommends having students write letters to the schoolmaster or to each other, and they will "frequently err against every rule of syntax" (vii). Fenning argues that, from his experience, "a Child will attend more carefully to the correction of an error made by himself, than to the correction of one made by another" (vii). His method appears to be an early form of peer editing.

Joshua Story provides exercises in *Introduction to English Grammar* (1783) to help a student memorize rules and correct his mistakes. He says a student needs to correct bad English through analysis and parsing. A student should memorize every rule so that the "Learner will be enabled to have more clear ideas of the use of the Rules," as well as "faithfully to retain them" (ix). The teacher should inculcate the principles and rules "soundly into the Children, and not be hasty in making them pass to other matters, which are higher, and more pleasing, but less proportioned to their strength." He warns that a child must learn the lesson well:

> A rapid and superficial manner may please the parent, and be of service to the masters, as it sets their scholars off to more advantage; but instead of bringing them forward, it throws them back considerable, and often prevents their making progress in their studies. It is with the first rudiments of science, as with the foundations of a building; if they are not solid and deep, the superstructure will soon tumble. It is better for Children to know but little, if they know it thoroughly and forever (9).

Story, like other grammarians of this time, supported the pedagogical view that if students saw the incorrect sentence, they would remember the correct version in both the written and spoken word. Grammarians, however, had no proof that correcting faulty sentences would improve a student's knowledge of grammar. It appears that no one, then or now, has paid much attention to the lack of student progress in the use of rote exercises because almost all modern grammar texts still list sentences for students to correct.

A final example, William Kenrick's *A Rhetorical Grammar of the English Tongue* (1784) looks more closely at how grammar and style connect orally. Kenrick recognizes that "The combination of words in sentences, follows different rules in different languages, agreeably to their variation in point of grammar and idiom," but "euphony" has the most influence on rhetorical discourse. He claims that languages were not "originally formed on philosophical principles, and therefore their "grammar and idiom vary widely" (28). Thus, "in ordinary discourse our words follow each other in some... habitual order." A person must first think about the "simple meaning of each sentence, according to its grammatical construction, and as it stands detached from every other part of the oration" (33). Then the speaker may proceed to examining all parts of the context of the sentence and the emphasis. He notes that "emphasis should ever be consistent with grammatical construction, and should serve to confirm and enforce the meaning of each particular sentence" while it connects to the whole (33).[23]

Writing instruction in seventeenth- and eighteenth-century England came in various forms, all of which served the needs of the rising classes. Models of business letters and other correspondence satisfied both writing instruction and vocational skills. Grammar books also used letter writing to teach composition in more realistic situations, a technique far more effective than writing artificial themes on honor or death. Some grammarians chose to incorporate traditional rhetoric as a means of teaching the basic skills in writing, such as using invention to discover ideas. The discussion over how much grammar to teach with writing instruction continued to be a source of contention with all facets of the academic community. Moreover, scholars never reached a consensus on how many years should be spent learning grammar before starting writing instruction. An examination of current writing pedagogy indicates that many of these controversies are still with us.

Notes

1 Michael (1987:269) claims that "Letter-writing, [was] always the most widespread application of rhetoric," but does not explain to what extent.
2 See Murphy (1974:194–268). Per Michael (1987:308), the "most frequently taught form of written composition was probably letter-writing, as the great number of manuals testify, from the seventeenth century to the twentieth." For further discussions of letter-writing, see Michael (1987:151, 154, 164, 269, 273, 304).
3 Angel Day's *English Secretary* (1586) may have been used for dictating letters. This manual, following the medieval tradition, designates thirty categories of letters that serve all purposes of correspondence and were still used in the seventeenth century. The most popular models were for letters requesting payment and for letters criticizing or praising someone.
4 All references in this paragraph and the next are from *Wit and Eloquence* (1697:A2).
5 All page references in this paragraph are from Johnson (1665:16).
6 Gordon instructs on measuring such things as building materials, structures, or geographical areas.
7 For more information on the history of business letters, see Locker (1985 and 1987).

8. See David P. French (1953:82).
9. Aristotle defines rhetoric as "the faculty of discovering the possible means of persuasion in reference to any subject whatever" trans. Freese (1926:1.2).
10. Abbott (1990:95–120).
11. Knox (1994:64–66) points out that rhetoric was not begun until a student reached maturity, that is, rationality. From the years seven until thirteen he acquired *ratio*, and then he moved toward *oratio*. Grammarians like Ralph Johnson and Charles Gildon do not make *ratio* a prerequisite, or at least not explicitly.
12. Green (1994).
13. Smith (1762–63:108–10).
14. Gerardus Vossius (1631); Georgius Macropedius (1580); Aphthonius (1531).
15. Although Ralph Johnson's *The Scholars Guide* was frequently reprinted, the recorded editions are (1665), (1677), (1679), and (1699). Johnson's work has not been studied by historians of seventeenth-century grammar, education, or writing instruction, nor is it included in Howell (1956).
16. For a discussion on the significance of the passions in relation to ethics in the classical tradition, see Harrington (1998).
17. Aristotle, *Rhetoric*, book III.
18. For a discussion of the authorship of *A Grammar of the English Tongue*, see Scheurweghs and Vorlat (1959:140). Although the text is, at times, referred to as "Brightland's Grammar," Brightland probably only contributed to Gildon's text. See also Mittens (1970).
19. Gildon (1723:123–34).
20. Ian Michael advises (1987:272) that "the term *composition* is liable to cause misunderstanding: its other sense in sixteenth- and seventeenth-century writing about language is the process by which compound words are formed." Indeed, Wilson (1553:Y4v) uses the term to mean "an apte joynyng together of wordes in such order, that neither the eare shall espie any ierre, nor yet any man shalbe dulled with overlong drawing out of a sentence, nor yet muche confounded with myngelyng of clauses, such as are nedelesse, being heaped together without reason, and used without number."
21. "The ease of conversation seems, in some cases, to require a relaxation of the severer laws of Grammar: at least, that, after the manner of the *French*, we take the liberty to drop some of the harsher terminations of words. For instance, who, in common conversation, would scruple to say, '*who is this for*,' or *where learnt* (or learned) *thou this*; rather than, *whom is this for*; or, *where learnedst thou this*" (46).
22. Grammarians like Charles Gildon and Michael Maittaire, however, placed as much emphasis on content as they did correctness.
23. John Walker's *Rhetorical Grammar* (1785) enforces the same principles as those of Kenrick. Walker illustrates how to vary style with compact sentences, sentences formed on conjunctions, antithetic sentences, sentences consisting of detached members, sentences in a series, sentences with rising inflections, and loose sentences. He provides copious examples of each type.

Chapter Four
Repairing Babel: Battles in Universal Language and Universal Grammar

I. Language Acquisition: Descartes and Locke

Until the seventeenth and eighteenth centuries, the linguistic aims of grammar instruction were not an issue. "Grammar" meant Latin grammar, a subject that along with logic and rhetoric had centuries of tradition behind it. By the early seventeenth century, however, grammar was the battlefield for controversies motivated by those who, for various reasons, wanted to control language. Latin usage among the educated was challenged by the increased use of the vernacular, especially by the rising classes, and the question of whether to use Latin or the vernacular was not the only linguistic controversy. Language planners argued for a universal language that people of all classes and nations would use for commerce, religion, and science. Moreover, grammarians were complicating matters further by introducing alternative models of language instruction.

The new models for teaching grammar arose partly from the debate on how children acquire language.[1] Linguists speculated on how much linguistic knowledge is present at birth, how children learn language, and how they solve the problem of ambiguity in communication. In the seventeenth century some grammarians took Descartes' model of innatism, the belief that humans come into the world equipped with knowledge, and applied it to linguistic knowledge. It held that language learning was merely the review of innate knowledge had been temporarily forgotten with the shock of birth. Such a selective model offered a rationale for the maintenance of the status quo, effectively privileging the upper classes. The lower classes would not be able to "recover" linguistic information because they were not exposed to the same instruction as their wealthier compatriots, and they therefore appeared to be naturally inferior. This implicit reinforcement of the existing class system made such a theory particularly appealing to those benefiting from that hierarchy.

As economic, social, and political conditions changed, the model of the mind changed with them. Educational reformers like Johann Amos Comenius and Samuel Hartlib argued for a greater degree of equality among students and demanded more vocational training. In this new model, pedagogues readily embraced John Locke's theory that a child is a blank slate (*tabula rasa*) with ability for linguistic learning.[2] Locke argued that language is not innate knowledge but rather a skill that a child acquires through sense experience and reflection. He disagreed with Descartes's position that the materials of knowledge – ideas – are innate.[3] Locke claimed that the theory of innate knowledge inhibits individual thought, promotes parties and factions, and encourages reliance on authority and second-hand opinions.[4]

Locke's view that one came into the world as a blank slate with a natural ability to learn was more congenial to an age of empiricism. Descartes' idea of innatism was too deterministic for most pedagogues and linguists to accept. Innatism lost out to Locke's theory of language acquisition, that students learn language by hearing it and using it, thereby building a foundation of linguistic skills. Locke's theory, however, did not distinguish between innate ideas and intuition.[5] By intuition, Locke meant the natural ability to learn or determine something with no prior knowledge of it.

In the midst of the debate on the theories of innatism and the blank slate arose the more weighty concern of undoing the effects of the Tower of Babel, or the confusion of languages. Language planners wanted to invent a universal language the entire world could speak and understand.[6] Grammarians agreed in theory that one could be devised, and they actually put forth a number of proposals for a universal language and a universal grammar.

II. Universal Schemes in Seventeenth-Century England

A variety of schemes for universal language and universal grammar were introduced in the seventeenth century. The purpose of this chapter is not to survey all of the schemes, but instead to describe how a few of them embody the controversies being fought during this time, and to discuss how they first developed in the seventeenth century and evolved in the eighteenth century. Early proponents for a common language in the seventeenth century argued that it would help the spread of religion. They also claimed that commerce would benefit if all nationalities spoke the same language. And, as the field of science was growing, so too was the demand for a language for communication among scientists. The perceived need for restoring man to pre-Babel times presented an opportunity for grammarians to think about adopting a universal language. Latin, the closest thing they had to a "universal" tongue, was losing ground to the vernacular. Diverse scholars, such as Francis Lodowyk (a London merchant) and Cave Beck (a Suffolk clergyman), found themselves in the role of language planners.[7] At first, they wanted to return to the language Adam devised under the inspiration of God, as it is described in the eighth chapter of Genesis when all the earth was "of one language and one speech."[8] If they could undo the effects of Babel by creating a universal language and restore Adam's linguistic sovereignty lost through human pride and the confusion of separate languages, they could unite the world. They began their quest by looking for Adam's original language. Their methodology was etymological or semantic, focusing on individual names for items. They quoted the second chapter of Genesis in which God, having created the world, brings before Adam the living creatures one by one for him to name.

In trying to undo Babel, grammarians naturally debated the language to be chosen. Some argued for the merits of such languages as Latin, Hebrew, and Chinese, while others maintained that the answer to finding a universal grammar was to create an artificial one. In creating these languages, grammarians tried to construct what they thought would be the most functional system with the least ambiguity. Some of these languages consisted of bizarre numerical combinations, difficult musical notes, or confusing symbols. Grammarians became so involved in creating artificial languages that they forgot to assess the practical aspects of how they would work in the everyday world. Borrowing from Descartes's theory of innatism, they argued that learning a new language would simply be a matter of knowledge recovery.

Several language planners devised universal characters, symbols that had the properties of natural objects and ideas.[9] Seth Ward and John Wilkins wrote in 1654 that a new language of real characters would enable one to convey something of the nature of things. They argued that every word is a definition of the thing it represents. Wilkins argued that Chinese would not work as a universal language because of the multiplicity of characters required and the complex structure of the language. He said that Chinese is not truly representative of things, and "there doth not seem to be any kind of analogy ... betwixt the shape of the characters, and the things represented by them, as to the affinity or opposition betwixt them, nor any tolerable provision for necessary derivations." Wilkins was unable to see differences in how cultures chose to represent character and viewed his own "universality" as the norm, as a way to unite people and promote commerce and spread religion. In *Mercury* (1641), Wilkins claims that a form of general character can be "legible to all Nations and Languages" (54). He suggests that since any list of radical (complex) words would inevitably be lengthy and cumbersome, a universal language should be modeled upon Hebrew since that language was thought to consist of fewer radical words than any other language. He urges that one use distinguishing marks to show radical words to convey case, conjugation, tense, and so on. In another chapter he even suggests showing language through musical notes.[10]

In the beginning grammarians and linguists had common goals for a universal language. They agreed that the language had to be superior to any other language, and it had to be practical. Language planners also insisted that a language be harmonious and that it signify the thing each word represented in the natural world. Each word was to incorporate the complex and abstract meanings of an idea. They experimented with numbers, symbols, signs, music, and pictures, thus producing some unusual systems. All these projects used the same grammatical principles, even though they built widely varying models of language.[11]

Francis Lodowyk, author of *A Common Writing* (1647), is credited with the first published project of universal character and language.[12] In it, Lodowyk creates an artificial language made up of signs, which, he argues, is a hieroglyphical representation of words that people can learn and communicate universally.[13] He promises, "what is once written with this writing, will be legible and intelligible, in all Languages whatsoever, although the reader in any Language, understood but his owne Language, provided as before, he understood this manner of writing" (A2r). His reasoning is "that this writing hath no reference to letters, or their Conjunctions in words, according to the serverall Languages" (A2r). His description of the hieroglyphical system, however, does not sound so simple:

> by so many severall Characters, for each word a Character, and that not at Random, but as each word is either Radical, or derivative, the Radical, have their radicall Characters, the derivatives beare the Character of the Radix of their descent, with some differentall addition, whereby they may be differenced, from other derivatives, proceeding from the said Radix (A2r–A2v).

Lodowyk selects radical words that he divides into root-words. He then moves to a second group that he divides into four sub-groups: substantives, pronouns, adjectives, plus one of adverbs, prepositions, interjections, and conjunctions. The radical words are made up of radical characters. Prefixes and suffixes of radical characters change the word to fit the sentence. A frequently used and easily understood example from Lodowyk's *Common Writing* is that of *to drink* with the root sign of / 𝒪 /. He applies "The signe of the six sorts of Nounes Substantive Appellative," / ⊃ /, by augmenting it and placing it to the right side of the radix, or noun:

ㅏ /	𝒪⊃ /	= the drinker
ㅋ /	𝒪⊐ /	= drink
ㄹ /	𝒪⊣ /	= the drinking
ㄹ /	𝒪⊒ /	= the drunkard
ㅋ /	𝒪⊒ /	= drunkennesse
ㅋ /	𝒪⊒ /	= drinking house (20)

Lodowyk devises other signs to be joined to the left side of the noun drinker:

/ ⌒ / proper noun	= /°𝒪⊃/
/ ⌒ / feminine gender	= /ᵛ𝒪⊃/
/ ᴄ / subordinal sign for young one	= /σ𝒪⊃/ (20)

Other signs are hard to distinguish. For example *they drink* would be / ⁺⁺⁺𝒪 /; *from me* / ⇑ /; and *from this* / ⇑2— / (23). His artificial language attempts to be an "expression or outward presentation of the mind" (21). Figure 4.1 gives an example of this attempt. As one would expect, Lodowyk's language scheme was not adopted as an international language because his method proved to be awkward and

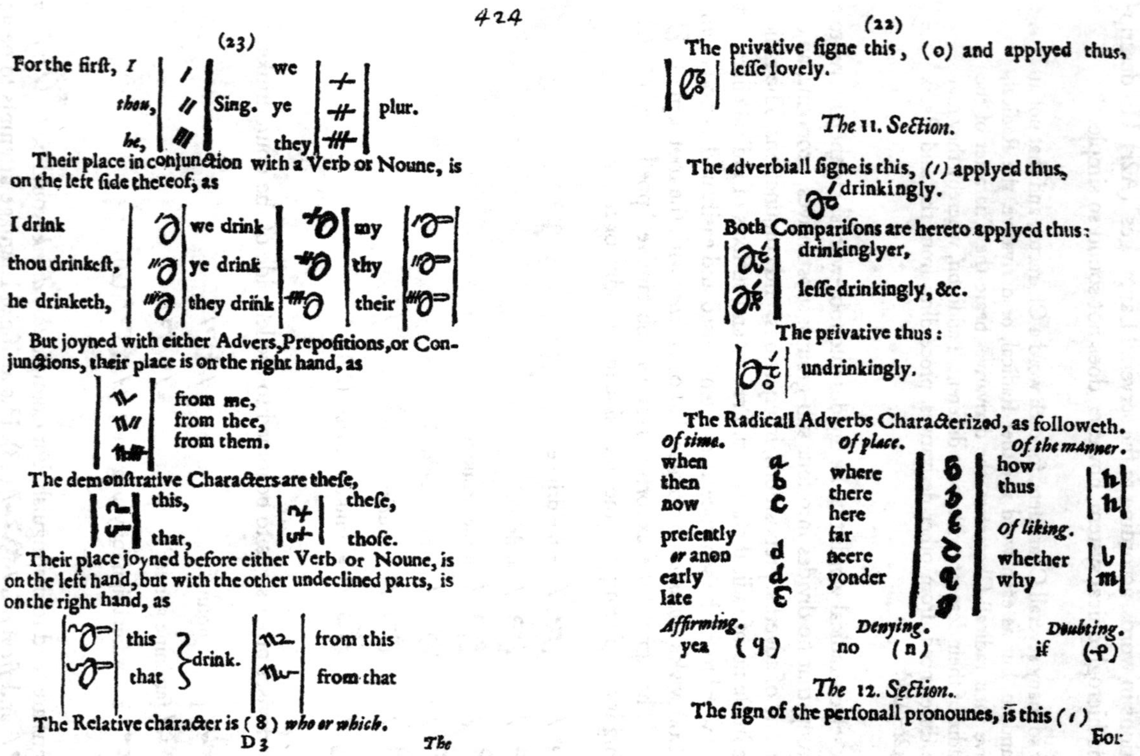

Figure 4.1 Francis Lodowyck *A Common Writing* (1647). Symbols for composing Lodowyck's writing scheme. Courtesy of William Andrews Clark Memorial Library, University of California, Los Angeles.

impractical. Although his proposal is an interesting exercise in language, users could not be expected to memorize all the characters and their variations.

In *The Universal Character* (1657), Cave Beck attempts to create an artificial language, one that is mostly an application of Latinate grammar, but based on a numerical system he believed to be superior to other symbolic schemes. He makes the same claims as other inventors of universal languages: it can be learned in a short time, it is free of ambiguities and redundancies, and it will be simple to use. The method, he states on the title page, "may be Attained in two Hours space, observing the Grammatical Directions," and "be Spoken as well as Written," and with it "all the Nations in the World may understand one another's Conceptions, Reading out of one Common Writing their own Mother Tongue." He proposes a universal character "to avoid all Equivocal words, Anomalous variations and superfluous synonyms (with which all Languages are encumbered and rendered difficult to the learner)" (A7r). His system was designed to solve language problems in teaching the mother tongue to native speakers, especially to children, and to foreigners. And Beck mentions other important concerns of the day in his support of universal character, those of commerce and religion: It "would much advantage mankind in their civil commerce and be a single means of propagating all sorts of Learning and true Religion in the World" (A7r–A7v).

Beck rejected obtuse, confusing symbols presented by symbolic writing and hieroglyphs. He instead chose a universal character of arithmetical numbers, hoping to bring order to his world, to simplify language by using symbols that are sequential and universal, and also to improve defects in spoken languages. He criticizes Egyptian hieroglyphics because the pictures distort the actual word: "the Picture shewing one thing to the eye, and a quite different sense imposed upon it, such as a misshapen cock being called a bull" (A8r). As a consequence, letters superseded the symbols or pictures, thus making hieroglyphics ineffective as a universal character. Beck was also critical of Chinese, complaining that the Chinese must start when they are children to learn how to draw the complex characters. Travelers, Beck observed, find Chinese too difficult and inconvenient to learn, but his own method could be learned perfectly in an hour or two (A8v). The advantage to travelers is that they will not need translators, will not be misunderstood, and will be not be deceived (B1r).

In reference to Comenius's *Janus linguarum reserata* (1652), Beck states that "a child of ten years old, learning five sentences a day, may in four months be perfect in the character" (B1r–B1v). Older people may "double the number, and consequently in half the time be master of it, for it having lesse then five thousand words, they will be comprehended in 500 sentences, allowing ten words to a sentence, one with another" (B1v). He also points out that his character "wil fright no Eye with an unusual shape" because figures are the most commonly known, and men can read their own languages into the numbers (B1v). He claims he has improved the universal method because God suggested that he do it (B2v).

Beck begins *The Universal Character* with typical rules of grammar, and then outlines the procedure for using his method. A glossary that covers a major part of the book uses a format that lists vocabulary words of the "Vulgar Language" on one page and the corresponding numerical character on the facing page. To numbers he adds letters to show part of speech, tense, case, gender, and number. He assigns as prefixes the consonants *p, q, r,* or *x* for nouns, followed by vowels to indicate case: *a* for genitive, *e* for dative, *i* for accusative, *o* for vocative, and *u* for ablative. Vowels *a, e, i,* at the beginning of a syllable signify the three persons of the pronouns, first, second, and third, respectively, and the consonants *b, c, d, f, g,* and *l* after them indicate the six tenses of the verbs: present, past, future, present perfect, past perfect, and future perfect (7–8). The base word *abate* with corresponding universal character 3 would yield the following noun forms:

Nominative	an abater	p3
Genitive	(of) an abater	pa3
Dative	(to) an abater	pe3
Accusative	(a or the) abater	pi3
Vocative	(o) abater	po3
Ablative	(from an) abater	pu3
Nominative	the abaters	p3s
Genitive	of the abaters	pa3s
Dative	to the abaters	pe3s
Accusative	the abaters	pi3s
Vocative	(o) abaters	po3s
Ablative	from the abaters	pu3s (12)

To make the nouns feminine, one would add /f/ to the vowels, as Nominative pf3, Genitive paf3, Dative pef3, and so on. For present tense verb forms Beck gives the following example (17):

I abate	thou abatest	he abates, or abeth
ab 3	eb 3	ib 3
we abate	ye abate	they abate
ab 3 s	eb 3 s	ib 3 s

The letter q indicates degrees of comparisons for adjectives (13):

bold	q 317
bolder	qq 317
boldest	qqq

Relative adverbs have the additional letter t set before their figures. At the end of the book, Beck has "An Example of writing and speaking the fifth Commandment" of "Honor thy Father and thy Mother." The numbers correspond to letters to create sounds for "universal speaking": 1 = ón, 2 = to 3 = re, 4 = fo, 7 = sén:

Write { leb 2314   p 2477 and   pf 2477 }
Speak { leb toreónfo, pee tofosénsen & pif tofosénsen }[14]   (M7r)

Beck complains that Latin requires years to perfect, and few are able to master it (A7v). To get away from the "evil" of learning Latin, he promises that his universal character can be attained within weeks and lead the learner from the "Laborinth of Languages" (A7v). But one might note that he has stayed with the Latin tradition in syntax and with the traditional rules of tenses, moods, and cases.[15] He also lists prepositions with their equivalent in Latin. As was the case with other universal language proponents, Beck did not recognize the inadequacies of his system. It was awkward, confusing, redundant, unwieldy, and hard to pronounce. He made claims about the superiority of his system, but in reality it did not work at all, given the massive number of figures one had to memorize to match words. George Dalgarno was later to accuse Beck of offering "an Enigmaticall waye of writing ye English Language" rather than devising a universal language (sloane ms 4377). Upon examining the system closely, one would have to agree with Dalgarno.

Some grammarians rejected artificial, nonsense language schemes and chose instead a system constructed from "real" character, that is, a system built from elements, symbols, and numbers of an existing language. Their idea of a universal language was that it would be systematic and rational. Language planners envisioned grammar as an organic entity capable of remaining rational, systemized, sensible, and organized. George Dalgarno and John Wilkins went beyond Beck's and Lodowyk's ideas of simply inventing symbols that stood for words. Dalgarno and Wilkins viewed language rationally and philosophically, and promoted systems that would force order on reality by setting up formulas to show shades of meaning. They began by combining meaningful units of characters to create a universal language. Next, they set up categories to organize words by genera, species, and specific differences, using properties of the "real character" to form letters and words. Dalgarno and Wilkins shared with their contemporaries a conviction that, if they could symbolize the order of things and notions (how the world is organized) in a universal language, they would have a greater understanding of their world.

In *Ars signorum* (1661) George Dalgarno describes his language as helpful for "civilizing barbarous Nations, Propagating the Gospel, and encreasing Traffique and Commerce" (Letter of Recommendation). Dalgarno's scheme may also be viewed as a philosophical language in that he sets up a system of classification as a rational means of ordering the universe, claiming that his "universal character and new Rational language" is superior to other systems of shorthand. The first

[95]

Lexicon Latino-Philosophicum.

Abacus *fran.*
Abbas *kaf.*
Abdicare *soskafisu, trud sosslem.*
Abdere *dit.*
Abire *bemprd.*
Abhinc *shub lol dan, bem lol dad*
Abhorrere *prebesu sumpron, trof*
Abjurare *scabe nimesu*
Ablactatio *sisfos, sofsum*
abolere *sosshantesu, grupesu, sosiauresu*
abominari *sumpronesu*
aboriri *pratesu sub danu*
abripere *dos don bemdep shekti*
abrogare *sosiauresu, soskebesu*
abrumpere *domesu donesu*
absolvere *konshon sis*
abstemius *sosprasemp*
abstinere *trus preb tim sodesu*

absurditas *shib prem sosros*
abundantia *sumu stodu*
abusus *shig*
abyssus *dadbas*
academia *dadtem santem dadtus*
accendere *numesu, sembsu num*
accidere *sakesu prk ded*
accingere *drod sitresu*
accipere *sprub*
acclivitas *blnmu*
accolere *stid shumbem*
accommodare *stop sitresu*
acervus *drotor, —— ind ut nusind*
acetum *stnm vel stem grusu*
acies *bnbu*
acqiescere *dram tup*
acqirere *stis synm*
aculeus *sabdik*
acumen *bnbu primu*
additamentum *shunu drese, tuno*
adeo *sum tolsus ses*

d $\mathbb{H}$ito

Figure 4.2 George Dalgarno, *Ars signorum* (1661). First page of Latin-universal character lexicon. Courtesy of William Andrews Clark Memorial Library, University of California, Los Angeles.

[118]

❦❦❦❦❦❦❦❦❦❦❦❦ : ❦❦❦❦❦❦❦❦❦❦❦❦

Primum Caput Geneseos.

1. DAN femu, Sava famesa Nam tɐn Nom.
2. Tɐn nom avesa sof-shana tɐn draga, tɐn gromu avesa ben mem suf basu : tɐn uv suf Sava damesa ben mem sof nimmi.
3. Tɐn Sava tinesa, gomu aveso : tɐn gomu avesa.
4. Tɐn Sava musesa gomu suma : tɐn Sava dosesa gomu dos gromu.
5. Tɐn Sava tonesa gomu Dan-gomu, tɐn tonesa groa, Dua-gromu, tɐn shem-gomu tɐn sem-gomu avesa dan-ve vasa.
6. Tɐn Sava tinesa, dad-dreku aveso bred brepu suf nimmi : tɐn doleso nimmi dos nimmi.
7. Tɐn Sava famesa dad-dreku, tɐn dolesa nimmi bren dad-dreku dos nimmi ben dad-dreku : tɐn lel-sas avesa.
8. Tɐn Sava tonesa dad-dreku, Nam : tɐn shem-gomu tɐn sem-gomu avesa dan-ve vasa.
9. Tɐn Sava tinesa, nimmi bren nam detoso bred dadu suma, tɐn granar metoso : tɐn lel-sas avesa.
10. Tɐn Sava tonesa granar Nom, tɐn tonesa deku

[119]

deku suf nimmi, Iffi; tɐn Sava musesa lolar suma.
11. Tɐn Sava tinesa, nom gypeso nab, neibeid gune rug, : tɐn rag-sneig gune rag, sos sugu lula, rug, suf lul tim bred lul ben nom : tɐn lel-sas rug, suf lul tim bred lul ben nom : tɐn lel-sas avesa.
12. Tɐn nom gunesa nab, neibeid gune rug sos sugu lula : tɐn sneig gune rag, rug suf lul tim bred lul, sos sugu lula : tɐn Sava musese lolar suma.
13. Tɐn shem-gomu tɐn sem-gomu avesa dan-ve vesa.
14. Tɐn Sava tinesa, gomu avesa bred dad-dreku suf Nam sham doleso dan-gomu dos dan-gromu : tɐn lelli aveso sas dannu, tɐn dan-vessi, tɐn dan-vussi.
15. Tɐn lelli aveso sas gomtru-bred dad-dreku suf nam, sham gomesu ben nom : tɐn lel-sas avesa.
16. Tɐn Sava famesa vn gomu soma, goma sama sham sudeso dan-gomu, tɐn gomu shuna sham sudeso dan-gromu : tɐn famesa alfi.
17. Tɐn Sava dadesa lelli bred dad-dreku suf nam sham gomesu ben nom.
18. Tɐn sham sudesu dan-gomu, tɐn dan-gromu, tɐn doleso gomu dos gromu : tɐn Sava musesa lolar suma.
19. Tɐn shem-gomu, tɐn sem-gomu avesa dan-ve vosa.
20. Tɐn Sava tinesa, nimmi sum-guneso neit, tɐn neip pɐ ne bired dad-dreku suf nam ben nom.

21. Tɐn

I 4

Figure 4.3 George Dalgarno, *Ars signorum* 1661. First chapter of Genesis in Dalgarno's universal character. Courtesy of William Andrews Clark Memorial Library, University of California, Los Angeles.

page of his Latin-universal character lexicon, shown in Figure 4.2, appears deceptively easy to learn, but in truth the lexicon is a difficult undertaking. When he applies the Latin-universal lexicon to the first chapter of Genesis, Dalgarno produces the pages shown in Figure 4.3.

Addressing another area of increasing interest during this time, Dalgarno advocated teaching deaf people to communicate with his symbols. He joined fellow grammarians in thinking they could represent reality by discovering the symbols of the properties of things and notions. This discovery, they said, would lead to truth about themselves and the universe. It would enable all men to speak with exactness and precision instead of ambiguities. Dalgarno, as well as other language planners, thought he could even improve on Adam's original language.

Language planner John Wilkins approached his language scheme in a more scientific manner than his contemporaries. In *Essay Towards a Real Character and a Philosophical Language* (1668), Wilkins develops a universal character and philosophical language with more careful attention to its linguistic foundation. He begins by recognizing in the "Epistle Dedicatory" that knowing many languages is not a remedy for the "Curse of Confusion," and by promoting that it is, nevertheless, possible to undo Babel. Wilkins, like his contemporaries, cites trade and religion as reasons for adopting his proposed design: "Besides that most obvious advantage which could ensue, of facilitating mutual *Commerce*, amongst the several Nations of the World, the improving of all *Natural Knowledge*; It would likewise very much conduce to the spreading of the Knowledge of Religion" (The Epistle Dedicatory).[16] He states that his universal character will be beneficial to God: "This design will likewise contribute much to the clearing of some of our Modern differences in Religion, by unmasking many wild errors, that shelter themselves under the disguise of affected phrases."

Wilkins intended to devise a universal language that one could use to observe the world and make sense out of it in a theoretical context.[17] A member of the Royal Society, he analyzed language empirically. In *Essay Towards a Real Character and a Philosophical Language* (1668), Wilkins lays out his purpose:

> ... definition of each species, that the *immediate form* which gives the particular essence to everything might be expressed; but this form being a thing which men do not know, it cannot be expected that it should be described. And therefore in the stead of it, there is reason why men should be content with such a description by *properties* and *circumstances*, as may be sufficient to determine the primary sense of the thing defined (289).

He classifies objects and ideas into forty generic groups by the way they are categorized in the natural world (e.g., rock, bird, fish, tree, etc.) and by their spatial orientation. He then applies symbols (he calls them "real characters") and spoken sounds to his classifications, as shown in the table in Figure 4.4 (387).

To each *genus* he gave a consonant and vowel and a corresponding written character. For example, all sounds from the genera that include vegetative matter,

Chap. I. *Concerning a Real Character.* 387

Transcend. { General / Rel. mixed / Rel. of Action	Animals { Exanguious / Fish / Bird / Beast	Action { Spiritual / Corporeal / Motion / Operation
Discourse	Parts { Peculiar / General	
God	Quantity { Magnitude / Space / Measure	Relation { Oecon. / Possess. / Provis. / Civil / Judicial / Military / Naval / Eccles.
World		
Element		
Stone		
Metal		
Herb confid. accord. to the { Leaf / Flower / Seed-vessel	Quality { Power Nat. / Habit / Manners / Quality sensible / Disease	
Shrub		
Tree		

The Differences are to be affixed unto that end which is on the left side of the Character, according to this order;

1 2 3 4 5 6 7 8 9

The Species should be affixed at the other end of the Character according to the like order.

1 2 3 4 5 6 7 8 9

And whereas several of the Species of Vegetables and Animals, do according to this present constitution, amount to more than Nine, in such cases the number of them is to be distributed into two or three Nines, which may be distinguished from one another by doubling the stroke in some one or more parts of the Character; as suppose after this manner, ―― ――. If the first and most simple Character be made use of, the Species that are affixed to it, will belong to the first combination of *Nine*; if the other, they will belong according to the order of them, unto the second Combination.

Those Radicals which are paired to others uppon account of *Opposition*, may be expressed by a Loop, or (o) at the left end of the Character, after this manner, o―

Those that are paired upon the account of *Affinity*, are to be expressed by the like Mark at the other end of the Character, thus, ―o

The double Opposites of *Excess* or *Defect*, are to be described by the Transcendental points, denoting *Excess* or *Defect*, to be placed over the Character, as shall be shewed after.

Ddd 2   Adje-

Figure 4.4 John Wilkins, *Essay Towards a Real Character and a Philosophical Language* (1668). Description of the real character. Courtesy of William Andrews Clark Memorial Library, University of California, Los Angeles.

Chap. III.   Concerning a Real Character.   415

That which at present seems most convenient to me, is this;

Transcend.	General	Ba	*Animals*	Exanguious	Za	*Action*	Spiritual	Ca
	Rel. mixed	Ba		Fish	Za		Corporeal	Ca
	Rel. of Action	Be		Bird	Ze		Motion	Ge
	Discourse	Bi		Beast	Zi		Operation	Ci
	God	Dα	*Parts*	Peculiar	Pα			
	World	Da		General	Pa		Oecon.	Co
	Element	De	*Quantity*	Magnitude	Pe	*Relation*	Possess.	Cy
	Stone	Di		Space	Pi		Provis.	Sα
	Metal	Do		Measure	Po		Civil	Sa
Herb confid. accord. to the	Leaf	Gα	*Quality*	Power Nat.	Tα		Judicial	Se
	Flower	Ga		Habit	Ta		Military	Si
	Seed-vessel	Ge		Manners	Te		Naval	So
	Shrub	Gi		Quality sensible	Ti		Eccles.	Sy
	Tree	Go		Disease	To			

The *Differences* under each of these *Genus's*, may be expressed by these Consonants B, D, G, P, T, C, Z, S, N.
in this order; 1 2 3 4 5 6 7 8 9.

The *Species* may be expressed by putting one of the seven Vowels after the Consonant, for the Difference; to which may be added (to make up the number) two of the Dipthongs, according to this order
{ α, a, e, i, o, υ, y, yi, yυ.
{ 1 2 3 4 5 6 7 8 9.

For instance, If (De) signifie *Element*, then (Deb) must signifie the first difference; which (according to the Tables) is *Fire*: and (Debα) will denote the first Species, which is *Flame*. (Det) will be the fifth difference under that Genus, which is, *Appearing Meteor*; (Detα) the first Species, viz. *Rainbow*; (Deta) the second, viz. *Halo*.

Thus, if (Ti) signifie the Genus of *Sensible Quality*, then (Tid) must denote the second difference, which comprehends Colours; and (Tida) must signifie the second Species under that difference, viz. *Redness*: (Tide) the third Species, which is *Greenness*, &c.

Thus likewise, if (Be) be put for the Genus of *Transcendental Relation of Action*, then (Bec) must denote the sixth difference, which is *Ition*; and (Becυ) will signifie the sixth Species, which is *Following*.

As for those Species under Plants and Animals, which do exceed the number of Nine, they may be expressed by adding the Letters *L*, or *R*, after the first Consonant, to denote the second or third of such Combinations. Thus, if Gαde be *Tulip*, viz. the third Species in the first Nine, then Glαde must signifie *Ramson*, viz. the third in the second Nine, or the twelfth Species under that Difference. So if Zana be *Salmon*, viz. the second species in the first Nine, then Zlana must signifie *Gudgeon*, viz. the second in the second Nine; or the eleventh Species under that Difference.

Figure 4.5 John Wilkins, *Essay Towards a Real Character and a Philosophical Language* (1668). Attribution of sounds in Wilkins's philosophical language to various categories of ideas. Courtesy of William Andrews Clark Memorial Library, University of California, Los Angeles.

herbs, bushes, plants, trees have initial letter g followed by either a, e, i, or o. Likewise birds, animals, fish, all have initial letter z followed by these same vowels in the same order (415). Figure 4.5 illustrates this. In *Universal Language Schemes in England and France 1600–1800*, James Knowlson explains Wilkins' method:

> In this way *genera* are represented by a systematically organized, basic set of letters and characters. Differences are made by adding the consonants B, D, G, P, T, C, Z, S, N, to the letters of the *genera* in the philosophical language. Thus, /Di/ is the basic generic sign for stone. If one adds a B /Dib/ marking the first difference of that *genus* one refers to a stone classified according to the first difference, that is, a vulgar stone. Species are then denoted by adding one of a number of vowels and diphthongs. Thus, /Diba/ will identify the stone even more closely as a "Rag," that is, a coarse-textured, vulgar stone. The process of identifying continues to narrow with symbols and characters.

In the real character, herbs, shrubs, and trees again are represented by similar written symbols (↭ ↯ ⊹) (395). Wilkins translates The Lord's Prayer into his symbols, as reproduced in Figure 4.6.

Wilkins claimed he could correct all the defects of language and therefore enable men to read and understand their world. The advantage of such a system, he argued, was that this process of identification defines the object or idea it signifies and establishes its relationship with other objects or ideas. His universal character, however, was not as logical or rational as he proposed it to be. He did not recognize that the rigidity of his system did not allow for many changes with the passage of time. The method was also impractical in conversations because people would not be willing to go through the logistics of figuring out what goes where. Fellow grammarians, nevertheless, recognized that his contributions to the systematic study of language made it a science for the first time. He eventually became known as the father of modern linguistics.

Although these grammarians were trying to invent a language that would visually represent the world, they instead created limited worlds. Dalgarno's and Wilkins's classifications, for instance, remained symbols of what they called reality and did not move beyond superficial categories. Both grammarians had intended for their universal language systems to be complete and functional, but that did not happen because their characters were not capable of breaking down the complex concepts into easily understandable units. Instead, these systems confused the listener and frustrated the speaker. Grammarians and linguists like Dalgarno and Wilkins had hoped to put an end to debates over the ambiguity of words, but they were not able to put their ideal systems into practice. They claimed that people could actually speak with coherence, but no one really succeeded in doing so. Moreover, these grammarians could not even agree about the type of universal language they wanted. This frustration parallels the fate, perhaps, of other language projects in the seventeenth century. Universal language schemes failed because the

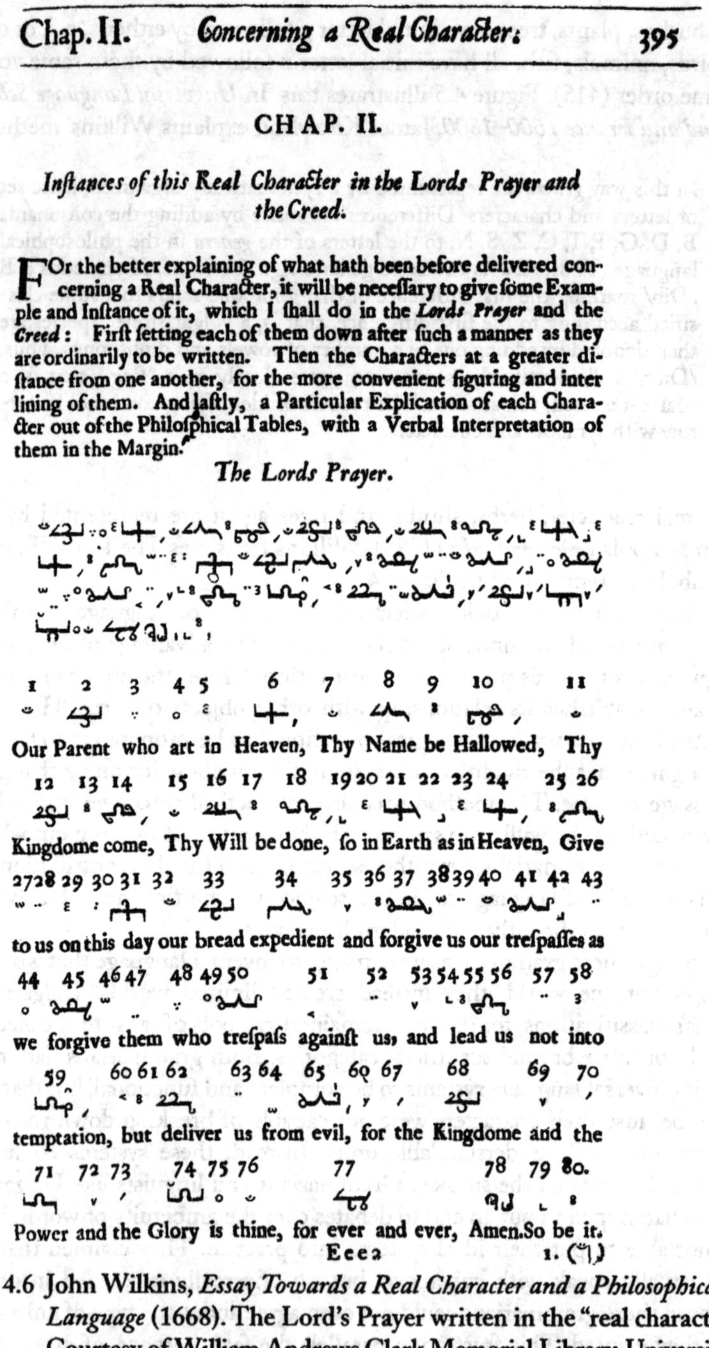

Chap. II. Concerning a Real Character. 395

CHAP. II.

Instances of this Real Character in the Lords Prayer and the Creed.

FOr the better explaining of what hath been before delivered concerning a Real Character, it will be necessary to give some Example and Instance of it, which I shall do in the *Lords Prayer* and the *Creed*: First setting each of them down after such a manner as they are ordinarily to be written. Then the Characters at a greater distance from one another, for the more convenient figuring and inter lining of them. And lastly, a Particular Explication of each Character out of the Philosophical Tables, with a Verbal Interpretation of them in the Margin.

The Lords Prayer.

[Real Character script]

1　2　3　4 5　　6　　7　　8　　9　　10　　11

Our Parent who art in Heaven, Thy Name be Hallowed, Thy

12　13 14　　15　16 17　　18　　19 20 21　22　23　24　　25 26

Kingdome come, Thy Will be done, so in Earth as in Heaven, Give

27 28 29 30 31 32　　33　　　　34　　35 36 37 38 39 40　41 42 43

to us on this day our bread expedient and forgive us our trespasses as

44　45　46 47　　48 49 50　　　51　　52　53 54 55 56　57 58

we forgive them who trespass against us, and lead us not into

59　　60 61 62　　63 64　65　66 67　　　68　　　69　70

temptation, but deliver us from evil, for the Kingdome and the

71　72 73　　74 75 76　　　77　　　　78　79 80.

Power and the Glory is thine, for ever and ever, Amen. So be it.

Figure 4.6 John Wilkins, *Essay Towards a Real Character and a Philosophical Language* (1668). The Lord's Prayer written in the "real character." Courtesy of William Andrews Clark Memorial Library, University of California, Los Angeles.

inventors were not practical. Grammarians invented innovative schemes based on theory, but when these language schemes were put into practice, people had a difficult, if not impossible, time learning the sounds and symbols.[18]

Several schemes of universal character, language, and grammar in the seventeenth century proved unsuccessful. Such efforts had appeared earlier in England, but by the seventeenth century the time was ripe for experimentation and innovation with language. Grammarians were drawn to the idea of creating a secret language, a universal scheme, or perfecting an already existing language. Even though the projects were not major influences on universal language, they still revealed much about a grammarian's attitudes, beliefs, and precepts. Many of the projects failed to meet the requirements that language planners had envisioned. For example, Comenius's "visible language" in *Orbis sensualium pictus* (1659) connects words with pictures to teach children grammar, vocabulary, science, religion, and many other subjects, but it failed to gain support in England. Universal language projects also prompted grammarians to come up with other systems like sign language in search of shorter, easier, clearer, more precise ways to communicate. Among the failures in these efforts was Samuel Botley's *Maximo in Minimo* (1674), a system of symbolical characters that proposed to teach the art of memory and simplified syntax. [19]

Toward the end of the seventeenth century, universal grammar and universal language projects shifted in focus to that of comparing the similarities of languages and of looking at the rationale or philosophy of language. In *Syncrisis* (1675) Elisha Coles has already recognized the approaching eighteenth-century view of universal grammar. He lists two principles:

> 1. That there is a certain Accord between the several Languages, and that therefore they are Attainable by Comparison.
>
> 2. That they are unquestionably Founded upon Reason, and therefore that must be made use of in the mutual Reference (The Epistle Dedicatory).

His conclusion is "that a Language with which we are already acquainted ... leads us to an Intimacy with those that were altogether unknown to us before." His grammar text marks a shift from universal language of invented character to a universal language of similarities.

Eighteenth-century grammarians continued to use the term "universal grammar," but not in the same way their seventeenth-century counterparts had used it. As the vernacular replaced Latin as the language of the educated, the more elaborate universal grammar schemes of the seventeenth century became the rational, practical grammars of the eighteenth century. Grammarians no longer used the term "universal grammar" to describe speculative systems but rather to describe language itself. To these eighteenth-century grammarians, universality meant combining the more traditional categories of the parts of speech, like nouns and verbs, with the philosophical rationale to represent universal language constants.

They thought of universal grammar in terms of analogies among languages, as a tool they would attempt to use to determine a doctrine of correctness. The vernacular did not have the voice of authority that Latin had carried with it, but if similar linguistic elements could be found in another language, then analogy could be used to determine what was correct.

III. Universal Language in Eighteenth-Century England

One of the earliest examples of the eighteenth-century concept of a "rational" or "universal" grammar to appear in England is Archibald Lanes' *Rational, Speedy Method of Attaining the Latine Tongue* (1695). On the title page Lane states that his goal is to present "Precepts as are common to all Languages." The work is also the first to put forward a system of grammar based on the vernacular rather than on Latin, an interesting early, but controversial, claim that English has the qualities of a universal tongue. In *Key to Art of Letters, or, English a Learned Language* (1700), Lane broaches an issue that would become a heated one: that European nations mistakenly think the purpose of learning grammar is to learn a new language. Instead, he promotes that grammar instruction should teach the mother tongue: "Whereas the true End and Use of Grammar is to teach us how to speak and write well and learnedly in a Language already known, according to the unalterable Rules of right Reason, which are the same in all Languages how different soever they be" (x). Lane reinforces the principles of universal grammar: if a student learns a rule in English grammar, he can apply it to Latin. He then supplies examples of how the practice works.

From about 1700 to 1750, activity in the field of universal grammar was no longer as much concerned with the creation of a new language as it was with the philosophical basis of language.[20] It also had to adjust to a new context: the emphasis on language as a social act of communication. English grammarians continued to argue about how to teach English grammar and about how and when to introduce Latin grammar, while the French continued to believe their language was superior to English. Daniel Defoe proposed an academy to regulate the English language. In *An Essay upon Several Projects* (1702), Defoe cites the Academy of Paris because it has been able "to Refine and Correct their own Language," and now it is "spoken in all the Courts of Christendom, as the language allow'd to be most universal" (228). He states, "The English Tongue is a Subject not at all less worthy the Labour of such a Society than the French, and capable of a much greater Perfection. The Learned among the French will own, That the Comprehensiveness of Expression is a Glory in which the English Tongue not only Equals but Excels its Neighbours" (228). The proposed English academy would "polish and refine the English Tongue, and advance the so much neglected Faculty of Correct Language, to establish Purity and Propriety of Stile, and to purge it from all the Irregular Additions that Ignorance and Affectation have introduc'd; and all those Innovations in Speech" (228). The British, however, did not warm to the idea of creating an academy to decide language questions the way the French had.

Eighteenth-century grammarians frequently clashed on the issue of teaching latin. Richard Johnson in *Grammatical Commentaries* (1706) argues the merits of Latin: "I know there be some, who think the Latin Tongue a thing of no such mighty Consequence, but that we might be well enough without: But surely a Universal Language (and such at present is the Latin Tongue) is a thing of mighty advantage" (A1v). He states that others think there are many languages to be learned, and many think that Latin is not necessarily the important one to be learned. However, Johnson suggests Latin should be learned because it is "common to Learned Men of all Countries; and it would be no small Trouble, if at all practicable, to establish another" (A2r). Other languages, he recognizes, could be chosen as a universal language, but none with the great richness of Latin.

For both practical and political reasons Johnson sees that the "Latin Tongue then is like to continue the universal Language: And as such, is well worth the preserving" (A2r). He argues that Latin is also pedagogically sound because "he that has got it by Grammar, may at any time recover it by Grammar; which having been once learned already, will come afresh to his Mind with a little Application" (A4v). The analogy principle in his argument should not be overlooked: "For he that has learn'd one Language, is so much the forwarder in his way to any other; there being a considerable deal in the Ratio of Language that is common to all." (A4r). Universal language to him emphasized how different grammars were constructed with similar rules of logic, not based on the linguistic ontology of corresponding categories that we see in the seventeenth century. He approaches language not by listing common rules but by placing words in the context of the world (3, 7–10). Johnson's definition reflects his emphasis on custom as a way of determining how we speak: "Grammar is the Art of Expressing the Relations of Things in Construction, with due Accent in Speaking, and Orthography in writing, according to the Custom of those, whose Language we learn" (3). Others followed the analogy principle in determining grammar.

Jenkin Thomas Philips states, in *An Essay Towards an Universal and Rational Grammar* (1726), that there are four kinds of words, that is, parts of speech, "sufficient to express all the Ideas of Things, and the Judgments we make upon them, and render them intelligible to others, by Writing or Discourse" (iv). Commenting on James Harris's *Hermes: A Philosophical Enquiry Concerning Universal Grammar* (1751), a major work on universal grammar, scholar Ian Michael states in his *Grammatical Categories* (1970) that Harris's book is "By far the most penetrating of all the works written in the name of universal grammar" (172). Harris takes each part of grammar from the basic word unit to the sentence and analyzes it in a philosophical way, explaining how each thing relates to its universe: "We may either behold Speech, as divided into its constituent Parts, as a Statue may be divided into its several Limbs; or else, as resolved into its Matter and Form, as the same Statue may be resolved into its Marble and Figure. These different Analysings or Resolutions constitute what we call Philosophical, or Universal Grammar" (2). Thus, beyond the idioms of a language, "Language, taken in the most comprehensive view, implies certain Sounds, having certain Meanings; and ... of these two Principles, the Sound is as the Matter, common (like other Matter) to many different things; the Meaning as that peculiar and characteristic Form, by which the Nature or Essence of Language becomes complete" (315). Language follows a universal principle – "that Words must of necessity be Symbols" and consequently that "all Language is founded in compact, and not in Nature" (337). Harris sees "Language [as] a kind of Picture of the Universe" (330), where words symbolize general ideas (341).

In *Lingua Britannica Reformata* (1749), however, Benjamin Martin disagrees with the analogy principle. In his book, probably the most thoughtful universal grammar written since Wilkins, Martin focuses on speech and linguistics, not so much on grammar and logic, and says that language is in a constant state of flux:

> I know of nothing that can be done; for as to the pretence of fixing a standard to the purity and perfection of any language, while the state of the people remains unchanged and unmix'd with others, is utterly vain and impertinent, because no language as depending on arbitrary use and custom, can ever be permanently the same, but will always be in a mutable and fluctuating state; and what is deem'd polite and elegant in one age, may be accounted uncouth and barbarous in another (111).

Martin was one of the few to recognize that using custom to dictate rules may produce some awkward, clumsy language.

Unlike Benjamin Martin, Daniel Farro argued for a doctrine of correctness based on analogy, or the common principles in a general system. In *The Royal Universal British Grammar* (1754) Farro designates universal grammar as a "System of a regular Digestion of Rules and Observations, which properly and absolutely appertain to each Part of a Language or Speech as is intended to be taught" (1). Farro believed that universal grammar could be used to determine what is acceptable in speech. He argued that a "doctrine of correctness" is reached through observing the elements of various grammars and then deciding what the consistent rule is. Farro writes, "If all languages share the same substantial Notion of Beings, Actions, and Passions," then English is "universal" (xv).

Joseph Priestley's *The Rudiments of English Grammar* (1761) marks a shift in the emphasis of the universal language debate. In the second half of the eighteenth century, controversies over grammar came to focus on the establishment of a codified, standardized grammar, even though England had no academy, such as the one in France, to decide language issues and protect it against change. Gone were the debates over finding Adam's original language or converting the world to a newly devised language scheme. Priestley and his fellow linguists were not tracing language to the original tongue, but methodically looking at the changes in language itself. Priestley did not believe in a "divine alphabet," even if language were once divinely given to Adam and Eve, claiming instead that human speech comes about naturally. With respect to the divine origin tradition, he states in *A Course of Lectures: On the Theory of Language, and Universal Grammar* (1762):

> Notwithstanding [that] the powers of speech might have been communicated, in a considerable degree, to the first parents of the human race; yet, since it is natural to suppose it would be only sufficient for the purposes of their own condition, we may perhaps conceive more justly of the manner in which language was improved, by supposing mankind to have begun from so small a beginning (237–38).

The power of language to communicate, he says, should be a primary factor in evaluating its history.

Priestley was, however, sympathetic to constructing a "philosophical language, which should be adequate to all the purposes of speech, and be without those superfluities, defects, and ambiguities, either in words or structure, with which all languages actually abound" (297). Such a language can promote "ease" and "precision," and it can become the language of the whole world. The most rational plan for this project, according to Priestley, was that of John Wallis.[21] But the universal languages of Dr. Wallis's time, the mid-seventeenth century, were no longer fashionable. Controversies over grammar in the eighteenth century centered on how the definition of universal grammar had changed, that is, on what elements grammarians thought most languages possess. Universal grammar, according to Priestley, became "a description of any particular mode of speech as [would] agree with the general practice of those who [use] it, without taking notice of those deviations which fall within the province of particular grammarians" (114). The eighteenth-century idea of universal grammar refers to social discourse, whereas that of the seventeenth century refers more to thought. For Priestley, language was not simply a philosophical, rational plan, but something that had to be viewed as changing, unplanned, and inconsistent (113).

Grammarians increasingly used universal grammar as a means of dealing with other language issues. In *Short Introduction to English Grammar* (1762) Robert Lowth, a prescriptivist, believed that language should follow traditional rules and not allow for corruption. He attempts to strengthen his position by claiming that universal language can be used to codify rules and standardize English. He states, "Grammar in general, or Universal Grammar, explains the Principles, which are common to all languages" (1). He continues to build his argument: "The grammar of any particular Language, as the English Grammar, applies those common principles to that particular language, according to the established usage and custom of it" (1). Lowth wanted a prescriptive grammar that designated what forms were correct. Although he claimed the purpose of grammar is to allow men to use it to understand each other, his goal was to publish a text on grammatical accuracy. He cites Jonathan Swift, who fifty years earlier, decried the imperfect state of language, in particular the "'many instances it offended against every part of Grammar'" (iii). Lowth believes that part of the problem is the ease with which one approaches the mother tongue: "Grammar is very much neglected among us: and it is not the difficulty of the Language, but on the contrary the simplicity and facility of it, that occasions this neglect" (vi). He argues, "Were the Language less easy and simple, we should find ourselves under a necessity of studying it with more care and attention" (vi).

Lowth, unlike earlier grammarians, focuses on accuracy or practice (words as words), not theory (words as ideas) as a way of repairing the state of grammar. English, to him, is an important tool of communication that must be consistent, accurate, and elegant. He concedes that it has been "polished and refined; it hath been greatly enlarged in extent and compass; its force and energy, its variety, richness, and elegance, have been with good success in verse and in prose, upon all subjects, and in every kind of stile" (2). But in spite of the improvements, he writes, English has made "no advances in Grammatical accuracy." Thus, Lowth's idea of universal grammar was to establish grammatical correctness, using English as a reference point. He did not support Priestley's idea that universal grammar establishes communication rather than correctness.

Lowth emphasizes his position through the use of analogy: "Grammar in general, or Universal Grammar, explains the Principles which are common to all Languages. The Grammar of any particular Language, as the English Grammar, applies those common principles to that particular language, according to the established usage and custom of it." (1). Lowth uses a building-a-foundation approach reminiscent of the seventeenth century school texts to reinforce his use of analogy: "Grammar treats of Sentences, and the several parts of which they are compounded. Sentences consist of Words; Words, of one or more Syllables; Syllables, of one or more Letters. So that Letters, Syllables, Words, and Sentences, make up the whole subject of Grammar" (2). He argues that to see the universal grammar of one language, one must compare it to another, in order to make generalizations. Universal grammar, he writes, "cannot be taught abstractly: it must be done with reference to some language already known; in which the terms are to be explained, and the rules exemplified" (1767 viii–ix). When a person has a "competent knowledge of the main principles of Grammar in general, exemplified in his own; he then will apply himself with great advantage to the study of any other Language" (ix). If universal grammar "explains the Principles which are common to all language," then English grammar "applies those common principles to that particular language, according to the established usage and custom of it" (1). English, for example, can be explained by knowing Latin models.

This belief that analogy could explain universal grammar and establish correctness for rules of grammar gained the support of most grammarians by the end of the eighteenth century.

Rowland Jones's attempt in the latter part of the eighteenth century to revive interest in a universal language characteristic of the seventeenth century presents a surprising anomaly. In *Circles of Gomer* (1771) Jones presents a type of system not seen since Wilkins, Lodowyk, and the "universalists" of the Royal Society. In *Hieroglyfic* (1768), Jones experiments with a universal grammar of primitive or "original" language. Jones's text should not be considered merely as a creative endeavor or a late attempt to repair Babel, but should instead be viewed as a text following eighteenth-century rational and philosophical principles. Jones defines grammar in a traditional manner, but adds the concept of signs and sounds corresponding with ideas: "Grammar of a particular language is the art of rightly speaking and writing it according to its own established and fixed rules. An Universal Grammar is the form and mode of rightly expressing our ideas by such signs and sounds as correspond with ideas and things, as their natural archetypes" (1). Jones describes his devised system: "Names consist of certain lines or chords, springs, circles, semicircles, surfaces, sides, divisions or parts, figures and letters, which as symbols and articulate sounds or voices, describe and represent the elements and parts of nature; their combinations into particles or syllables of two letters; models of names of two particles or three letters, with an elision of the other; and decomposites or still larger combinations of these in names, phrases, and sentences" (1). His effort to describe a universal language came too late to be taken seriously, but it is does demonstrate another attempt for a means of codifying the English language in the eighteenth century.

Toward the end of the eighteenth century, many grammarians continued to examine universal grammar from philosophical and rational perspectives. In *Dissertations Moral and Critical* (1783) James Beattie points out that people of all countries have similar ways of thinking in their languages. In "The Theory of Languages," Beattie states: "In the most antient histories we find, that the modes of thinking and acting, of believing and disbelieving, of approbation, are perfectly similar to what we experience in ourselves and in the world around us" (382). The following statement seems to revisit the Locke-Descartes debate in the seventeenth century about whether language is innate or learned, but in an updated social context:

> Now, as human thoughts discover themselves by language, and as the thoughts of men in one age and nation are similar to those in another, is it not probably, that there may be in all human languages some general points of resemblance, in structure at least, if not in sound? Since, for example, all men in all ages must have had occasion to speak of acting, and of being acted upon, of good and of bad qualities, and of the various objects of outward sense, must there not in every language be verbs, and adjectives, and nouns? (382-83).

For example, Beattie notes that nations may have a "hippopotamus" and that they may use "different names," "yet this animal is known and spoken of, and words to express its qualities" are used in similar ways (383). He argues, "Languages, therefore, resemble men in this respect, that, though each has peculiarities, whereby it is distinguished from every other, yet all have certain qualities in common" (383). And finally, he defines his terms: "The peculiarities of individual tongues are explained in their respective grammars and dictionaries. Those things, that all languages have in common, or that are necessary to every language, are treated of in a science, which some have called Universal or Philosophical Grammar" (383). In the second volume of *Dissertations Moral and Critical* he reinforces the idea of universal grammar: "May we not then infer, that in every language there must be nine or ten species of words; or, to express it otherwise, that Articles, Nouns, Pronouns, Adjectives, Verbs, Participles, Adverbs, Prepositions, Interjections, and Conjunctions, must be in all languages?" (2). Beattie then concludes, "Thus shall we unfold the principles of Universal Grammar, by tracing out those powers, forms, or contrivances, which, being essential to language, must be found in every system of human speech that deserves the name" (2).

As the eighteenth century came to a close, the prevailing kind of universal grammar promoted by grammarians such as Lowth and Farro supported the codification of English and, consequently prescriptivism. Historians of the English language have long canonized Lowth as being a central, founding father of grammar books. This assertion is problematic because Lowth needs to be understood, not in isolation, but in the context of his period. He comes after a century of discussion about universal language, and reaps the benefits of his predecessors. His grammar book is a result of many decades of successes and failures, of experimentation and controversy by those who came before him.

Universal grammar changed in its principles and practice from the beginning of the seventeenth century to the end of the eighteenth. It was also a topic that brought issues on religion, commerce, education, science, foreigners, politics, and language to the discussion table. At the beginning of the seventeenth century, grammarians were idealists who thought they could discover Adam's original language and repair the effects of the Tower of Babel. It was an age of empiricism, a time when people observed phenomena and then experimented with ideas to explain them. Grammarians were innovators who created entirely new, artificial languages and tried to put them into practice. It is amusing to us now that they thought their universal language schemes would actually work and be accepted. None of the schemes gained popular, financial, or academic support because they were too impractical, but while the universal language schemes did not prove feasible, they did influence the emerging science of linguistics. The various schemes forced grammarians to look for consistent elements in language, codify and standardize language, and view it as accessible to empirical observation. The eighteenth century was equally the beneficiary of new universal language theories.

Grammarians searched for rules that could be transferred from one language to another, using analogy or common elements. The new definition of universal grammar, in terms of elements common to all languages, gave impetus to the codification and standardization of the English language and a kind of prescriptivism that we see to this day.

Notes

1 The seventeenth century marked a period when people wanted to know about the history of their language. They started tracing their linguistic roots to European languages, establishing criteria for determining linguistic relationships, and discovering the origin and history of the English language.
2 Locke (1690). For modern scholarship on Locke, see Aaron (1937, repr. 1971:25-53, 156-65), Ayers (1991:I.83-101), Woolhouse (1983:1-56).
3 Woolhouse (1983:5-6) observes in *Locke* that Descartes's *Rules for the Directions of the Mind* (1628), *Mediations on the First Philosophy* (1641), and *Principles of Philosophy* (1644) were influential in the seventeenth century and in the following decades. He states "Though, as we shall see, Locke disagreed with Descartes on many matters, Lady Masham reported 'the first books, as Mr. Locke himself has told me, which gave him a relish of philosophical things, were those of Descartes.'"
4 See Gewirth (1967:257-62), Kenny (1967:234-37).
5 For a discussion on intuition, see Woolhouse (1983:42-69).
6 Knowlson (1975:3-4) cautions readers not to confuse artificial languages developed during the seventeenth and eighteenth centuries with those constructed by modern linguists.
7 See Salmon (1985:129-56) notes that language planners attempted to find the underlying principles to all languages, teach them in the mother tongue, and then teach the "accidental" differences in a "target" language. See also Padley (1985: 221-3) and such primary texts as Webbe (1622) and Daines. According to Daines (1640:A3v), "The perfection of all Arts (whereto the knowledge of Tongues ought to be reduced) consists as well in the Theory, as the Practice ... and this Theory [consists] in the ... knowledge of Universals; wee are, as well in this, as all other Tongues or Languages, to have recourse to Grammar, as the generall fountain."
8 Cohen (1977:38-42) discusses Locke's concept that adamic naming and signification played a role in language planning.
9 Bright (1588) lists English words in tables to suggest they were similar to Chinese ideographs.
10 Besnier (1675:23-25), who invented a system for language learning based on musical notes, claims that one can master all languages by knowing one. His two stated aims are to show that a student learns grammar when "an accord between several languages makes them attainable by comparison" and to show that languages are founded upon reason.
11 For early writing schemes, see Knowlson (1975:44-64).

12 Salmon (1972:3, 15) credits Lodowyck as being the first to attempt at publishing a universal character, and Francis Bacon as the first English scholar to discuss in any detail the topic of universal character.
13 According to Sloane MS 897 f32r, "Carracter is the signe of some sound or thing or the affections of things. When applyed to sounds — I meane those we call articulate sounds — then is it called a vocall Carracter. Such are the alfabetall letters a, b, d, etc. When applyed to things they are called Reall Carracters, from *res* or thing, in distinction from the former vocall carracters ... These Reall Carracters are either those which represent the thing it standeth for, as the picture of a man is the carracter of a man, and which all that have seen men will know what it signifieth; or those which only signifie by concent the thing it standeth for."
14 See Knowlson (1975:63) for an explanation of this example.
15 Knowlson (1975:66) also makes this observation.
16 Comenius and his religious motivations for a universal language are discussed in chapter 2.
17 Knowlson (1975:98–107) discusses Wilkins's methodology at length.
18 The boundaries of this discussion do not permit a detailed discussion of Wilkins's scheme. It is also not possible to discuss Leibniz's formulation of a universal character in Knowlson (1975:107–111).
19 Other books that deserve mention are Theophilus Metcalfe's *Short Writing* (1645); John Farthing's *Short-Writing Shortened* (1654); Elisha Coles's *The Newest, Plainest, and Best Short-hand* (1674); and George Ridpath's *Shorthand yet Shorter* (1687).
20 Modern scholarship has largely ignored developments in universal grammar from 1700 to 1750, but for a brief discussion of this transitional period, see Cohen (1977:99–102).
21 Not all plans for grammar include a scheme universal language, but Wallis (1653:68) is one of the most rational, pointing out common technical terms shared between classical languages and English.

Chapter Five
Regulating Social Position

The task of grammarians was not only to teach grammar, but also to prepare students for life in their vocations and in their domestic roles. Grammarians also had the power to create, assign, and reinforce identities for marginal social groups. Foreigners, for example, had a moral and national identity imposed upon them through the requirement that they learn the language and so prove they accepted their new country and its customs. Grammar texts also tell us how much learning was considered appropriate for women. Education for women was limited to the domestic realm. If they crossed the line of what they were expected to learn, they risked being labeled immoral. While foreigners and women had an identity thrust upon them, the middle class, by contrast, generated its own identity focusing on morals and literacy. When grammarians assigned identities to marginal groups, they reinforced their designated status.

I. Grammar for Foreigners: A Moral and National Identity

Although English-as-a-foreign-language (EFL) instruction is common today, in the early seventeenth century in England the notion of English as a foreign language was an innovation. Latin was still the language of the educated, and the vernacular had not yet been completely accepted as language for official business. Foreigners, though, needed to master English, since England was already importing and exporting goods to and from many foreign parts, and vernacular communication was a necessity for trading. To complicate the language problems, foreigners began moving to England with their businesses, and grammarians began to get nervous about the corruption of the English language. In their nervousness about the language, grammarians wanted the newcomers to learn English properly before they attained any degree of mobility. Teaching English to foreigners, then, was a means by which the British imposed a moral and national identity on the new residents. We might think of English grammarians' attitudes toward foreigners as passing through three points of transition: from confidence to arrogance, from arrogance to nervousness, and from nervousness to conformity.

From Confidence to Arrogance At the beginning of the seventeenth century, British grammarians were gaining confidence in the use of the vernacular, even though it had not yet been accepted as the language of the educated.[1] The growing acceptance of the vernacular also survived the challenges from seventeenth-century universal grammarians who were creating new (albeit wildly different) languages. To grammarians, however, it was one thing to create new languages or to make charts of their similarities, and quite another to have one's native language threatened with corruption by incoming foreigners. Thus, in this respect, warring grammarians who would have otherwise parted company over their theories of language banded together to keep foreigners from corrupting the English language. The confidence in the vernacular came from a growing sense of the superiority of the mother tongue, one that would eventually feed the arrogance that British grammarians began to feel toward their language. English was spoken in all parts of the world, they thought, because of its inherent superiority.

As early as 1582 Richard Mulcaster asserts the superiority of the English language when he asks in the preface of *The First Part of the Elementarie*, "Will all kindes of trade, and all sorts of traffik, make a tunge of account?" He claims that English dominates in usage all over the globe: "If the spreading sea, and the spacious land could use anie speche, theie would both shew you, where, and in how manie strange places, theie have sene our peple, and also give you to wit, that theie deall in as much, and as great varietie of matters, as anie other peple do, whether at home or abrode." Because English is so widely known, Mulcaster argues, it is the superior language for universal use: "Which is the reason why our tung doth serve to so manie uses, bycause it is conversant with so manie peple, and so well acquainted with so manie matters, in so sundrie kindes of dealing." This is a time for the English language to grow, he explains, because "Now all this varietie of matter, and diversitie of trade, make both matter for our speche, and mean to enlarge it." He does caution, however, that "For he that is so practised, will utter, rather then he will stik in his utterance, will use the foren term, by waie of premunition, that the cuntrie peple do call it so, and by that mean make a foren word, an English denison" (Preface). If English is to be dominant, Mulcaster warns, it must be used correctly and carefully.[2]

Mulcaster was not the only grammarian to be simultaneously smug and nervous about the dominance of the English vernacular. In *Grammatica Anglicana* (1594), a practical grammar intended as a guide for native and foreign speakers, Paul Greaves complains about the grammar of native speakers and aims his text at his fellow countrymen.[3] He also takes the opportunity to focus on the grammar of foreigners, by which, he actually means their perspicuity in speech (4). The idea of concentrating more on perspicuity than on grammar itself was unusual for the end of the sixteenth century when learning grammar was stressed more than learning style. Alexander Gill also argues in the introduction to his book the same point as Greaves. Ivan Poldauf considers Gill's *Logonomia Anglica* (1619) to be "the first thorough grammatical work in English" (4). It was also the first grammar text with an extensive syntax and prosody.[4] Grammarians even thought they could improve diplomatic relations between England and other countries by teaching foreigners English. In his posthumously published *English Grammar* (1640), Ben Jonson attempts to help foreigners learn English and to adjust to a new linguistic environment. Jonson notes that "The profit of Grammar is great to Strangers, who are to live in communion, and commerce with us."[5] On this issue, other grammarians like James Harris (1751) and Guy Miège (1688) agreed that foreigners should learn the same system of grammar with the same rules so that there would be some consistency.

Grammarians argued that if foreigners, both immigrants and expatriates, learned the English language, they were proving their loyalty and patriotism to their new home. In *Tutor to True English* (1699) Henry Care mentions that foreigners are welcome in England if they can "be Masters of Our Language," and, like other Englishmen, be "Expert for the Negotiation and Conduct of their Affairs" and have "Christian Ethics and Morality" (A1v–A2r). In *Compleat School-Master* (1700) Thomas Tryon provides instructions to help foreign traders use the English language to keep shop in England (23). Grammarians even went a step further by complaining that when Englishmen went abroad for commercial trading ventures, foreigners impeded business transactions because they could not speak English. However, these grammarians ignored the fact that foreigners who did not speak English were going to have a difficult time understanding the British grammar texts.

From Arrogance to Nervousness Although grammarians arrogantly thought of their language as superior, they also began to feel nervous about the integrity of English.[6] These feelings were prompted by the number of foreigners who had acquiesced to the British dictate that they learn the English language. Throughout the seventeenth century, as foreigners were learning the "mother tongue," the vernacular was also becoming the language of the educated, and thus arose a new fear for grammarians that foreigners would corrupt the newly enfranchised English language. Grammarians had a responsibility to guard the language by teaching foreigners the rules with accuracy.

Jeremiah Wharton tells foreigners who wish to learn English that his book, *The English-Grammar* (1654), "will bee the most certain Guide, that ever yet was existant" (A5). In a sense concurring with the predominant grammarians of the seventeenth century who advocated the teaching of English grammar to prepare a student for Latin, he also claims that it is easier to learn English than Latin: "Likewise to strangers that desire to learn our language, it will bee a special help; which they shall finde not to bee barbarous, confused, and irregular ... but familiar, orderly and easie, equal to the Greek, and beyond the Latine for Composition, yea happie above them both in this; not that it cannot bee reduced to any: but that indeed it needeth little or no Grammar at all" (A6r–A6v). He illustrates the differences between Latin and English: "For whereas in the Latine-tongue there are threescore Variations of the Terminations of Nouns, and six hundred of Verbs, and in the English there is little or no variation at all; and therefore needeth not any Declensions of Nouns, any Conjugations of Verbs, any Rules of Concord or

Construction, wherein the difficultie of any language doth consist, and which in the Latine and Greek cost much labor and toil." Also, children and foreigners, who he says needs the most instruction, are better able to transfer linguistic knowledge from English to Latin because of the structural parallelism between the two: "it will bee a notable Preparative to the learning of the Latine, or any other Grammatized language; because the Rules in *this*, for the most part may bee applied unto *that*" (Avi). Wharton said he wrote an *English Grammar* because he wanted a text that would emphasize the common elements of the native tongue and Latin. Wharton was able to reduce some his nervousness about English by using analogy in applying rules of grammar.

Guy Miège, an immigrant himself, also wanted to protect the English language. Miège, who was born in Lausanne in 1644 and moved to England in 1661, said he would preserve the purity of English and help foreigners to speak correctly.[7] He was distinguished as a lexicographer after his publication of his *New Dictionary of French and English* (1679), later enlarged to *The Great French Dictionary* (1687–88). He published several grammars: *A New French Grammar* (1678); *Nouvelle méthode pour apprendre l'Anglois* (1685), and *English Grammar* (1688). This last text, as R. C. Alton notes, "has the distinction of being the only grammar of English written in English by a non-native speaker" (1969, introductory note). In it Miège claims that his "aim is to satisfy the Curious, and to advance the Illiterate into the knowledge of the Grounds of their Language ... Neither will it be improper for the Use of Forreiners, especially the French, that have already got some Smattering of the English Tongue." It is somewhat misleading, though, to think of Miège as a foreigner writing in England. Though he was a native of Lausanne and a Protestant, he came to England while still a teenager and lived there most of his life, facts which attenuated the influence of French upon him. Thus, when he claims to appreciate the beauty of the English language, it is not entirely from a foreigner's point of view:

> When Substance combines with Delight, Plenty with Delicacy, Beauty with Majesty, and Expedition with Gravity, what can want to the Perfection of such a Language? Certainly such is the Mixture of the English, that one may frame his Speech majestical, pleasant, delicate, or manly, according to the Subject of all which Advantages inherent to the English Tongue Foreiners are at last become very sensible (A6).

The operative word here is "sensible" because a foreigner who recognizes the virtues of English is, according to Miège, wise. He claims that the excellency of the language consisted of four elements: "facility, copiousness, significancy, and sweetness." It was not enough for a foreigner to learn English; he had to learn to use the language with refinement, a quality that other grammarians did not emphasize. Perhaps Miège did so because he was foreign-born and he appreciated language more than native-speaking grammarians, who concentrated on teaching foreigners grammar just for the sake of accuracy. As a foreigner-turned-British, Miège secured his position among English grammarians by claiming that English language was the superior tongue and that all people of all nations should learn it fluently. In *English Grammar* (1688), he even contrasts English to his native French tongue: "And, whereas the French is stinted, and grown barren through its exceeding Nicety; the English on the contrary is grown mighty Copiousness, by its innate Liberty of making such Compounds and Derivatives as are proper and suitable to abridge the Expression" (A5). As an example of such compounding, Miège offers the pairs: after and afternoon, forth and forth-coming, off and off-spring; (20–21) the grace of such compounding "is one of the greatest Beauties... in a Language" (A5–A6).

Miège praises English people for the extent to which they had improved their native tongue, saying "that those amongst Forreiners who understand the Genius of it are in a maze to see this Language so far outdo their own, and to find many of their Words transplanted here, throve better in England than in their proper and natural Soil" (A7). Even foreign languages, apparently, were better in English. He also claims that foreigners who used to resist learning English as an "Insular Speech" with "groundless prejudice" are now admirers of the language, especially since he has provided help for them (6).

However, reflecting the growing nervousness among grammarians, Miège warns both native speakers and foreigners not to incorporate any more foreign words. He observes that "now the English is come to so great Perfection, now 'tis grown so very Copious and Significant, by the Accession of the Quintessence and Life of other Tongues, 'twere to be wished that a Stop were put to this unbounded Way of Naturalizing foreign Words" (A9). If grammarians are going to add foreign words to English usage, it should be done only with "Judgement and Authority," and grammarians should improve on what they have rather than to continue adding to the language: "Were this Nation contented to improve what Grain they have already, without over-stocking themselves from other Parts, and putting their Language on a perpetual Motion, it would be much for the Credit of it" (A9). By arguing against the corruption of English by foreigners, he gained more status among native English grammarians because he supported their linguistic beliefs.

From Nervousness to Conformity British grammarians overcame their nervousness about foreigners corrupting the English language by insisting that they conform to rules. But many foreigners could read neither English nor Latin, and so there developed a need for texts which taught English as a second language.[8] These texts were designed not only to make it easier for foreigners to adjust to a new language and culture, but also to reassure grammarians that the newcomers would conform to the mother tongue.

In *A New English Grammar, prescribing as certain rules as the language will bear, for forreners to learn English* (1662), James Howell writes a grammar for English, Spanish, and Portuguese, with additional sections devoted to English literature, English proverbs, and English history. Howell goes to far greater lengths than other authors to teach foreigners the English language. Although the book is trilingual, it resembles the format of Charles Hoole's earlier bilingual Latin grammar in which students had English on one side and Latin on the other. In the introduction Howell specifically states that the purpose of his book is for foreigners to use it to learn English:

> Now, touching this new English Grammar, let not the Reader mistake, as if it were an English Grammar to learn another language, as Lillie is for latin, and Littleton for French, etc. No, This is a meer Grammar of the English it self, for the use of Forreners; With a modest reserche into som solecisms that are in the orthography and speaking (3–4).

This book was astonishing for its time because it was one of the only English-as-a-second-language text of its type. Up to this point, foreigners were expected to use regular grammar texts to learn English and do the best they could, even though they might speak no English. Howell acknowledges that it is a hard task to make a

> Grammar of a Mother Toung, A harder task to make one of a Dialect, But to make an exact Regular Grammar for all parts of a Subdialect (as the English is) is a task that may be said to be beyond the reach of human understanding, the subject being not capable of it: Mr. Ben Jonson a Weighty man, and one who was as patient as hee was painfull in all his composures confess'd, the further hee waded herin the more he was still gravelled (4–5).

Howell describes what he thought would be the easiest and most efficient textbook for foreigners to use in learning English. First, he suggests a "new English Grammar prescribing as certain Rules as the Language will bear for Forreners ... to attain the knowledge of the English" (8). Second, he recommends that some of the superfluous words not used in English be omitted, "whereby the language will be more easily for Forreners to learn: as also of som Solecisms us'd in the common practice of speech" (9).

Howell advises foreigners that they must be able to read, speak, and pronounce the English tongue if they are going to live and work in England. Too often, he says, a foreigner underestimates the effort it takes to learn the language: "He may be said to do his Mother Tongue a good office, who makes her the more docile and easy to be learnt by Forreners: Now, ther is not any thing which tends more to the easy attaining of a Language, and to allure a stranger to the study thereof, as when the writing and pronunciation of words do both agree." Howell recognizes a problem that existed for both native and foreign speakers: how the word looks is not necessarily how it is pronounced. Foreigners, he counsels, may get discouraged with learning a difficult language like English, but they should stay with it. "I have known divers Forreners much affect the English Toung, but when they went about to study her, and found such a difference betwixt the printed words and the pronouncing of them, (which proceeds from the superfluous letters) they threw away their books in a kind of passion and dislike" (83). Howell, by the way, was telling foreigners the above information in English, an act that excluded students who did not know English.

Howell reiterates the advantages of foreigners learning the English language; to prove it, he counts letters and words. English, he claims, "hath som things (that other Toungs have not) which tends much to the advantage and ease of the Forren Lerner, for all Verbs terminat alike in the singular and plural, through all the Moods, except in the second and third person singular" (87). Howell cites an example and claims that "ther are above 27 letters sav'd, and the words made fit to be pronounc'd by an Forrener being written as they are utter'd." The purpose of showing the "letters sav'd," he argues, is to promote the use of the English tongue: "Now, as ther was a hint given before, He doth his native Toung a good office, who finds a way to spread her abroad, and make her better known to the world" (87). No better advocate than Howell can be found for convincing foreigners to learn English.

Grammarians also argued that foreigners needed to conform to the rules of English in order to demonstrate they were accepting the culture of their new country. Part of the embedded message for foreigners was that accepting the culture also meant being able to read the Bible and other doctrinal material. It was an unsettling idea that foreigners might not speak the language; worse yet that they might not accept the other parts of British culture. In *Grammatica Linguae Anglicanae* (1653) John Wallis urges foreigners to learn English in order to read theology.[9] He did not stress the cultural or commercial benefits of learning English but rather the religious ones.[10] One of the primary goals of grammarians like Wallis was to teach students how to read the Bible. Other grammarians like Christopher Cooper cited social and cultural reasons for foreigners learning English. Cooper's *Grammatica Linguae Anglicanae* (1685) is a practical grammar designed to help foreigners assimilate the ways of their new country. The book advertises on the title page that it is a practical one for non-native speakers. Cooper places demands on foreigners that native countrymen could not always meet. In the preface Cooper outlines four reasons for foreigners to learn English: to practice their trades, to communicate, to understand the culture, and to be knowledgeable in art and science. Cooper set out the ideal program for a citizen, whether he be native or foreign, to become proficient enough to perform in all aspects of his life.

Grammarians cite other problems getting foreigners to adapt to the language of their new country. In *The English Grammar* (1693) Joseph Aickin complains about the length of time it takes foreigners to learn English: "I have known some Foreigners who have been longer in learning to speak English and yet are far from it: the not learning by Grammar, is the true cause" (A2v). Archibald Lane was amazed that any foreigner would even question the reasons for conforming to the ways of the English language. Since English-as-a-second-language was still a new concept in grammar books during this period, grammarians were still trying to convince people of its value. Lane in particular made the argument to foreigners that English is valuable and that they should learn it as quickly as possible when entering England. He claims on the title page of *A Key to the Art of Letters* (1700) that this text is a "an Essay to enable both Foreiners, and the English Youth of either Sex, to speak and write the English Tongue well and learnedly, according to the exactest Rules of Grammar." Like Howell, he sets forth what he believes to be the best and easiest methods for helping foreigners adjust to a new country. He tries a rational approach to make language acquisition easier and faster for non-English-speaking people.

Grammarians believed that foreigners should have enough literacy to read newspapers, essays, and other literature. In helping foreigners learn English, grammarians continually focused on literacy. James Greenwood writes in *An Essay Towards a Practical English Grammar* (1722) that his reason for following Dr. Wallis's work is that "Foreigners might be assisted to understand our Language, and read the many excellent Books which have been wrote" (28). Grammarians also came up with another way to help foreigners learn English, by advertising a compendium of grammar in a dictionary. In *The Royal English Dictionary* (1763) Daniel Fenning tries to sell foreigners on the virtues of his book. Fenning says that "these compilations are not confined to the use of the natives; the inhabitants of all the globe are compelled to avail themselves of their help, and are obliged to make use of them as keys to unlock the treasure of our language" (Preface).

Grammarians equated the integration of foreigners into the British culture with their conformation to the rules of the language. John Rice argues in *An Introduction to the Art of Reading* (1765) that foreigners are not part of their new surroundings and are not accepted until they can speak idiomatically (362). The first qualification for any reader in any language, he says, is to have the "Idiomatical Order of its Words in common Discourse and simple Narration. Indeed, the grammatical construction of modern Tongues, depends so much on this Order of Succession in the Words, that they will by no Means admit of arbitrary Transposition; without being rendered equivocal or unintelligible" (358). A reader or auditor has knowledge of this arrangement and uses this knowledge to anticipate the meaning of the speaker. According to Rice, it is hard to anticipate the meaning of foreigners when they lack such knowledge, because "even after having acquired a *copia verborum* and a tolerable Pronunciation of particular words, [they] speak in a very different Manner from the Natives" (360). Thus, "it is necessary that they should be instructed in the particular Influence, which the Idiomatical Order, and the Transposition of our Words, have on the grammatical Construction of the Sentence they compose" (362).

Insisting that foreigners learn English as part of their accepting their new country is surprising for a time when the vernacular was just acquiring its own identity. English traders, after all, did not accord the same privilege to people in other countries, but instead demanded that foreigners abroad conduct business in English, even in their own countries. Grammarians were both confident in and arrogant about the newly established vernacular, yet nervous about the pedagogy for teaching English. In a move to combat this nervousness, grammarians insisted that foreigners could only establish their moral and national identity by conforming to the English language.

II. Grammar for the "Weaker Sex": How Much is Morally Appropriate?

The discussions about women in seventeenth- and eighteenth-century grammar books tell us to what extent learning was considered appropriate for them.[11] If they learned more than what was considered appropriate, they were deemed immoral. Their responsibility in society was to be a good wife and mother, and they were thought to be mentally and physically incapable of taking on rigorous academic tasks. Sometimes authors even thought that women possessed no more than the same diminished intellectual capacity as children. They were allowed to learn only enough to stay within their social spheres, and going beyond those limits was considered morally reprehensible.[12] Since grammar was a subject partially within those limits, grammar books helped regulate the moral identity of women.

Overall, both rhetoric manuals and grammar texts of the early modern period envisaged a "valuable" woman, both socially and commercially. Grammar texts, however, patronized their female readers far less than did rhetoric texts, and grammar provided for the middle classes what rhetoric did for the upper classes. Modern scholars have made little comment on the treatment of females in grammar and rhetoric.[13] Early modern rhetoric and grammar books reflected ideas about the moral identity of women in three ways: misinformation about their physical capabilities, prescriptions for their subservient status, and stereotypical notions about their emotional stability.

Misinformation about Physical Capabilities Women were generally thought to be physically inadequate to do tasks related to grammar.[14] This attitude carried over from the sixteenth century, although it had developed in much earlier periods. Women who were intelligent were even considered physically unattractive.

Martin Luther said, "There is no gown nor garment that becomes a woman worse than when she will be wise."[15] Early modern rhetoric texts were generally directed to the more elite male audiences and to the occasional upper-class female. Those few texts directed to females were patronizing because the authors assumed that females were weak and deficient, both physically and mentally. This was, after all, a time when school meant long hours on hard benches, and physical stamina was a pedagogical issue. In 1524 Richard Hyrde cites from his translation of Vives's *Instruction of a Christian Woman* that women are "frail, and if they [are] disposed to the reading of Latin and Greek and the eloquence of writing it, they [can] easily fall to vice, upset their stomachs, and may become unstable".[16] Hyrde, however, recognizes the importance of women receiving an education. He asks "what is more fruitful than the good education and order of women, the one half of all mankind" (Watson 167). Women, as maternal caretakers, have the majority of influence over the development of young children, according to Hyrde. In contrast, in his *Arte of Rhetorique* (1533), Sir Thomas Wilson sees women as inferior: "Order is of two sorts, the one is when the worthier is preferred and set before. As a man is set before a woman" (54).

Although the female intellect gained respect during Queen Elizabeth's reign, in *The First Part of the Elementarie* (1582) grammarian Richard Mulcaster takes Vives's position that women's role in life does not require an education (18).[17] Because men governed, Mulcaster argues, they had exclusive rights to education, meaning that education was "framed for their use" and "most properly belonged to them" (18). Mulcaster says, however, that men should, as a courtesy, educate women. He admits that women have the intellectual capabilities to learn (51). Women would not get technical training, as they did not need the same kind of knowledge that men did. He stresses that women should learn "within certain limits" because of the differences between men's and women's vocations. The vocational training of men was to be "without restriction either as regards subject-matter or method" (52-3). Women were restricted mostly to their duties at home, and, therefore, their education also had to be limited.[18] In fact, under King James, women were accorded respect for diminished intellects. The King asked for sanctions against women who did not obey their husbands, and dismissed the question of whether they could write Latin and Greek in favor of a much more pressing concern: whether they could spin (Wilson 54).

These attitudes did not change in the seventeenth century. Bathsua Makin, one of the few authors to write about the education of women, and one of even fewer of these authors who was a woman, reacted to the injustice in denying them an equal education.[19] In the introduction to *An Essay to Revive the Antient Education of Gentlewomen* (1674), she condemns the "barbarous custom to breed women low" and the belief that "women are not endued with such reason as men, nor capable of improvement by education" (3). In her anonymous essay she adopts a male persona, a fact that explains why her argument is, at times, more conservative than would be expected. In the guise of a man, "he" tries to convince "his" supposed brothers that men would not be troubled by having educated wives and daughters, that women are intellectually competent, and that society suffers by not recognizing what women are capable of learning and accomplishing.[20]

The Lady's Rhetoric (1707) is an example of the tone and terminology that male authors used to express their perception of female inadequacy. The anonymous author of this text claims to teach young Sophia how to write elegantly, but he spends much of his time apologizing to her for using big words and expounding difficult ideas. The author tells Sophia that she probably cannot understand his explanations of Ciceronian rhetoric, or for that matter, use it if she did. He reiterates his conviction that women are academically limited, incapable of thinking as men do. Upper-class females were not expected to do serious scholarly work.[21]

Grammar texts, on the other hand, appear to be less concerned with female inadequacies than are rhetoric texts, although the strictures for moral identity remain. These grammar texts were addressed to the middle-class female who did not have the option of a rigorous classical education. She learned to read and to write to help her children and husband. Her duties included cooking, sewing, gardening, and caring for children, as well as working in the family business. Grammar books, such as Ralph Johnson's *The Scholar's Guide* (1665), provided a no-frills approach that was less patronizing than rhetoric texts. Surprisingly, however, these same grammar texts did include some watered-down versions of Ciceronian rhetoric that a female, along with her middle-class male counterpart, was expected to master.

Although Samuel Hartlib thought females were not physically strong enough for the classroom, he nonetheless also felt that women needed to be educated so that they did not corrupt their own children's language. Hartlib thought it appropriate for women to read not Horace but home economics texts, and to avoid educational attainments that might make them dangerously attractive, lest they become "objects of lust and snares unto young Gentlemen."[22] The polarized fears that intelligent women might be "dangerously attractive," or alternatively, ugly, emphasizes the ambiguity men felt toward educated women. A moral education for women, he said, should be reformed so that their education will "fit them for the true end of their life in a Christian Commonwealth, to become modest, discreet, and industrious house-keepers" (21).

Grammar books were more aggressive than rhetoric books in proclaiming what they thought was appropriate for women to learn. Archibald Lane (1700) recognizes that young women have been discouraged from learning and that they should have the opportunity to learn grammar:

> Our Young Gentlewomen, who have generally been discouraged from good Learning (their more nice and tender Constitution not being able to endure those rugged and thorny Difficulties in the Methods hitherto practiced)

> may, if they be not wanting to themselves, attain to a perfect knowledge of the Art of Grammar in the method here proposed, by which they may become as learned as those excellent Greek and Roman Matrons recorded in History; which will contribute much more to the good of their Children and Families afterward, than all those inferior attainments which take up so much of their best time and which are generally useless to them in the remaining part of their lives. And if any of them have a generous ambition of understanding the Greek or Latin Tongue, they may now do it at a much easier rate than some excellent English Ladies of our own time (xvi).

Lane claims that although females may be weak, they should have an opportunity to learn grammar.

Prescriptions for Subservient Social Status A woman's moral identity was determined by a preconceived notion about her mental growth. Women were expected to work and produce for the good of the household, but even those acts would not allow them the kind of identity that men or even foreigners had. In directing grammar books to middle-class females, grammarians were cautious about privileging females more than society would allow. Thus, even though girls were filling classrooms and attending school alongside their brothers, females were not considered to have any capacity to be scholars. Girls were expected to learn only those skills that would benefit their families; they were to be of service to others, and not serve themselves with learning. In the introductions to their textbooks, authors still expressed the widely-held view that females did not have the strength or intellect to pursue advanced studies. Females were, however, supposedly fully capable of keeping accounts, tending shop, and writing bills and receipts.

In *The Academy of Eloquence* (1654), Thomas Blount reaffirms what he sees as the subservient position of women. In "Women Commended" he explains why women are inferior: "Women, being of one and the self same substance with man, are what man is, only so much more imperfect, as they are created the weaker vessels" (101). He places them in either of two categories, saints or evil doers. In the pages that follow he describes women of virtue, beauty, peace, and love; they are "Angels, clad in flesh" (103). In "Women discommended" Blount paints a frightening picture of the alternative to "angels":

> Loose Women are whoops, proud birds, which have nothing but crest, and naturally delight in ordures; they are Bats, which cannot endure one little ray of light, but seek to hide themselves under the mantle of night; they are Horseleeches, which draw blood from the veins of a House and State, where they exercise their power. They are Syrens of the earth, which cause shipwracks without water. They are Lamia, who have Hosteries of cutthroats, that kill men under pretext of good usage. They are Harpies, who surprise even from Altars, and in the end become envenomed Dipsades, which enforce an enraged thirts upon those whome they once bitten (113).

His details about the evil women project more energy and imagination than do the ones on the saintly women. The reader may even get the impression that Blount delights in describing "Her tongue" as the "sting of a Scorpion," or that "A Woman is the unnecessary Parenthesis of Nature" (116).

Johann Amos Comenius, in spite of his progressive plans for educational reform, assumed that a woman's proper social role was to serve in a male-dominated world. His choice of language placed women firmly in subservient roles. He believed that females should learn to become good, "carefull housewives, loving towards their husbands and their children when God shall call them to be married" (1650, 38). Women do not need to be educated in such a way that their "natural tendency to curiosity" be developed, but rather in such a way that their "sincerity and contentedness may be increased" so that they "can accomplish womanly tasks" (1657, 68).[23] The pictures and language in Comenius's *Orbis sensualium pictus* (1658) is male dominated, except for a few domestic scenes. For example, men are interacting at school, work, church, and social occasions, but women are limited to domestic scenes in the roles of wives, mothers, or other caretakers.

The social role of a woman was to educate her children, not the world. In *A New Method of Educating Children* (1695) Thomas Tryon presents a plan for rearing children from age three, but he describes it with instructions to the "Breeding Women" about their diet. In *Compleat School-Master* (1700) Tryon argues that women should be educated so that they can care for – and tutor – children properly (Preface). Note the key word here is *tutor*, not simply to cook and sew, but to have the responsibility for teaching children. This advice sounds like Quintilian's counsel that only those women who speak properly be allowed contact with a future orator. Quintilian's women, though, were cast in a passive role. They were required merely to use good speech around the children, not to take an active role in pedagogy. Early modern women, by contrast, were expected to help their children acquire some fundamental knowledge about their mother tongue before they entered school.

For grammarian Michael Maittaire, the moral identity of a woman rested on her position in the family, that is, the ability to reproduce and care for her family. In *English Grammar* (1712) he points out, nevertheless, that women have been excluded too long from getting an education and from preparing properly for a trade. He criticizes this exclusion, stating that it is "cruelty or ignorance, to debar them from the accomplishments of speech and Understanding; as if that Sex was ... weak and defective in its Head and Brains" (v–vi). Despite his apparent respect for the intelligence of women, however, he is not above using animal imagery to describe girls, noting for example, that "much effort is put into caring for females," "in the variety of breeding, some for the feet, some for the hands, others for the voice" (v). Thus, even though Maittaire advocates education for women, he still refers to females as if they were animals being bred for their physical characteristics, a practice that was not uncommon at that time.

In *Essay upon Study* (1731), pedagogue and grammarian John Clarke approaches the topic of education for females by "humbly request[ing] the honour of their Attention, and that they would not be alarmed with the apprehensions of rough Usage, now they are going to fall into the Hands of a School-Master" (245–46). Clarke has "pleaded long and much, for more gentle and generous Usage of their Sons and Brothers," and now he has taken much trouble to write the present treatise "with a very particular View to [ladies'] Service" (246). He pledges, "I design not to lay any great Burdens upon them, because I consider they have other Burdens to bear, which ought to recommend them to the most soft and tender Usage" (246). He argues that "It has been often complained of, that the Ladies are too much neglected in their Education; but yet there have been no great Endeavours used, that I know of, to remedy the Grievance" (247). He is not going to "enquire into the Causes of that Neglect of so precious a Part of Human Race":

> The Apprehensions of wary politick Men, jealous of their own Power and Pre-eminence, that the Advantages of a proper Education, added to all the other Charms of Ladies, might give them a Superiority over the Gentlemen, or at least render it difficult Business for the latter to maintain the Dominion they were born to (247).

Clarke does not describe how to educate a lady or how to cultivate her mind; instead, he directs her to "useful Reading." He claims ladies can "apply themselves a little more to Books and Study, than they usually do" (248). However, he is not "advising them to pore upon Books to the prejudice of their Eyes and Features, and giving them a Stiffness and Sowrness, usually observable in profound Philosophers, and Criticks" (248). What would be even more intolerable is "to spend all their Time in Dress, Visits, Balls, and Assemblies. For those are not the business of Life, but Diversions only" (249). When young women become wives and mothers, they "should have something else to do, than to spend all their Time rambling and Tea-Table Chat" (249).

Clarke makes several suggestions for women. They "should understand their own Language so well, as to talk and write it properly and handsomely" (249–50). Ladies are accomplished in conversation, but do not do so "well for the writing it, with that Propriety and Exactness, which would be very becoming in a Gentlewoman" (250). Surprisingly Clarke goes into quite a lot of detail of writing instruction for ladies: "The Gracefulness of a Good Style, lies pretty much in a due and proper Connection of the several Clauses of long Periods, which there is not much Room for in common ordinary Chit-Chat; but which are unavoidable in Writing, or at least necessary in some Measure, to the Beauty and Perfection of it" (250). Clarke does not recommend grammars to take care of the deficiency, but asks women instead to read *Tatlers*, *Spectators*, and *Guardians* in order to write "justly and prettily." He recommends to them the same practice he does to schoolboys: read the newspaper several times and then try to write an imitation of it (251). It will be entertaining for the ladies, but also ensure that they will not be swayed by "Follies and Vices."

Clarke argues for women to be "well accomplished in their own Language," but does not concede more than that: "I judge it not proper they should be troubled with any more ... it is ... a great Absurdity in the Education of Ladies, to teaze them with Learning the French Tongue, which they have no more real Occasion for, than Welsh or Wild-Irish" (251–52). He adds: "It's plain they want it not at all, either for the purpose of Talking or Reading." Women need to spend their time conversing with their own and reading, "For their Business in Life does not require a profound Knowledge in Philosophy, Mathematicks, or any other abstruse Parts of Literature" or that they would need French. Clarke is "at a loss to imagine, upon what pretence it is, that our fine Ladies, Ladies of Rank and Fortune, must needs be instructed in French forsooth" (252). If they are going to learn a language, he argues, Latin will more useful than French. Clarke recommends readings in history, such as *Mr. Eachard's Roman History, Prideaux's Connection of the History of the Old and New Testament, Historys of England,* and other such books. He recommends, especially to the unmarried ladies, Locke's *Essay Concerning Human Understanding,* unless the idea of philosophy frightens her. She should leave the book lying on her table to give a good impression to her suitors, because "it is more in the Power of Ladies, than Princes themselves, to promote good Letters in the World" (256). Clarke sees no reason for women to carry their studies beyond what he has outlined, unless a woman is "stubbornly resolved against Holy Matrimony" (257). Unmarried women have nothing to do except "to read and think, for the Improvement of their Minds," if they are not to follow Saint Paul's words: "Marry, bear Children, and Guide the House." His feelings about women and learning seem to be more obvious here: "Such Ladies therefore as out of Laziness, or an Unnatural Aversion for the Male Sex, decline that Good Work, can scarce have any thing else of Importance to do in Life, but study, and pour forth the Wisdom they imbibe thereby, to the Benefit of the Publick; by employing their Tongues, or their Pens, or both, in the Way of administering Advice, Consolation, or Instruction, as they see Occasion" (258). Clarke recognizes that women are prohibited from holding professional ranks or positions in trades. To "Old Maiden-Ladies" who are "resolved to have no Pity upon any Man living," Clarke recommends they study languages, philosophy, mathematics, and any other field of accomplished scholars (259). Clarke adds, wittingly or not, that men should like learned ladies; however, the ladies will not have to worry about men talking to them because "few would care to meddle with those that are much wiser than themselves upon equal terms. I may add to that the forbidding Airs, which a severe Application to Study may give them, will be a further Security to what they are so much concerned to preserve, their Virginity" (259).

In *The Pleasing Instructor: Or, Entertaining Moralist* (1756), the anonymous author speaks at length about education for females. He begins with the problematical situation that "Grammatical Learning is at present, perhaps, too much out of Fashion, especially among the Ladies" (vii). He blames the English grammars for being "so dependent upon the Latin, that they appear only Translations of them, introducing many needless Perplexities; as superfluous Cases, Genders, Moods, Tenses, &c. Peculiarities which our Language is exempt from" (vii). He admonishes schoolmasters for teaching "mere" scholars material they do not understand, and he criticizes scholars and learned men for English Grammar being "neglected or so lightly esteemed." No one, he states, can read and write correctly who is "ignorant" of grammar. He purposes "a Practical English Grammar" such as Ann Fisher's *English Grammar* (1750) because it is "independent of the Latin, except in such Articles as are common to both" (viii). To be educated in writing or conversing, a student must have "a Taste for the Beauty and Propriety of their Mother Tongue; and which they can never have, without learning it, so as to know the Nature and Kinds of Words with their Connections and Dependencies upon one another" (ix). Women cannot read and write because they have not learned "Connections and Dependencies":

> [They] thereby apply Relatives to wrong Antecedents, Verbs to wrong Names, particularly when there is a Genitive Case between a Nominative Word and the Verb, mistake Things for Persons and Persons for Things, and are thereby misled in the Sense of what they are about to trace, especially in circumstantial Authors, or such as the Generality call dark and obscure Writers, meaning those who by Transpositions, &c. deviate from the general Order of the Language (viii).

Women "feel an Entanglement" and are "blind to the Beauties and Idioms of Language" because they are "left lame in their Learning" (ix). They are "incapable of further improving themselves" until they are able to remove the "Obstacle" of understanding grammar. But even after that obstacle is taken away, there is yet another one:

> And still to aggravate the Case, they are mostly put to Sewing or similar Articles, under the Care of some Mistress, who is perhaps either utterly incapable of assisting them in the Pursuit of Knowledge, or who, from a Crudity of Scholars, wants Time to point out or explain to them such Places or Subjects in Books as are best adapted to their several Wants, or even to direct them in their Choice of Books. Others there are who have not a Book in their Schools, or such only as are no way suitable for Youth. These Impediments are very lamentable, especially as they occur in the very Nick of Time a young Lady should be taught to think, reflect, and form a Taste of Life in (ix).

The unknown author, however, backtracks somewhat in that he does not want to liberate women too much with the idea of education. He does not "mean to recommend Reading at the Expence of Sewing, but would only make a Principle of the former. There are several Governesses doubtless who are very capable of instructing young Ladies in both, which would form an agreeable Variety, by relaxing or relieving them from one by the other" (ix). The plea in this text for better education for women is still a somewhat lukewarm one: women should learn grammar but not at the expense of their household duties.

Statements on women's education also appear in James Buchanan's *The British Grammar* (1761). He observes, "It is greatly to be lamented that the Fair Sex have been in general so shamefully neglected with regard to a proper English Education" (xxix). In looking at the treatment of females, he wonders why "Many of them, by the unthinking Part of the Males, are considered and treated rather as Dolls, than as intelligent social Beings" (xxix). Buchanan argues, "though in Point of Genius they are not inferior to the other Sex, yet due Care is not always taken to cultivate their Understandings, to impress their Minds with solid Principles, and replenish them with useful Knowledge" (xxix). His statements about the education of females are surprisingly strong for 1761. Should a lady of "Birth or Fortune," he asks, "be cruelly deprived" of being able to attain the "Capacity of expressing herself with Fluency and Accuracy in speaking or writing her Mother tongue," an attainment that would distinguish her? (xxix). He points out, "Males are not only highly interested in, and derive much social Happiness from the right Education of Females," being they are "the sole Arbitrators of what constitutes a proper [education]," but the responsibility for their education "falls more immediately under the Inspection of Mothers" (xxx). Because of the seriousness of women's education, he questions why "Fathers are at all exempted from superintending what is most interesting and essential; of which they are supposed to be more competent Judges" (xxx). Fathers should, he states, "be embracing every Opportunity of enlarging their [females] Minds, and improving those Talents which the God of Nature has conferred upon them" (xxx). If men take care of "these more beautiful Pledges," they will "become dutiful Children, good Wives, good Mothers, good Friends, ornamental to their Sex, and, in their several Stations, useful Members to the Community" (xxxi).

Stereotypical Notions about Emotional Stability The learned woman's proper place in society was thought to be where she would do the least harm. Bathsua Makin complains *An Essay to Revive the Antient Education of Gentlewomen* (1674) that "[a] learned woman is thought to be a comet, that bodes mischief whenever it appears" (3). She reports that male authors believe that to offer women a liberal education is "to deface the image of God in man," and it will make women "so high and men so low, [that] like fire in the house top it will set the whole world in a flame." Contrast her language with that used earlier by Richard Mulcaster in

1581. He gives priority to the schooling of boys over girls because the "male is more worthy and politically he is more employed" (Mulcaster 132). He says that girls have a natural weakness, "their brains be not so charged as boys," and "like [an] empty cask they make the greater noise." Mulcaster treats women as mere containers, while Makin treats them as human beings.

In *The Young Man's Companion* William Mather (1695) not only discusses grammar but makes assumptions about what a good wife should be in marriage. "A Vertuous Woman," he claims, "is a Heavenly Gift, bestowed upon Man, as well for the Refreshment of his Youth, as the Repose and Sollace of old Age" (211–12). He sees a wife as one "Linked to us [husbands] by such Obligations of Love and Duty" and "wholly Assigned to her Husband, on whom she soly depends" (212). Mather also makes claims about the dangers of women. He says, "many Women are to blame" for men leading men astray:

> The Gorgeous Attire of Women do make Men more dissolute, careless, and bent to Lust, and other Evils, (saith the said Author) namely when they build wide Windows for their Breasts, and give their Eyes liberty to wander; the high Towers (or whorish Attire above their fore-heads) the frizzled Hair, and especially the wanton Eye, and Lascivious or Shameless Countenance are the forerunners of Adultery (214–15).

Mather states, "It is a great Abuse … for a Woman to seek to please her Husband, rather in her Apparel, than her Virtues; for to be chaste, discreet, diligent, and faithful to her Husband, is far more to be esteemed, than to be well Apparelled, Comb'd, Decked and Painted" (215). Moreover, an "honest" woman was not to use her education "to meddle in the Affairs of the Common-wealth, much less to meddle with making of Marriages, unless for her own Children and Servants, wherein she must refer her Sister to the discretion of her Husband, lest she incur the name of a Harebrain" (215). A wife, Mather argues, worthy of "Commendation" is one who "meddleth only with her Household Affairs, that loveth her Husbands Bed, and keepeth her Tongue quiet" (215). Mather seems to prefer a wife who is obedient rather than learned.

Jonathan Swift's comments about language ability of women in *Proposal for Improving the English Tongue* (1712) are questionable. In addressing the Earl of Oxford, Swift cautions against attempting to correct language with "the least qualified Hands." If the choice were left up to Swift, he states: "I would rather trust the Refinement of our Language, as far as it relates to Sound, to the Judgment of Women, than of illiterate Court-Fops, half-witted-Poets, and University-Boys. For, it is plain that Women in their manner of corrupting Words, do naturally discard the Consonants, as we do the Vowels" (28). After a brief description of an experiment with men and women, he observes: "I would by no means give Ladies the Trouble of advising us in the Reformation of our Language; yet I cannot help thinking, that since they have been left out of all

Meetings, except Parties at Play, or where worse Designs are carried on, our Conversation hath very much degenerated" (29). Not an advocate for their intellectual participation in the language discussions, Swift seems to suggest merely that women's presence will keep the men from becoming ungentlemanly.

In his *Reflections on Dr. Swift's Letter* [1712], John Oldmixon's shows that he misunderstands what Swift is trying to say, seeing only that Swift would let women have linguistic control when the language is "corrected, enlarg'd and ascertain'd" because they are "softer mouth'd, and are more for Liquids than the Men" (2). He asks how "the Two Universities would give up so Essential a Branch of their Privileges to the Ladies, and take from them the Standard of English" (3). Oldmixon cannot resist adding that the plan reminds him of "Fontenelle's way of learning a language... having an Intrigue with some Fair Foreigner; and beginning with the Verb *I Love, You Love, &c.*" (3). He adds sarcastically that "It is well enough from Him, a Papist, or Layman, but for a Protestant Divine to erect an Academy of Women to improve our Stile, is very extraordinary and gallant, and little agrees with the cruel Quotation of Author of the *Tale of a Tub*" (3).

Charles Gildon also dismisses the mental capacity of women in *A Grammar of the English Tongue* (1712). This text was written for the grammatical instruction of children, women, and other persons unfamiliar with Latin. Gildon angered women by calling them "ignorant, of those call'd the Learned Tongues" but tempered his words by saying that women might "learn to Read and Write English with as great Justness and Exactness as the Learned may be suppos'd as to do" (A6r). This text is one of the first grammars directed to women, but Gildon's comments are not flattering to their intellect: "We ought to make our Grammar as plain, obvious, and easie, as the Nature of the Thing will permit." He claims his purpose in the book is to help women become educated to help at home and in the family business. Unlike rhetoric texts that proposed to educate and refine women, grammar texts prepared them for the working-class world.

Grammar texts did not turn out to be all that simple because they conflated both a practical grammar and a philosophical theory of grammar. In *A Grammar of the English Tongue* (1712) Gildon makes extensive use of traditional rhetoric by including large sections on logic and rhetoric. He follows the method of going through invention, disposition, eloquence, and delivery, and suggests using the passions as well as tropes and figures to enhance an argument. Girls without any classical background or training probably would have had difficulty understanding Gildon's lengthy sections on logic and rhetoric.

In *A Treatise on Education* (1743) James Barclay reinforces the idea that what females learn in the home will help them be worthy human beings. "Ladies," he states, "are generally much at home, and have leisure to improve in musick, poetry, and painting. Such pleasures fill up every vacant hour, make time unheeded pass, and heighten every charm" (235). His portrayal of women does suggest intellectual work: "Each tender note, both moves the heart, and softens every look.

The features always speak the temper of the mind, and, from the emotions of the soul, assume a harsh or milder air" (236). Barclay sets out a recommended study plan of history and philosophy for women, because they are "equally capable of imitating the illustrious examples of antiquity; and the labour of attention, will soon be lost in the pleasure of every valuable discovery" (236). Ladies, he advises, cannot live in "continual diversion," but reading will "reform the subject of female conversation, and teach them to improve the happy leisure they enjoy" 236). Men, however, are "born to labour; and, after much fatigue, can scarce at last obtain one moment to retire," whereas women are expected to be "in calm repose, wanting only instruction to make them as happy as mortals can be" (236–37).

Barclay suggests particular works for women to read, but he introduces each one with an emphasis on emotion rather than intellect. History, he explains, "heightens every tender passion, and teaches a moving softness they never knew before" (237). The stories he chooses all represent some aspect of being an attractive female. For example, Andromache "increases the fondness of the kindest wife, industry grows in conversing with Penelope, and wanton luxury is taught to blush at the examples of Lucretia and Octavia" (237). Barclay states that the female who reads these histories will find that the "charms of the mind will also adorn the body. While the heart is warmed by so many tender passions, the face must wear such an air of mildness as softens every beauty" (237). He cleverly appeals to the vanity of his female audience to read and improve themselves so that will not lose their husbands: "Tis perhaps this mark of internal goodness, which chiefly raises admiration, and preserves the husband's esteem, long after the devastations of fickleness and age" (237). He denounces the amount of money "spent in the education of boys" without thinking of the "fair sex." No one knows "how much they suffer by such neglect, or what dangerous passions they may acquire. But they certainly weary, and are often at a loss how to dispose of those moments which might otherwise be spent to better advantage" (237–38). In other words, educating women is less important as a means of challenging their intellects than as a means of subduing their emotions.

Female readers were also addressed in *The Royal English Dictionary* (1763) with its compendium of grammar. Daniel Fenning states that the "fair sex, as well as foreigners, might not lament the want of a Grammar, adapted to the Genius of our language" (Preface). He advises that he has "prefixed a new Grammar, which ... is plainer (if not more comprehensive) than any that yet appeared" and that it is "suited to the meanest understanding." Even the newer, more forward-thinking kinds of publishers recognized the need to include marginal groups only with the provision that they were not going to overly tax the intellects of these groups.

One woman who transcended the moral identity assigned to her was Anne Fisher, who at first assumed a male pseudonym. Against convention, she wrote and published *New Grammar* (1757), a text that went through several editions.

Fisher's book taught middle-class boys and girls not only grammar, but the amenities of letter writing and polite conversation. Books like Fisher's, however, number few because women did not have the avenues, nor were they encouraged, to write books. Authorship was a man's territory, so much so that if a woman wrote a book, the gender of her name (as with Bathsua Makin) had to be disguised in order to sell the text. As late as the eighteenth century, most men still thought women incapable of performing complex cognitive tasks.

Grammar books can tell us much about the moral and intellectual identities assigned to women in the early modern period. These books prescribed what was appropriate for them to learn, what they were to do with that learning, and how they were to conduct themselves. Male authors during this period considered females to be delicate creatures with little stamina or intellect. Rhetoric books were directed to the leisured classes, and while grammar texts, written for middle classes, were generally less patronizing to women, nevertheless, these texts portrayed women as mentally, physically, and socially inadequate. A woman's language was significant only to the extent that it influenced her children or was useful in the family business.

III. Self-Generated Identity: The Middle Class and Birth of the "Language Police"

Foreigners and women had an identity thrust upon them; the middle class, by contrast, conspired in generating its own identity. The aspiring class stressed two elements in its identity: morals and literacy.[24] The upper classes did not have to emphasize these two elements because they saw themselves already as moral and literate. Members of the middle class, however, were responsible for educating children of less affluent parents.[25] A logical place for the schoolmaster to teach middle-class children language and religion was in grammar books, because all students had to take grammar.

Some educational reformers took the position that grammar and religion were inseparable in the classroom. In The Reformed School (1642) Johann Amos Comenius states that the primary goal in education should be to train boys and girls to "know God in Christ, that they may walke worthy of him in the Gospell and become profitable instruments of the Common-wealth in their Generations" (41).[26] To accomplish this goal, they must be taught the way of "Godliness, wherein every day they are to be exercised, by prayers, reading of the word, catecheticall Institutions, and other exercises subordinate unto the life of Christianity" (41). The grammarian George Snell also believed that schoolmasters should assume the responsibility of religious instruction along with teaching grammar. In *The Right Teaching of Useful Knowledg* (1649) Snell designates religious instruction as a significant part of classroom teaching (26). The primer, according to him, should "conduct the learner to the sacred Scriptures, and to the Grammar for English: of which the former must bee an exercise alwaies concurrent with all other studies; and to the later hee is to bee lead" (26).

Grammarians also had religious motives in that they wanted students to learn the mother tongue before Latin so that they could read the Protestant doctrine. In *Syncrisis, Or The Most Natural and Easie Method of Learning Latin: By comparing it with English Together with the Holy History of Scripture-War* (1675), Elisha Coles states that students should be familiar with "the whole Mother-Tongue" because it "assists ... in the introducing [of] any other that is foreign" (A1v). Coles mentions the principle that one should "consider what there is in one, which may assist us in the Learning of the other" (A1v). He explains there are common elements to languages that help students learn both the native tongue and a foreign one. However, consistent with his title, one of the main reasons for teaching the vernacular was to enable students to read Scripture. Like Comenius, Coles accomplishes his purpose by illustrating the concepts with pictures.

In *Nolens Volens: Or You Shall make Latin whether You will or no* (1675), Coles tells students to learn the mother tongue so that they can read the Scriptures. In the subtitle he purposes to teach grammar with *the Youths Visible Bible: Being An Alphabetical Collection (from the whole Bible)*. Of interest here is the connection of grammar and religion in establishing the correlation of language and character. The idea that a man is as good as his word or that a person with good grammar is a good person takes root in texts such as these. He again cites *syncrisis* in teaching English and Latin grammars: "The Principle I go upon, is that most Rational One of syncrisis; that is, Comparing of one Language with another. And I call it Rational, because it is most Natural" (A3r). Coles combines religion and grammar to provide an opportunity for various skills to reinforce each other. One skill is the ability to acquire morals from reading selections in the Bible, while another is the ability to translate Latin through reading Bible stories. The child also learned vocabulary because Coles chooses quotes to illustrate each principle, thus combining the skills of grammar, spelling, pronunciation, and reading. He places an English word next to a small drawing of the object on the left page of the book. On the right side of the book, he uses the word from the picture in a quote from the Bible, first in Latin then in English. This text was particularly successful with middle-class parents who wanted their children to learn grammar and morals.

Besides the biblical teachings, many grammarians included other instructions in morality. Edward Leedes, in *New English Examples Turned into Latin* (1685), makes the connection in the preface between good men and scholars. In *English Examples of Latin Syntaxis* (1686) William Walker states he has "cast in some short and smart Moral and Prudential Sentences" to make students good men (Preface). He continues to say that "Learning without Religion" may save time, but it makes men the "more desperately debauched, and the more mischievously wicked." In the *Compleat School-Master* (1700) Thomas Tryon follows Leedes's example by stating that education ensures that one will become a better Christian. He offers proverbs, moral training essays, and a catechism.

In *Grammatical Commentaries* (1706) Richard Johnson uses his text to criticize learned men with "a great deal of Learning without a great deal of Latin." These poor Latinists have not been able to convert Catholics because of the "small Number of Latin Books that have been written among us in so many Years" (B1v). Although, he says, there are many excellent Treatises in "Divinity and Morality, beside other Subjects," some would have been in Latin if men had learned the language. He argues that the "general Good of Mankind wou'd have prompted them to have put them into that Language which is most communicative," namely, Latin (B1v). According to Johnson, learned men have missed their chance at furthering their religious crusade against Catholicism:

> The eager Desire of converting Roman Catholicks, which has appear'd for so many Years, wou'd in all likelihood have been much more furthered by this means. Some of those Books wou'd in all Probability have lighted into the hands of some such Learned Men abroad, as wou'd have considered them impartially, and have been convinc'd by them. And what a Number of Proselyts wou'd such a Conversion have brought in after it? The common Soldiers seldom stand out long when the Chiefs surrender. But suppose it has miss'd of this great England, it wou'd however have establish'd the Glory of our Church abroad, and gain'd her a Reputation, which wou'd at one time or other have been serviceable to her, and of which she may come at one time or other to stand in need. At least our Casuistry and Devotion wou'd have been serviceable to many poor Souls there, as having the Advantage of what they find there in point of Honesty and Piety, which if we are in earnest, we should be as desirous of saving as our own (B1v–B2r).

In spite of his stand on learning Latin, he still argued in favor of learning the mother tongue first.

In *The English Scholar Compleat* (1706) the unknown author takes time from his grammar and rhetoric material to go into a tirade against "Papists." He starts his outburst by blaming any faults one has "chiefly upon the Papists" (A4v). In this section he plans "to expose their horrid, erroneous, ridiculous and base Religion, and to beget an early inbred Abhorrency and Aversion to it in the Children" he teaches (A4v). He then tells a story about how "Thousands of Strangers ... desire rather Protestant Divinities be present, and especially the English" (A5r–A5v). The author states in the tale that "none of the Reformed were admitted; knowing full well that their Cause was better founded on Scripture than their own" (A5v). He ends by saying that it is "A Story worthy to be written in all the Annals and Language of Christendom, to the eternal Infamy of Papists and their Cause" (A5v). The commentary about Catholics in *The English Scholar Compleat* is one of the strongest appearing in grammar school texts.

In his plea to stop the English language from deteriorating, Jonathan Swift states in *Proposal for Improving the English Tongue* (1712) that religion plays an influential role in determining fluency and keeping standards in language. In a letter to the Lord High Treasurer, Swift states, "if it were not for the Bible and Common Prayer Book in the vulgar Tongue, we should hardly be able to understand any Thing that was written among us an hundred Years ago" (32). In terms of learning grammar, he explains, "those Books being perpetually read in Churches have proved a kind of Standard for Language, especially to the common People" (32). He questions the worth of changes in language and laments the loss of "Simplicity." And, he praises the "Translators of the Bible" because they were "Masters of an English Style much fitter for that Work, than any we see in our present Writings" (33). John Garretson also focuses on the Bible for literacy and morals in *English Exercises for School-Boys To Translate into Latin* (1719). In his various lessons, he teaches boys and girls to be virtuous and dutiful to God. He tries "to intermix some useful admonitions relating to the Duty of Children towards God, or Man, or themselves, because they can never have Principles of Virtue or Prudence suggested to them too soon; considering the natural Forwardness of young ones to Vice, and the many evil Examples which tempt them thereto" (33). Instruction in grammar and religion at the same time would make a child a good person.[27]

Thomas Dilworth is precise about his religious intentions in *A New Guide to the English Tongue* (1751). In the Epistle he addresses the promoters of the charity schools in Great Britain and Ireland. He recognizes their concern for the "Salvation of Souls" in educating children and for saving "so many poor Creatures from the Slavery of Sin and Satan" (iii). Their attempts will "save these little Ones from utter Destruction" and will promote the preferred religion: "Your Preference of the Protestant Religion is herein gloriously discovered by those Principles of that best constituted Church, as professed in the Church of England, which You cause to be taught, and in grafted in the tender Age of Your Pupils" (iii). Next, Dilworth makes his patriotic statement when he mentions the "Public Good of these Nations, united in the true Faith of Christ." In the preface he continues to make religious statements, claiming that with the Reformation "Ignorance has gradually vanished at the increase of Learning amongst us, who take the Word of God for a Lantern to our Feet" (iv). He states his strong feelings on his religious position: "Since the Sunshine of the Gospel of Jesus Christ has risen amongst us: since we are loosed from the Bands of Ignorance and Superstition; since every Protestant believes it to be his Duty to promote Christian Knowledge; certainly it will be confessed, that all Improvement in Learning ought to be encouraged" (iv). He reminds the reader of what Solomon said: "Train up a Child in the Way he should go, and he will not depart from it" (iv). Dilworth fills the text with morals and readings from Scripture.

In the self-generated identity of the middle class, grammar and literacy were seen as necessarily connected.[28] In fact, the term "literacy" came to encompass grammar, reading and writing, and refinement, but all from a moral perspective. The middle class continued to think of a man as being as good as his word. If he did not speak the word correctly, he was not a good person. Literacy, therefore, was an important means for establishing a person's moral standing.

Most importantly, middle-class men defined literacy as the absence of corrupt language.[29] One of the first ways of protecting themselves from deteriorating language was to empower the William Safires of the seventeenth and eighteenth centuries. Grammarians like A. Lane (1700) and Richard Johnson (1706) were watching changes in usage, while Jonathan Swift (1712) and Samuel Johnson (1747) tried to fix the English language. The middle class was not secure with vague rules or changing usage; they wanted consistency so that they would not make mistakes. The upper-class student, in contrast, came from a privileged background where he had learned rules and followed them when he chose to do so. A student from the lower ranks had to work at learning rules and acquiring refinement. He would be entering a world where a knowledge of literature, elocution, and logic had little value and was seldom used. He learned to read and write among hoards of other students who were all struggling to learn practical skills they would use later as apprentices. For the working class, refinement remained a distant relative on the educational family tree. The working class, instead, strove for literacy.

The idea of literacy for the middle class took some odd turns. One theorist insisted that if the middle class understood the physiological process of speaking, they would, themselves, learn to speak correctly. In *Discourse Concerning Speech* (1668) Geraud de Cordemoy appeals to an interest in science and empirical studies. He provides a Cartesian analysis of speech with a physical description of vocalization to prove that words are "signs of our thought" (2). His idea is that people who could understand the physical working of the voice would also have a greater understanding of meaning of words and the act of speaking itself. He explains that meaning or signifying originates from the windpipe where the difference of sound occurs. Agitation of air upon the ear determines the signification of words (55). Cordemoy then moves from the physiological aspects to the mental, instructing the student to be a good orator. The orator can strengthen memory by putting things in a natural order (102). As for eloquence, a person must use it only "to manifest truth" (103). It is a "violation of the most sacred right that is amongst men, to employ, for the leading of them into error, or for persuading them to evil, such endowments as ought to serve only to make them know what's true or just" (103–4). An orator ought to be "a man of integrity" (105). Thus, Cordemoy moves from a physical description to a discussion of integrity and speaking style. Several grammarians and linguists tried to explain the acquisition of good language through this type of physical description.[30]

Other grammarians took a more practical approach by arguing that grammar is necessary for literacy. A. Lane argues that the best way to be educated in a refined way is to learn grammar. In *A Key to the Art of Letters* (1700) he says that grammar is a necessity because it "polishes and perfects those noble Faculties of Reason and Speech, by which Men are distinguished from Brutes" (vii). Lane argues, as do some of his contemporaries, that culture comes from learning one's mother tongue and then using it by reading good literature. Language orders our lives, prompts our linguistic exchanges, and makes us part of the social structure. He even claims that culture is directly tied to grammatical purity: "Were we as industrious in improving and cultivating our Language, as the Greeks and Romans were, we might equal if not succeed them" (vii).

Members of the middle class also chose to define literacy for themselves by battling colloquialism, incorrectness, and archaism. By determining the criteria by which refined speech was to be judged, they hoped to avoid the stigma of incorrect usage, outdated forms, and substandard language. For example, they rejected "power-coding," that is, indicating through speech another person's social status. They adopted the use of the *you* of the mannered upper class people rather than the *thou* of working-class people.[31] The rejection of a term of inequality marked the desire of the rising classes to have a more democratic voice. What is interesting in this shift is that the middle classes did not designate any distance from the lower classes, perhaps reacting to an egalitarian ethic. The rejection of *thou* also safeguarded against offending people. With the increasing material status of some middle-class entrepreneurs, one did not want to risk using a lower-status term of address to someone of higher socio-economic standing.

In the eighteenth century, members of the middle class became more aggressive in creating criteria for what they perceived to be a literate person. In *Common and Courtly Language: The Stylistics of Social Class in Eighteenth-Century Literature* (1986) Carey McIntosh identifies the role of grammar texts in this process. According to McIntosh, many "shopkeepers and lower-rank servants might be confined in their everyday existence to English identical to that of illiterate speakers, but they had access to higher dialects, perhaps in school or from their superiors, perhaps through one of the thousands of handbooks and pamphlets sold to the lower middle classes to enable them to become more upper class" (37). Indeed, some grammarians made attempts to help the lower ranks raise their standards of literacy. Thomas Dilworth's *New Guide to the English Tongue* (1740), for example, was intended "to enable such as are intended to rise no higher, to write their Mother-Tongue intelligibly, and according to the Rules of Grammar" so they could read *The Spectator* and *The Tatler*, not "Grubstreet Papers, idle Pamphlets, lewd Plays, filthy Songs" (viii–ix). The rising classes did not want to be branded by their use of the kind of uneducated language that Moll Flanders spoke. This rejection of Flandersean speech was typical of the neoclassical period when the prevalent values were correctness, elegance, ease, wit, refined taste, and gracefulness. People wanted speech that was elegant and pure, and they rejected anything that seemed barbaric or corrupt.

The middle classes also discovered that reading was not only part of being literate, it also had some status attached to it.[32] The ability to acquire books and to read them added a degree of status to the middle-class home. Authors were eager to respond with an "art of reading" text to inform people how to read, what books were desirable, and why they would reap many benefits in the process. The popularity of how-to-read books was similar to the Evelyn Woods courses offered today; everyone wanted to improve quickly and easily. A book that sold well was Isaac Watts' *Art of Reading and Writing* (1721). Watts worries that reading comprehension for the general public is inadequate, and claims that he has written this book to remedy the problem:

> There are Multitudes who can read common Words true, can speak every hard Name exactly, and pronounce the single or the united Syllables perfectly well, who yet are not capable of reading six Lines together with a proper Sound, and a graceful Turn of Voice, either to inform or to please the Hearers (xvi).

It is also significant that a pedagogue is giving instructions to teachers on how to teach reading. Watts advises the teacher to spell or read the lessons he assigns in front of the students so that the children will imitate a good example (47). Modeling the correct practice is superior to correcting faults without examples. He then suggests ten rules for developing speech: do not guess at words, do not pause or drawl, do not hurry, do read loudly, pronounce words correctly, use proper stops and points, put accent on proper syllables, adapt voice to the topic, listen to good readers, and practice (53).

Watts is one of the few grammarians who argues that people should read to enjoy the experience rather than merely to pursue culture. One argument for reading books, he says, is that they are one of the greatest blessings that God has bestowed on Men. Through books man can preserve what memory loses in a few days, and he can "lay up a rich Treasure of Knowledge for those that shall come after us" (153). Watts also says that with books one can "sit at home and acquaint [himself] with what is done in all Parts of the World, and find what [his] Fathers did long ago in the first ages of Mankind." A third advantage of literacy is seen in the Briton who holds "Correspondence with his Friend in America or Japan, and manages all his Traffick" (154). Watts' final argument for letters, or reading, is that

> The greatest of advantage of being able to read is the Knowledge of the Holy Scripture, wherein God has appointed his Servants in antient Times to Write down the Discoveries which he has made of his Power and Justice, his Providence and his Grace, that we who live near the end of Time may learn the Way to Heaven and everlasting Happiness (154).

Letters provide a "sort of Immortality in this World, and they are given us in the Word of God to support our immortal Hopes in the next" (154–55). He sums up his argument with the warning that if we "Neglect Knowledge," we "live and die in Ignorance both of the Things of God and Man" (155).

John Clarke makes the same argument as Watts: reading liberates or makes a person independent in thought and action. In *Essay upon Study* (1731) Clarke reminds his audience they can do well in society by acquiring taste in reading good literature, writing with style, and speaking with "good figures." Nothing, he says, becomes a Gentleman more "than to be able to reason closely, and speak handsomely upon all Occasions, that fall within the Compass of his Business in Life" (227). The rising classes were to aspire to be "Persons of Fashion, and a suitable Education," who could be "distinguished thereby from the rest of Mankind that want those Advantages, as in their Fortunes." To be autonomous and to lead others, one must be literate to be qualified: "As their Business in the World, is to guide and govern their fellow-Cityzens, of inferiour Rank, without being Masters of Reason and Language, they must needs be but indifferently qualified for it" (228). Those members of the aspiring classes were to look to the educated person as a model: "Blundering and Nonsense in a Gentleman, are shameful and scandalous, in the next Degree to Lying; and if such will not take Care to clear their own Minds, and see for themselves, they must be obliged to stoop below their Rank, and give Place to Men of inferiour Fortunes" (228–29).

Other pedagogues reinforced the connection of grammar to morals and literacy. In *Treatise on Education* (1743) James Barclay provides a method of acquiring language and "Reflections on Taste ... and ... Moral Precepts" (preface). He complains that boys do not get enough help in grammar and therefore are not able to read words in their mother tongue (64). He claims that boys who learn the mother tongue will be able to "observe the beauty of the moral world and the whole rational creation" (219). Barclay asks: "Our passions and desires, are they not subject to the same uniformity and variety, which occasions all the different scenes of human life? Yet all agree in promoting the publick welfare, and combine in performing those duties that are the bonds of society" (219). He claims that in educating youth, "systems of human nature and happiness" are "superior to the rules of language" (219). By these systems, "stormy passions are subdued, and mankind raised to original perfection .... What observations in grammar can be compared with that which describes the origin and end of human minds!" (219). Barclay's view of education includes God's universe: "The precepts of such philosophy are not confined to particular persons, virtues or vices; but comprehend the whole of man, his powers, affections and faculties, as he is in himself, in his relation to God and his neighbour" (219).

In *British Education* (1756) rhetorician Thomas Sheridan suggests that communication skills could improve society, that "a revival of the art of speaking, and the study of our language, might contribute, in a great measure," to the cure of the "evils of immorality, ignorance and false taste" (11). Sheridan wanted to promote the study of grammar "in order to refine, ascertain, and fix the English language." In *The Art of Reading* (1775) Sheridan tells a student how to read orally with expression (43). A grammatical basis of sound and syllables is presented in the first half of the book to ensure accuracy of delivery. To illustrate his discussion, Sheridan uses sermons. It was in church that the art of speaking with style was particularly important.[33]

Few grammarians stressed in their texts that being literate also meant understanding the words and comprehending the meaning. John Rice protests in *An Introduction to the Art of Reading with Energy and Propriety* (1765), "among the numerous Writers on the Arts of Speaking and Writing, there are few or none who have treated professedly on that of Reading" (B1). He argues that just because a person can pronounce words does not mean that he understands them. He notes many books exist that treat pronunciation in a cursory way, but one arrives at the actual pronunciation of a language by hearing it and practicing it every day. It is possible that a person can look at a word and pronounce it correctly, yet he may have no comprehension of the meaning nor be able to read it.[34] People are wrong, Rice says, if they say they can speak a language but do not understand it. He said, "to speak well one must be a good actor and a good writer." The art of reading depends on the "art of pronunciation in general, or that of intelligibly and emphatically repeating or rehearsing what is written in any Language" (B3). Thus, Rice's work is proof that as early as the seventeenth and eighteenth centuries, someone was arguing for the correlation of reading, writing, and speaking.[35]

Grammarians in the seventeenth and eighteenth centuries worked within the practical contexts of grammar books. They responded to the ethos of their middle-class audiences by including material relevant to their everyday lives. These grammar texts demonstrate how grammarians often drew from other fields, such as business and theology, to teach the things that society felt was useful and necessary. Schoolmasters, in fact, had the responsibility of using the texts to prepare students to be independent, productive citizens, and these texts demonstrate what a powerful influence the printed material had on an audience. Grammar texts communicated to foreigners that they had to learn the English vernacular in order to prove that they accepted their new country and its customs. Through the act of learning the English language, foreigners were allowed to assume the national identity. The texts also defined how much knowledge was appropriate for women so that they would not stray into territory reserved for men. If women went beyond the intellectual limits allowed them, they were learning too much and they risked being perceived as "immoral." Moreover, grammar books instructed the aspiring classes in morals and literacy. Whereas the grammarians assigned an identity to foreigners and females, the aspiring classes generated its own. The middle classes used grammar books to teach the skills they thought were important in building a strong national identity: reading, writing, and speaking correctly. They also encoded other values like honesty, hard work, and morals. Within the context and purposes set by grammarians, grammar books served these many functions for the marginal groups like foreigners, women, and the lower classes.

Notes

1 For discussions on foreigners learning the English language, see Padley (1985); Poldauf (1948, repr. 1961); Webster (1974).
2 See Jones (1974:247–48), who quotes Alexander Gill's theory in *Logonomia Anglica* (1619) that the desire to speak with eloquence and learning has caused many strange terms to be deposited into the English language, enough to make the tongue hardly recognizable as having descended from the Angles and Saxons.
3 Greaves (1594:4) complains of even learned authors who "in aliis linguis accurate omnia dictitant" ["in other languages say all things accurately"], but Greaves complains about everything.
4 Funke (1941:38).
5 Jonson (1640:46). An earlier attempt is recorded around 1620, but the manuscript was lost in the fire that burned Jonson's library. He rewrote *English Grammar* and first published it in 1634; the citation here is from a later edition.
6 See Jones (1974:337–71).
7 Per Salmon (1996:21), "the teaching of English to foreigners was therefore largely responsible for the outstanding development of phonetics which characterized seventeenth-century England."
8 For discussions of early ESL books, see Cohen (1977); Salmon (1996).
9 "Hujusce autem linguae Grammaticam institutionem ideo aggressus sum, quod ipsius cognitionem videam ab exteris non paucis maxime desideratam: quo possint varia illa & maximi momenti scripta intelligere, quae apud nos nostro exstant idiomate. Multi nempe sunt, praesertim ex Theologis exteris, qui Theologiam Practicam, prout a nostris tradi consuevit, summopere cupiunt intueri; qua in re Concionatores nostros, faventibus Divini numinis auspiciis, profectus non vulgares fecisse in confesso est" (Wallis [1653:A6–A7]).
10 Vorlat (1975:63).
11 Wrightson (1982, repr. 1998:190–1) notes that girls were even more discriminated against than boys. The education of boys was determined by family wealth; girls were not only limitated by poverty, but schools, beyond the petty school, were mostly closed to them. See Jordan (1990) for an extended, helpful discussion of female status in the Renaissance. For an excellent description of women's status, education, writings and autonomy, see Grundy and Wiseman (1992). For discussions of female literacy, see especially Travitsky and Seeff, eds. (1994:219–40, 265–79). For further background information on early modern women, see Amussen (1988) and Matchinske (1998). For further discussions of the education of women in the seventeenth century, see Brink (1980); Clark (1919, repr. 1968); Miller (1973); Reynolds (1920); Hilda Smith (1982); Cressy (1980).

12 For a contemporary discussion of women's education, see Astell, ed. Springbourg (1997), Astell, ed. Hill (1986). For secondary commentary on Astell, see Perry (1986), Sharrock (1992).
13 Ezell observes (1993:135) that "our notion of seventeenth-century female education is that opportunities were extremely limited, even among upper classes," yet visionary and Fifth Monarchist Anna Trapnel, the daughter of a shipwright, was educated. As Trapnel (1654:3) says, "I was trained up to my book and writing." Ezell provides examples of such other women as Margaret Fell's daughters, who were tutored by William Caton, and whose maids in turn were educated (p. 136). She also notes that "the number of Quaker women writers, supposedly drawn mostly from the lower middle classes, suggests that there is still work to be done on the extent and nature of women's literacy in the seventeenth century. In this group, at least, it does not appear that one can simply take for granted that the women were illiterate because of their social status" (p. 136). Ezell (1987:12–15) describes the importance of education for all Quakers, both male and female.
14 For a discussion of how early modern English women were perceived, see Kamm (1965).
15 For the restrictions placed on female education, see McKnight (1928; rev. 1956:253).
16 See Hyrde (1524:167). Hyrde translated this edition from Juan Vives (1523). See also Vives, ed. Foster Watson (1912).
17 Ezell (1987:9) stresses this concept: "The characteristic features of domestic patriarchalism as it is presently defined involve two important aspects of human life: education, which shapes one's self and the world, and marriage, in which social values are confirmed and transmitted to the next generation. Women in a patriarchal system, it is maintained, were educated differently from men and were restricted to studies that did not permit them to challenge masculine authority." Ezell argues that as patriarchial authority over females increases, opportunities for education beyond the domestic front decrease. Ezell also cites Fraser (1984:121) as supporting this argument: "The prejudice against education for girls – and its dreaded end-product, the learned woman – had derived fresh impetus from the presence of a male sovereign after 1603." Both Ezell (11) and Fraser (333) observe that women were thought disfigured in some way if they were educated beyond their domestic responsibilities, especially in post-Restoration society.
18 Mary Astell was an exception in seventeenth-century women's education. She chose the difficult life of a female intellectual, remained unmarried, and argued for equality for women. For a fuller description of Astell, see Smith (1982:88–97).
19 Myers (1985:175–80). See also Smith (1982:102).
20 Makin (1674:41–42) not only learned to read and write foreign languages but also discussed methods of teaching them. She also argued for an academic education for girls. See also Salmon (1996:239–60).
21 Alexander Pope plays with this idea of a female's limited abilities in a letter supposedly written to Mrs. Arabella Fermor at the beginning of the *Rape of the Locke* (1713): "I know how disagreeable it is to make use of hard words before a Lady; but 'tis so much the concern of a Poet to have his works understood, and particularly by your Sex, that you must give me leave to explain two or three difficult terms." Ed. Wimsatt (1964:86).

22 See Hartlib (1653:21). Milton also plays with this idea in book 9 of *Paradise Lost*.
23 See Milton's treatment of Eve in *Paradise Lost*, book 9.
24 According to Wrightson (1982:198), "the growing vernacular literature of the age was above all a religious literature and the books possessed by the growing minority of testators whose inventories listed books were above all bibles, prayer books, psalm books and devotional works." Literacy made it possible for the masses to read the Bible.
25 Wrightson (1982:191) points out that literacy and prosperity were closely related, as was illiteracy and poverty. For further discussion of literacy during this period, see Spufford (1981).
26 See also Comenius (1632, 1652) for an outline of how religion is incorporated into curriculum.
27 Herries (1773) provides a manual of equations for success and popularity in the later eighteenth century.
28 In his preface to his edited *Orbis* Charles Hoole's complains about the literacy of tradesmen. He complains that a great number of them "write such false English, that none but themselves can interpret what they scribble, in their Bills and Shop-Books" (Johann Amos Comenius, *Orbis sensualium pictus*. London: (1659), sig. A8r).
29 Ben Jonson (1640: 33–42) has a humorous discussion of this topic in *Timber: Or, Discovery*.
30 For a similar discussion, see Besnier (1675:22–79).
31 See Leith (1983:108) for a more extensive discussion.
32 Wrightson (1982:190–95) notes that in the latter part of the sixteenth century, "Educational expansion had produced not a literate society, but a hierarchy of illiteracy which faithfully mirrored the hierarchy of status and wealth." He attributes three reasons for education acting as a stimulus for social change: greater cultural cohesion among the upper classes; increasingly literate popular culture, and growth of middle-class literacy. In the early seventeenth century, however, the illiterate had to deal with a growing world that incorporated popular cultural and other printed material as part of a daily routine. The social divide widened, and, at the same time, a conflated notion of education including morals, wealth, intelligence, and privilege became even more vivid. Literacy was also more than an act of reading; it also was a factor promoting independency or liberation. The citizen who could read had more power and freedom in manipulate or control his world.
33 For a discussion of preaching theory in the Renaissance and the seventeenth century, see Lares (2001), chapter two.
34 Rice (1765:B2). "We have, indeed, many Books which treat cursorily of the Pronunciation of Particular Languages: But the Pronunciation, or Method of Sounding the particular Words of a Language, is acquired by Habit, and not by Art: And it is possible (at least we may conceive) that a Man may be able to pronounce every Word of a Language in the most unexceptionable manner, who might, nevertheless, be incapable of Reading any Language whatever."
35 Twentieth-century pedagogues are still spending a great deal of money and energy to reinvent the wheel by proving this assertion.

Afterword

In describing the controversies embodied in seventeenth- and eighteenth-century grammar texts, I may have inadvertently entered into some controversies of my own with two different kinds of readers: those who are looking for a more theoretical approach, and those who doubt that the preceding chapters can be put to any practical use. Those looking for more theory may feel my approach to battles over linguistics, pedagogy, composition and rhetoric, universal language, and social mobility is too open-ended, while those actively engaged in teaching grammar or making decisions about current usage may wonder what any of the foregoing has to do with them. The following discussion is aimed at first one and then the other kind of readers, though my answers will often speak to both.

Those looking for more theory are perhaps the most easily answered, as they themselves can probably see the potential for further research in what I have here only sketched out, and can imagine that their own labor would not go unrewarded if they also sorted through dusty, crumbling old editions of grammar texts – or their microfilm equivalents. There are gold nuggets buried among the pages for the patient scholar. The range of discussion in these texts is fascinating in itself, moving sometimes quickly from conjugating verbs to such seemingly unrelated topics as making wine and treating breast cancer, suggesting that grammar was felt at the time to occupy a more central position in its society than it does today. More importantly, a careful study of these texts will do much to challenge the assumption that English grammar "began" with the canonical texts of Bishop Robert Lowth (Short Introduction to Grammar [1762]) and Lindley Murray (English Grammar [1795]). Historians cannot afford to dismiss the evolution of grammar texts during the seventeenth and earlier eighteenth centuries.

Indeed, much remains to be done. We still need to examine issues that have been almost completely ignored in current studies: the pervasive impact of religious doctrine on grammar pedagogy, the specific ways in which grammar was taught to the middle class, the contentious connection between grammar and composition that begins in the seventeenth century, and the acrimonious relationship between grammar and literature that leads to their ultimate divorce. To the degree that these issues can be researched, our understanding of language in early modern England will be enhanced, and therefore our own continuity with those who helped shape our modern thinking about language and society, surely a crucial issue in our own Information Age.

Those looking for more practical applications may best be persuaded by the usefulness of the foregoing information to their own tasks. Those whose job it is to set or enforce language standards should benefit from an understanding of grammar's less recent history, and particularly the extent to which class anxiety drives the concern for "correct" grammar, even though some of the "rules" of that grammar are ahistorical and only date from a few centuries ago. This middle-class concern, combined with thrift, led to the "combined grammars" that are the direct ancestors of the modern usage guides and composition texts being written today. Often overlooked by modern academics, Ralph Johnson's popular classroom text, *The Scholars Guide* (1665), went through nine editions and could easily be called the prototype for the modern handbook. One can imagine Johnson cutting and pasting sections from several grammars to make a more comprehensive single text for his village schoolroom. Several other authors followed similar formats to include what they thought the middle-class student should know: grammar, rhetoric, logic, composition, elocution, poetry, reading, and letter writing.

Those in the classroom may benefit from going back to the actual sources of contemporary language pedagogy. Many of the questions we ask today about the practice of grammar were first asked, and often answered, in seventeenth- and eighteenth-century texts, questions on issues such as whether to follow custom or authority for determining correctness. Teachers may also benefit from seeing that grammar has been a heated topic for some time. I know from my own experience that arguments over minor points of usage can be acrimonious even among friends and classmates. It was no less so in the past.

Another legacy of seventeenth- and eighteenth-century grammar wars is that different social classes approach rhetoric and grammar differently. The long tradition behind the pedagogical use of letter writing instruction in the seventeenth century followed class lines; those class differences still continue today. Letter writing instruction of the early modern period satisfied business needs and simple social duties of the middle class; more elaborate models accommodated the professional and social demands of the upper class. Today, texts aimed at the upper class still stress eloquence; those aimed at middle and lower classes continue to stress plain-spoken pithiness. Finally, I have only begun to examine the growth of dictionaries, another important issue in this period. The ways in which lexicographers chose material and presented it was not solely about which words should be preserved, but about who controlled language, which social classes could join the elite, and which classes were excluded. As a result, dictionaries contained overt emotional appeals to their audiences. In the sixteenth and early seventeenth centuries, many controversial issues, such as teaching Latin with English, had been decided in school texts, and crude dictionaries had little influence. During the latter part of the seventeenth century, as dictionaries became more powerful and reached more people, lexicographers began to claim linguistic authority. Lexicons reflected values of society and standards of current language usage. They might or might not reach out to include women, foreigners, and lower social classes. They might reflect political or religious views. Lexicographers followed the examples of grammarians and negotiated controversial cultural issues through usage rules designed to reinforce correct speech, through ideological definitions and through didactic illustrations.

When making lexicographical decisions, lexicographers were also driven by rhetorical concerns. Their initial definitions often represented brief arguments for their linguistic theories, and they needed to adopt suitable voices for themselves and raise appropriate emotions in their readers to make these arguments work. They also had to determine what level of style would be most effective for their entries. In order to serve a diverse audience, successful lexicographers adopted a variety of pedagogical practices used successfully by grammarians and rhetoricians, such as pictorial illustrations for some definitions (modeled by Comenius), citations from literature and the Bible, and mnemonic etymologies. These practices demonstrate that the successful lexicographers were aware of audience and occasion; the texts they produced were remarkably useful and understandable.

Lexicographers are explicit about their debts to the other verbal disciplines. Henry Cockeram attempted in *The English Dictionarie* (1623) to help the user obtain "an elegant perfection of the English Tongue." In *New World of English Words* (1658) Edward Phillips included terms of theology, philosophy, logic, rhetoric, and ethics, and in the *New English Dictionary* (1702) John Kersey even referred the reader to Gildon's *A Grammar of the English Tongue* (1712) for poetry, rhetoric, and logic. Nathan Bailey used his interest in proverbs to appeal to a reader's sense of morality in *An Universal Etymological English Dictionary* (1721), a technique that was also a pleasant diversion to readers. In *Bibliotheca Technologica* (1737) Benjamin Martin directed his lengthy entries on rhetorical terms to informed, intelligent readers. By using words and pictures to explain concepts, by providing linguistic tags for correct usage, by adding emotions to definitions through story telling, and by selecting details to persuade the user of an opinion, lexicographers made pedagogical decisions that reflected rhetorical concerns. Although we take the organization and contents of dictionaries for granted, we see that the decisions lexicographers made in the early modern period were informed by a remarkable and innovative synthesis of rhetoric and pedagogy, and their contributions to the linguistic efforts of the early modern period are fully as worthy of discussion as the topics covered in this book.

Bibliography

Aicken, Joseph (1693). *The English Grammar, or, the English tongue reduced to grammatical rules containing the four parts of grammar, viz., orthography, etymology, syntax, prosody or poetry: being the easiest, quickest, and most authentick method of teaching it by rules and pictures . . . composed for the use of all English-schools.* London

Allestree, Richard (1675). *The Art of Contentment. By the Author of the Whole Duty of Man &c.* London

Anonymous of Bologna. *The Principles of Letter-Writing* (1135 A.D.). Trans. by James J. Murphy in *Three Medieval Rhetorical Arts*, ed. James J. Murphy, 5–25. Berkeley: University of California Press

Aristotle (1982). *The "Art" of Rhetoric* Trans. John Henry Freese. Loeb Classical Library. Cambridge: Harvard University Press

Ascham, Roger (1570). *The Scholemaster or plaine and perfite way of teaching children, to understand, write, and speake, the Latin tong, but specially purposed for the private brynging up of youth in gentlemen and noble mens houses, and commodious also for all such, as have forgot the Latin tonge, and would, by themselues, without a sholemaster, in short tyme, and with small paines, recover a sufficient habilitie, to understand, write, and speake Latin.* London

Ash, John (1763). *Grammatical Institutes; or grammar, adapted to the genius of the English Tongue.* London

___ (1775). *The New and Complete Dictionary of the English Language . . . To which is prefixed, a compendius grammar.* London

Bailey, Nathan, (1730). *Dictionarium Britannicum: or a more compleat universal etymological English dictionary than any extant. Containing . . . words . . . from the antient British, Teutonick, Dutch Low and High, Old Saxon, German, . . . The second edition with numerous additions and improvements.* London.

___ (1755). *A New Universal Etymological English Dictionary: containing not only explanations of the words in the English language but also their etymologies from the ancient and modern languages: and accents directing to their proper pronunciation; shewing both the orthography and orthoepia of the English tongue. A historical account of the English language and a compendious grammar of the English tongue.* London

___ (1721). *An Universal Etymological English Dictionary: comprehending the derivations of the generality of words in the English tongueü. And also a brief and clear explication of all difficult words Together with a large collection and explication of words and phrases us'd in our antient statutes . . . and processes at law; and the etymology and interpretation of the proper names of men, women and remarkable places in Great Britain: also the dialects of our different counties To which is added a collection of our most common proverbs.* London

Ballard, George, ed. (1752). *Memoirs of Several Ladies of Great Britain, who have been Celebrated for their Writings or Skill in the Learned Languages, Art, and Sciences.* Oxford.

Barclay, James [Rector of Grammar Schools at Dalkeith] (1743). *A Treatise on Education: or an easy method of acquiring language, and introducing children to the knowledge of history, geography, mythology, antiquities &c. With reflections on taste* ... Edinburgh

Barclay, James [Curate of Edmonton] (1774). *A Complete and Universal English Dictionary on a New Plan: including not only I. A full explanation of difficult words and technical words ... II. A pronouncing dictionary; ... To which are prefixed, a free enquiry into the origin and antiquity of letters: ... a new compendious grammar of the English language: and to the whole is added, an outline of antient and modern history.* London

Barlow, Frederick (1772). *The complete English Dictionary: or, General repository of the English language Containing a copious explanation of all the words in the English language; together with their different significations To which will be prefixed, a complete English grammar.* London

Baskerville, John (1765). *A Vocabulary or Pocket Dictionary. To which is prefixed, A Compendious Grammar of the English Language.* Birmingham

Bathe, William (1615). *Ianua Linguarum, siue Modus maxime accommodatus, quo patefit aditus ad omnes linguas intelligendas. In qua, totius linguae vocabula, quae frequentiora, & fundamentalia sunt, continentur: cum indice vocabulorum, & tranlatione Anglicana eiusdem tractatus.* London

Bayley, Anselm (1771). *The English Accidence teaching by an easy method the pronunciation of English and the parts of speech.* London

___ (1758). *An Introduction to Languages, Literary and Philosophical; especially to the English, Latin, Greek and Hebrew; exhibiting at one view their grammar, rationale, analogy and idiom.* London

___ (1772). *A Plain and Complete Grammar of the English Language: to which is prefixed the English accidence: with remarks and observations on A Short Introduction to English Grammar.* London

___ (1771). *A Practical Treatise on Singing and Playing with Just Expression and Real Elegance, being an essay on I. Grammar II. Pronunciation; ... III. Singing.* London

Beattie, James (1783). *Dissertations Moral and Critical. On memory and imagination. On dreaming. The theory of language. On fable and romance. On the attachments of kindred.* London

Beck, Cave (1657). *The Universal Character, by which all the nations in the world may understand one anothers conceptions, reading out of one common writing their* own mother tongues. An invention of general use, the practice whereof may be attained in two hours space, observing the grammatical directions. London

Besnier, Pierre (1675). Henry Rose (trans.) *A Philosophical Essay for the Reunion of the Languages, or, the art of knowing all by the mastery of one.* Oxford

[Bible] (n.d.) *The Holy Bible The Text Conformable to That of the Edition of 1611 Commonly Known as the Authorized or King James' Version.* Philadelphia: A.J. Holman,

Bird, John (1639). *Grounds of Grammar Penned and Published.* Oxford

Blair, Hugh (1790). *Lectures on Rhetoric & Belles Lettres.* London

Blount, Thomas (1654). *The Academy of Eloquence. Containing a compleat English rhetorique, exemplified, with common-places, and formes, digested into an easie and methodical way to speak and write fluently, according to the mode of the present times, together with letters both amorous and moral, upon emergent occasions.* London

Boad, Henry (1799). *The English Spelling-Book and Expositor: Being a new method of teaching children and adult persons to read, write and understand the English tongue, in less time, and with much greater ease, than has hitherto been taught.* London

Botley, Samuel (1674). *Maximo in Minimo.* London

Boyer, Abel (1699). *The Compleat French-master, for ladies and gentlemen. Being a new method, to learn with ease and delight the French tongue, as it is now spoken in the court of France. In three parts. I. A short and plain grammar. II. A vocabulary; ... III. Four collections ... of proverbs ... of new songs.* London

Brady, Nicholas (1712). *The Construction of the Westminster-Grammar, for the use of the young beginners in Richmond school.* London

Bright, Timothy (1588). *Charac[terie.] An ar[te] of shorte, swift[e], and secrete writing by character.* London

Brightland, John. (see Charles Gildon)

The British Letter-Writer: Or Letter-Writer's Complete Instructor ... To Which is added, A Plain and Easy Grammar ([1765?]), London

Brinsley, John (1612). *Ludus literarius: or, the grammar schoole; shewing how to proceede from the first entrance into learning, to the highest perfection required in the grammar schooles, with ease, certainty and delight both to masters and scholars; onely according to our common grammar ... Intended for the helping of the younger sort of teachers.* London

Brown, David (1638). *The Introduction to the True Understanding of the Whole Art of Expedition in Teaching to Write. Intermixed with rare discourses of other matters, to shew the possibilitie of skill in teaching, and probabilitie of successe in learning ... For removing a vulgare opinion against his native countery of Scotland, he sheweth that it hath moe excellent prerogatives than any other kingdome. Whereby it will rather follow, that a Scotishman is so much the more able to prosecute whatsoever hee undertaketh, and therefore so much the more to bee respected, by how so much he is more ingenuous than one of another nation.* London

Brown, George (1779). *The New English Letter-Writer; Or, Whole Art of General Correspondence. Consisting of a series of the most important, instructive, and interesting entire new letters, on every occurrence in life: by which any person who can use the pen, may write letters on every subject, with propriety and elegance of stile . . . To which is added, a course of cards, or notes of compliments . . . Together with the universal petitioner . . . Including also a new English grammar; or, the English language made perfectly easy to every capacity.* London

Brown, Richard (1701). *The English School Reformed containing, firstly, rules shewing the nature of vowels, consonants, syllables, dipthongs, dividing of syllables, and of stops and points . . . lastly, an accidence adapted to our English tongue.* London

Buchanan, James (1762). *The British Grammar: or, an essay, in four parts, towards speaking and writing the English language grammatically, and inditing elegantly. For the use of the schools of Great Britain and Ireland, and of private young gentlemen and ladies.* London

___ (1753). *The Complete English Scholar. In three parts. Containing a new, short and familiar method of instructing children and perfecting grown persons in the English tongue, and of learning grammar in general, without the help of Latin.* London

___ (1766). *An Essay towards Establishing a Standard for an Elegant and Uniform Pronunciation of the English Language, throughout the British Dominions.* London

___ (1773). *The First Six Books of Paradise Lost rendered into Grammatical Construction.* London

Bullokar, William (1586). *A Short Introduction or Guiding to print, write, and reade Inglish speech: conferred with the olde printing and writing: deuises by William Bullokar: and he that doubteth in any part thereof, shall be more fully satisfied by a booke devised by the same author at large, for the amendment of ortographie for Inglish speech, which shall be imprinted shortly, which booke at large answereth all obiections, and openeth all doubts in this amendment of ortographie. So that this pamphlet is printed for a short proofe of the same work at large . . . by the helpe whereof a ruled grammer for Inglish is made (not yet in print): to the great helpe of a perfite dictionarie in time to come, and already purposed . . . hereunto also is added (at the end) the use of the same ortographie in writing easie to be followed of all writers.* London

Burgh, James (1761). *The Art of Speaking. Containing I. An essay, in which are given rules for expressing properly the principal passions and humours, which occur in reading or publick speaking. II. Lessons taken from the antients and moderns with notes of direction referring to the essay.* Manchester

Butler, Charles (1633). *The English Grammar, or the institution of letters, syllables, and words in the English tongue. Wher'unto is annexed an index of words lik' and unlik'.* London

Campbell, George (1963). Lloyd F. Bitzer, ed. *The Philosophy of Rhetoric.* 1776. Carbondale: Southern Illinois University Press

Care, Henry (1699). *The Tutor to True English: or brief and plain directions, whereby all that can read and write may attain to orthography, (or the exact writing of English) as readily as if bred scholars. Very much conducing likewise to the due sounding and perfect reading all sorts of words used in the English tongue. With an introduction to arithmetic; more easie than any yet extant. And several other observations of general use; especially for the youth of either sex, and forreigners.* London

Carter, John (1787). *Exercises, instructive and entertaining, in False English.* London

Cawdrey, Robert (1604). *A Table Alphabeticall, conteyning and teaching the true writing, and understanding of hard usuall English wordes, borrowed from the Hebrew, Greeke, Latine, or French, &c. With the interpretation thereof by plaine English words, gathered for the benefit & helpe of ladies, gentlewomen, or any other unskilfull persons. Whereby they may the more easilie and better understand many hard English wordes, which they shall heare or read in scriptures, sermons, or elsewhere, and also be made able to use the same aptly themselves.* London

[Cicero?] (1981). Harry Caplan (trans.) *Ad C. Herennium de ratione dicendi.* Loeb Classical Library. Cambridge: Harvard University Press

Cicero (1970). *De Oratore* J. S. Watson (trans.) as Cicero on *Oratory and Orators.* Carbondale: Southern Illinois University Press

___ (1971). H. M. Hubbell (trans.) *Orator.* London: Heinemann

Clare, William (1690). *A Compleat System of Grammar English and Latin: wherein that most excellent art is plainly, fully and distinctly taught, and practically manag'd thro' every part thereof. In a method which renders it easie to all capacities, and by the use whereof the learner may attain to the perfect knowledge of the Latin tongue in less than one quarter of the time usually spent therein, and those who have lost their Latin may hereby soon repair it.* London

Clarke, John (1632). *Formulae Oratoriae in usum Scholaru[m].* London

___ (1651). *Dux grammaticus Tyronem scholasticum.* London

Clarke, John (1731). *An Essay upon Study. Wherein directions are given for the due conduct thereof, and the collection of a library, proper for the purpose, consisting of the choicest books in all the several parts of learning.* London

___ (1740). *An Introduction to the Making of Latin, comprising, after an easy, compendious method, the substance of the Latin syntax, with proper English examples, most of them translations from the classick authors, in one column, and the Latin words in another. To which is subjoin'd, in the same method, a succinct account of the affairs of ancient Greece and Rome; intended at once to bring boys acquainted with history and the idiom of the Latin tongues; with rules for the gender of nouns.* London

___ (1736). *An Essay Upon the Education of Youth in Grammar-schools. In which the vulgar method of teaching is examined, and a new one proposed, for the more easy and speedy training up of youth to the knowledge of the learned languages, together with history, chronology, geography, &c.* Dublin

Cleland, John (1766). *The Way to Things by Words, and Words to Things; being a sketch of an attempt at the retrieval of the antient Celtic, or, primitive language of Europe.* London

Cocker, Edward (1704). *Cocker's English Dictionary: interpreting the most refined and difficult words . . . With an explanation of those hard words, which are derived from other languages. To which is added. An historico-poetical dictionary.* London

___ (1715). *Cocker's English Dictionary: interpreting the most refined and difficult words . . . With an explanation of those hard words, which are derived from other languages. To which is added. An historico-poetical dictionary.* London

Cockeram, Henry (1626). *The English Dictionarie: or, An Interpreter of hard English Words: Enabling . . . the understanding of the more difficult Authors already printed in our language, and the more speedy attaining of an elegant perfection of the English tongue, both in reading, speaking and writing.* London

___ (1632). *The English Dictionarie: or, An Interpreter of hard English Words: Enabling . . . the understanding of the more difficult Authors already printed in our language, and the more speedy attaining of an elegant perfection of the English tongue, both in reading, speaking and writing.* London

Coles, Elisha (1674). *The Compleat English School-master.* London

___ (1692). *A Dictionary, English-Latin, and Latin-English; containing all things necessary for the translating of either language into the other. To which end, many things that were erroneous are rectified, many superfluities retrenched, and very many defects supplied. And all suited to the meanest capacities, in a plainer method than heretofore: being (for ease) reduced into an alphabetical order, and explained in the mother tongue. And, towards the compleating the English part, (which hath been long desired) here are added thousands of words, phrases, proverbs, proper names, and many other useful things mentioned in the preface to the work.* London

___ (1674). *The Newest, Plainest, and Best Short-hand, containing 1. A brief account of all the short-hands already extant; with their alphabets, and fundamental rules. 2. A plain and easie method for beginners, less burthensome to the memory than any other. 3. A new invention for contracting words, with special rules for contracting sentences, and other ingenious fancies both pleasant and profitable unto all, let their character be whose or what it will.* London

___ (1675). *Nolens Volens: or you shall make Latin whether you will or no. Containing the plainest directions that have yet been given on that subject. Together with the youths visible bible: being an alphabetical collection (from the whole bible) of such general heads as were judg'd most capable of hieroglyphicks.* London

___ (1675). *Syncrisis, Or The Most Natural and Easie Method of Learning Latin: By comparing it with English together with the holy history of scripture-war.* London

Collyer, John (1735). *The General Principles of Grammar.* London

Comenius, Johann Amos (1896). M. W. Keating (trans.) *The Great Didactic.* 1632. London: Adam and Charles Black

___ (1652). *Janua linguarum reserata: sive, omnium scientiarum & linguarum seminarium: id est, compendiosa Latinam & Anglicam, aliasque linguas & artium etiam fundamenta addiscendi methodus; una cum Januae Latinitatis vestibulo. Autore viro J.A. Comenio. The gate of languages unlocked: or, A seed-plot of all arts and tongues; containing a ready way to learn the Latine and English tongue. Formerly translated by Tho. Horn: afterwards much corrected and amended by Joh. Robotham: now carefully reviewed by W.D. to which is premised a portal. As also, there is now newly added the foundation to the Janua, containing all or the chiefe primitives of the Latine tongue, drawn into sentences, in an alphabeticall order.* London

___ (1901). Franz von Lützow (trans.) *The Labyrinth of the World and the Paradise of the Heart.* 1640. New York: E. P. Dutton

___ (1659). Charles Hoole (trans.) *Orbis sensualium pictus. Hoc est, omnium fundamentalium in mundo rerum . . . Commenius's Visible World. Or, a picture and nomenclature of all the chief things that are in the world; and of mens employments therein. A work newly written by the author in Latine, and High-Dutch (being one of his last essays, and the most suitable to childrens capacities of any that he hath hither-to made) & translated into English, . . . for the use of young Latine-scholars.* London

___ (1631). J. Anchoran (trans.) *Porta linguarum trilinguis reserata et aperta. The gate of tongues unlocked.* London

___ (1642). Samuel Hartlib (trans.) *A Reformation of Schooles, designed in two excellent treatises: the first whereof summarily shewth, the great necessity of a generall reformation of common learning. What grounds of hope there are for such a reformation. How it may be brought to passe. The second answers certain objections ordinarily made against such undertakings . . . now upon the request of many translated into English, and published by Samuel Hartlib.* London

___ (1938). E. T. Campanac (trans.) *The Way of Light.* 1668. Liverpool: The University Press

The Complete Letter-Writer: or, Polite English Secretary. Containing directions for writing letters all occasions, in a polite, easy, and proper manner; with a great variety of examples, from the best authors on business, duty, amusement, affection, courtship, love, marriage, friendship, etc. . . . To which is prefix'd, an easy and compendious grammar of the English tongue. With instructions how to address persons of all ranks, either in writing or discourse; and some necessary orthographical directions; with a spelling dictionary of such words as are alike in sound, but different in sense, very useful to the English scholar (1756). London

Cooke, Thomas ([1788?]). *The Universal Letter-Writer; or, new art of polite correspondence. containing a course of interesting original letters on the most important, instructive, and entertaining subjects, which may serve as copies for inditing letters on the various occurences (sic) in life. To which is added, the compete petitioner; containing great variety of petitions on various subjects, from persons in low or middling states of life, to those in higher stations. Also a new, plain, and easy grammar of the English language. And directions for addressing persons of all ranks, either in writing or discourse. Likewise forms of mortgages, letters of licence, bonds, indentures, wills, wills and powers, letters of attorney, &c. &c. &c. as they are now executed by gentlemen of distinguished abilities in the law.* London

Cooper, Christopher (1687). *The English Teacher, or the discovery of the art of teaching and learning the English tongue.* London

___ (1685). *Grammatica Linguae Anglicanae.* London

Coote, Charles (1788). *Elements of the Grammar of the English Language, written in a familiar style: accompanied with notes critical and etymological; and preceded by an introduction, tending to illustrate the fundamental principles of universal grammar.* London

Coote, Edmund (1614). [*The English Schoole-maister*]. London

Corbet, James (1743). *Introduction to the English Grammar.* Glasgow

Cordemoy, Louis Gerard de (1668). *A Philosophicall Discourse Concerning Speech, conformable to the Cartesian principle.* London

Cotgrave, Randle (1650). *A French-English Dictionary . . . whereunto are newly added the animadversions and supplements, &c. of James Howell.* London

Cox, Leonard (1899). *The Arte or Crafte of Rhetoryke.* 1532. Frederic Ives Carpenter, ed. Chicago: University of Chicago Press

Curray, Edward (1732). *Sententiae Selectae. Or, a collection of miscellaneous sentences, divine, moral, and istorical, in prose and verse, English and Latin. Excerpted from the works of many learned and judicious authors and digested into alphabetical order, for the use of schools.* London

Dalgarno, George (1661). *Ars signorum vulgo Character Universalis et Lingua Philosophica.* London

___ (1680). *Didiascalocophus, or the Deaf and Dumb Mans Tutor.* Oxford

___ The Sloane M.S. 4377, in the British Library

Daines, Simon (1640). *Orthoepia anglicana: or, the first principall part of the English grammar.* London

Day, Angel (1586). *The English Secretorie. Wherein is contained, a perfect method, for the inditing of all manner of epistles and familiar letters, together with their diversities, enlarged by examples under their severall tytle. In which is layd forth a pathwaye, so apt, plaine and easie, to any learners capacity, as the like wherof hath not at any time heretofore beene delivered.* London

Defoe, Daniel (1702). *Essays upon Several Projects: or, effectual ways for advancing the interest of the nation.* London

Descartes, René (1955). E. S. Haldane, G. R. T. Ross (trans.) *Philosophical Works*, 2 vols., Cambridge, 1911: reprinted New York: Dover Press

Devis, Ellin (1775). *The Accidence.* London

Dilworth, Thomas (1751). *A New Guide to the English tongue: In five parts. Containing . . . III. A short, but comprehensive grammar of the English tongue, delivered in the most familiar and instructive method of question and answer; necessary for all such persons as have the advantage only of an English education.* London

Dixon, Henry (1728). *The English Instructor; or, The Art of Spelling.* London

Donatus (1926). *De partibus orationis ars minor.* Trans. Wayland Chase, *The Ars Minor of Donatus: For One Thousand Years the Leading Textbook of Grammar Translated from the Latin, with Introductory Sketch.* University of Wisconsin Studies in the Social Sciences and History 11. Madison: University of Wisconsin Press

DuBois, Dorothea (1771). *The Lady's Polite Secretary, or new female letter writer. Containing an elegant variety of interesting and instructive letters, . . . to which is prefixed a short, but comprehensive, grammar of the English language.* London

Dury, John (1649). *The Reformed School.* London

Dyche, Thomas (1707). *A Guide to the English Tongue. In two parts. The first proper for beginners, shewing a natual and easy method to pronounce and express both common words, and proper names; . . . the second . . . containing observations on the sounds of letters and dipthongs.* London

___ (1731). *The Spelling Dictionary; or, a collection of all the common words and proper names made use of in the English tongue.* London

___ (1731). *Youth's Guide to the Latin Tongue.* London

Dyche, Thomas and William Pardon (1735). *A New General English Dictionary . . . Wherein the difficult words, and technical terms . . . are not only fully explain'd but accented on their proper syllables . . . To which is prefixed, a compendious English grammar . . . Together with a supplement of the proper names.* London

Eachard, John (1671). *The Grounds & Occasions of the Contempt of the Clergy and Religion.* London

Elephinson, James (1765). *The Principles of the English Language Digested: Or, English Grammar Reduced to Analogy.* Two volumes. London

Ellis, Tobias (1680). *The English School.* London

Englands Thankfulnesse, or An Humble Remembrance presented to the Committee for Religion in the High Court of Parliament. (1642). London

The English accidence, being the grounds of our mother tongue: or, a plain and easy introduction to an English grammar. (1733). London

The English Guide to the Latin Tongue: Or A Brief System of All the Most Necessary Rules for the Initiating of Youth in the Rudiments of Grammar. (1675). London

The English Scholar Complete. Containing I. An English Grammar, or rather Accidence. II. A Catalogue of all the chief Latin Roots. III. An Explanation of such Words. IV. Several Select Latin Sentences. V. An History of select Proper Names. VI. An English Rhetorick. VII. A Catalogue of all such Greek Roots, as Greek-English Words are derived from, with the Explanation. (1706). London

Entick, John (1765). *The New Spelling Dictionary, teaching to write and pronounce the English tongue with ease and propriety in which each word is accented according to its just and natural pronunciation; the part of speech is properly distinguished . . . a complete pocket companion . . . to which is prefixed, a grammatical introduction to the English tongue.* London

___ (1728). *Speculum Latinum: or, Latin made easy to scholars, by an English grammar only; neither tedious, nor obscure; composed on natural principles, and instructing the young beginner in Latin, by English rules, adapted to the meanest capacities, for the use and benefit of schools and families.* London

Evelyn, John (1650). *The English Grammar.* London

Farmborow, Nickolas (1690). *Fundamenta grammatices: Or the Foundation of the Latin Tongue in two parts. The first being an explanation of the eight parts of speech; with a most easie method for the declining of nouns, terminating the declensions, comparing of adjectives, conjugation of verbs, &c. The second being . . . with the meaning of all the rules in syntaxis, with the particular examples of each rule applied; with a dictionariolum or index thereunto annexed, for the more ready use, benefit and ease of all those that desire to be instructed in the Latin tongue.* London

Farnaby, Thomas (1641). *Systema grammaticum.* London

Farroe, Daniel (1754). *The Royal Universal British Grammar and Vocabulary. Being a digestion of the entire English language into its proper parts of speech.* London

Farthing, John (1654). *Short-Writing Shortened: or, the art of short-writing reduced to a method more speedy, plain, exact, and easie, than hath been heretofore published. In which, the principal difficulties and discouragements that have been found in short-writing, particularly the burthening of memory with, and inconvenient joining of many characters, are removed; and the whole art so disposed, that all usual words may be written with aptnesse and brevity.* London

Fell, John (1784). *Essay Toward an English Grammar. With a dissertation on the nature and peculiar use of certain hypothetical verbs.* London

Felton, Henry (1713). *Dissertation on Reading the Classics and Forming a Just Style.* London

___ (1715). *Dissertation on Reading the Classics and Forming a Just Style.* London

___ (1723). *Dissertation on Reading the Classics and Forming a Just Style.* London

Fenning, Daniel (1771). *A New English Grammar of the English Language; or an easy introduction to the art of speaking and writing English with propriety and correctness.* London

___ (1761). *The Royal English Dictionary or a treasury of the English language containing, a full explanation of all the terms made use of . . . to which is prefixed, a comprehensive grammar of the English tongue.* London

___ (1756). *The Universal Spelling-Book: . . . containing . . . a very easy and approved guide to English grammar, by way of question and answer.* London

Fisher, Ann (1773). *An Accurate New Spelling Dictionary, and expositor of the English language. Containing a much larger collection of modern words than any book of the kind and price extant: . . . .* London

___ (1762). *The New English Tutor: of modern preceptor. Consisting of orthography . . . Observations on the particular powers of letters, . . . also, a practical abstract of English grammar.* London

___ (1750). *[A New Grammar, with Exercises of Bad English.] A New Grammar: being the most easy guide to speaking and writing the English language properly and correctly. To which are added, exercises of bad English, ... Designed for the use of schools, &c.* London

Fisher, Daniel (1750). *The Child's Christian Education: or, spelling and reading made easy. Being the most proper introduction to the profitable reading the Holy Bible, &c. In five parts. ...* London

Fisher, George (1742). *The Instructor: or, young man's best companion. ...To which is added, the family's best companion: ... and also, a compleat treatise of farriery;. ...* London

___ (1700). *Fisher's New Spelling Book, being the most easy, speedy and pleasure way to learn to read, and write true English. Fitted to all ages, and religions, proper for schools and private families. With many other things of use.* London

Fleming, Abraham (1581). *The School of Skill.* London

Fordyce, David (1790?). *The New and Complete British Letter-Writer ... with a concise and familiar English grammar.* London

Fox, George (1660). *A Battle-Door for Teachers and Professors to Learn Singular and Plural: you to many and thou to one: singular one, thou; plural many, you. Wherein is shewed ... how several nations and people have made a distinction between singular and plural. And first, in the former part of this book, called by the English battle-door, may be seen how several people have spoken singular and plural; ... how emperors and others have used the singular word to one; and how the word you came first from the Pope. Likewise some examples, in the Polonian, Lithuanian, Irish and East-Indian, together with ... Sweedish, Turkish, ... tongues. In the latter part of this book are contained severall bad unsavory words, gathered forth of certain schoolbooks, which have taught boys in England. ...* London

Free, John (1788). *An Essay toward an History of the English Tongue. The fourth edition with additions. Divided into five preliminary dissertations. ...* London

Gardiner, Jane (1799). *The Young Ladies' English Grammar; adapted to the differential classes of learners.* York

Garretson, John (1719). *English Exercises for School-Boys To Translate into Latin.* London

Gentleman, R. (1788). *The Young English Scholar's Complete Pocket Companion in Six Parts.* London

Geoffrey of Vinsauf (1791). *Poetria nova.* Jane Baltzell Kopp (trans.), in *Three Medieval Rhetorical Arts,* James J. Murphy, ed., 31–108. Berkeley: University of California Press

Gildon, Charles and John Brightland (1711). *A Grammar of the English Tongue, with notes, giving ground and reason of grammar in general. To which is added, a new prosodia; or the art of English numbers.* London

___ (1712). *A Grammar of the English Tongue, with notes, giving ground and reason of grammar in general. To which is added, a new prosodia; or the art of English numbers.* London

___ (1721). *A Grammar of the English Tongue, with notes, giving ground and reason of grammar in general. To which is added, a new prosodia; or the art of English numbers.* London

Gill, Alexander (1619). *Logonomia Anglica.* London

Gordon, William (1765). *Every Young Man's Companion: Containing... directions for reading, and writing English. ... Together with a great variety of cuts and tables.* London

Gough, James (1754). *A Practical Grammar of the English Tongue.* Dublin

Granger, Thomas (1616). *Syntagma Grammaticum, or an easie, and methodicall explanation of Lillies grammar, whereby the misterie of this art is more plainely set forth, both for the better helpe of all schoolmaisters, in the true order of teaching, and the scholars farre more easie attainement of the Latine tongue.* London

Greaves, Paul (1594). *Grammatica Anglicana.* London

Greenwood, James (1722). *An Essay Towards a Practical English Grammar. Describing the genius and nature of the English tongue: giving likewise a rational and plain account of grammar in general, with a familiar explanation of its terms.* London

___ (1737). *The Royal English Grammar, containing what is necessary to the knowledge of the English tongue. Laid down in a plain and familiar way. For the use of young gentlemen and ladies. To which are added, lessons for boys at school, shewing the use of the parts of speech, and the joining words together in a sentence.* London

Hammond, Samuel ([1760?]). *A Complete and Comprehensive Spelling Dictionary of the English Language, on the newest plan; for the use of young gentlemen, ladies, and others ... to which is prefix'd, a compendious English grammar; with a history of the language.* Nottingham

Harris, James (1751). *Hermes: A Philosophical Enquiry Concerning Language and Universal Grammar.* London

Harrison, Ralph (1777). *Institutes of English Grammar; comprising, I. The different kinds, relations, and changes of words. II. Syntax, or the right construction of sentences. With exercises of true and false construction. Adapted to the use of schools.* Manchester

Hartlib, Samuel (1653). [*The Advancement of Learning*] *The true and readie way to learne the Latine tongue. Attested by three excellently learned and approved authours of three nations: viz. Eilhardus Lubrinus, a German, Mr. Richard Carew, of Anthony in Cornwall; the French Lord of Montaigne. Presented to the unpartiall, both publick and private considerations of those that seek the advancement of learning in these nations.* London

___ (1654). *The True and Readie Way To Learne the Latine Tongue. Attested by three excellently learned and approved authours of three nations: viz. Eilhardus Lubinus, a German; Mr Richard Carew, of Anthony in Cornwall; the French Lord of Montaigne.* London

Henson, John ([1760?]). *A Compendium of English Grammar, containing chiefly the two parts, etymology and syntax: in which the rules and examples . . . will give [children] a sufficient knowledge of grammar in general, whereby they may be prepared for learning the Latin, French, or any other language, without burden to the memory.* Nottingham

Hill, J. (1689). *The Young Secretary's Guide or, a speedy help to learning. I. Containing the true method of writing letters upon any subject; whether concerning business, or otherwise: fitted to all capacities, in the most smooth and obliging style; with about 200 examples never before published. As also instructions how properly to entitle, subscribe, or direct a letter to any person of what quality forever. Together with full directions for true pointing, and many other notable things. II. Containing an exact collection of acquitances, bills, bonds, wills . . . letters of attorney . . . with notes of directions.* London

Hoole, Charles (1702). *The Common Accidence examined and explained by short questions and answers . . . conducing very much to the ease of the teacher, and the benefit of the learner. Being helpful to the better understanding of the rudiments and grounds of grammar.* London

___ (1667). *The Common Rudiments of Latine Grammar usually taught in all schools delivered in a very plain method for young beginners . . . : with a synopsis of the matter and an index of words belonging to each of them written heretofore.* London

___ (1651). *The Latine Grammar Fitted for the Use of Schools. Wherein the words of Lilie's Grammar are (as much as might bee) retained; many errors thereof amended; many needless things left out: many necessaries, that were wanting, supplied; and all things ordered in a method more agreeable to children's capacitie.* London

___ (1660). *A New Discovery of the old Art of Teaching Schoole, In four small Treatises.* London

Hoskins, John (1935). Hoyt H. Hudson, ed. *Directions for Speech and Style. 1600.* Princeton: Princeton University Press

Houghton, John (1766). *A New Introduction to English Grammar: In the simplest and easiest method possible.* London

Howell, James (1662). *A New English Grammar, prescribing as certain rules as the language will bear, for forreners to learn English.* London

Huise, John (1624). *A Perfect Survey of the English Tongue, taken according to the use and analogie of the Latine. And serveth for the more plaine exposition of the grammatical rules and precepts, collected by Lillie, and for the more certaine translation of the English tongue into Latine.* London

Huish, Anthony (1670). *Priscianus embryo et nascens: Being a Key to the Grammar-School. In two parts. I. The Embryo, presenting a distinct and methodical praxis on all the rules of the common accidence, consisting of short, proverbial, sententious, or phraseological examples on all the Latine declensions, adjectives, degrees of comparison, pronouns, verbs, and participles in their order, no former example intrenching on any rules not learned, excepting the verb substantive, or some such for the filling up of the sense. All which may serve indifferently for any Latine grammar. II. The Nascens, tendering a short and familiar introduction into the rules of the Latine syntax, drawn up after the English idiom, or propriety of speech; with many of the English particles explained. Very much conducing to the more facil and secure translating either English into Latine, or Latine into English, than formerly hath been shewn; it being also a praeludium to the Priscianus Ephebus, which is an explanation of this, and a comprehension of most of the difficulties of the Latine syntax. Both parts tending to the very great ease and delight, both of the master in teaching, and the scholar in learning. Moreover, all the examples of both parts are in an appendix by themselves exactly construed and parsed, with necessary rules to nouns, verb, &c.* London

—— (1668). *Priscianus ephebus: or a more full and copious explanation of the rules of syntax: heretofore briefly delivered and printed under the name of Priscianus Nascens, offering certain rules directing to a more facile and sure way of translating English into Latin, or Latin into English, than hitherto hath been given: together with variety of choice examples, moral, and others; with the exceptions to the several rules. In all things clearing and smoothing the way to the syntax, both English and Latin, of the usual grammar, commonly called Lilies Grammar. With divers necessary indexes for the more ready use of this book; the one of them being a parallel of the rules of this book, with the rules of Lilies Grammar; together with a preface, shewing the practice and benefit of both the Priscians, Nascens, and Ephebus.* London

Hume, Alexander (1617). *Of the Orthographie and Congruitie of the Britan Tongue.* London

Hunter, John (1711). *A New Method of Teaching the Latine Tongue; compiled in such a natural order, as a child may learn that language, more speedily than by any other grammar yet extant.* London

Hyperius, Andreas Gerhard (1577). John Horsfal (trans). *Of Framing of Divine Sermons, or Popular Interpretation of the Scriptures.* 1553. London

Joel, Thomas (1770). *An Easy Introduction to the English Grammar Composed for the Conveniency of Children under Seven Years of Age.* Chichester.

Johnson, Charles (1779). *The Complete Art of Writing Letters. Adapted to all classes and conditions of life. Designed not only to finish the education of youth in general; but for every person that wishes to write letters well. . . . to which is prefixed, a compendious and useful grammar of the English language.* London

Johnson, Ralph (1665). *The Scholars Guide From the Accidence to the University: or, short plain, and easie rules for performing all manner of exercise in the grammar school, etc. Rules for spelling, orthography, pointing, construing, parsing, making Latin, placing Latin, variation, amplification, allusion, imitation, observation, moving passion. As also rules for making colloquies, essays, fables, prosopopoeia's, characters, themes, epistles, orations, declamations of all sorts. Together with rules for translation, variation, imitation, carmens, epigrams, dialogues, echo's, epitaphs, hymns, anagrams, acrostichs, chronostichs, &c.* London

Johnson, Richard (1706). *Grammatical Commentaries: being an apparatus to a new national grammar: by way of animadversion upon the falsities, obscurities, redundancies, and defects of Lilly's system now in use in which also many errors of the most eminent grammarians both ancient and modern particularly Sanctius, Scioppius, Vossius, Messieurs de Port Royal, etc. are corrected, and their defects supply'd with an alphabetical index of words and matter necessary for schools as a comment upon the present grammar and such as would attain to the true knowledge of the Latin tongue.* London

Johnson, Samuel (1755). *A Dictionary of the English Language: in which the words are deduced from their originals, and illustrated in their different significations by examples from the best writers. To which are prefixed, a history of the language, and an English grammar.* London

___ (1747). *The Plan of a Dictionary of the English Language.* London

Johnston, William (1772). *A Pronouncing and Spelling Dictionary: to which is now added, a short, and plain grammar of the English language.* London

Jones, Hugh (1724). *An Accidence to the English Tongue, chiefly for the use of such boys and men, as have never learnt Latin properly, and for the benefit of the female sex.* London

Jones, J. (1704). *The New Art of Spelling. Design'd chiefly for persons of maturity, teaching them how to spell and write words by the sound thereof, and to sound and read words by the sight thereof, rightly, neatly, and fashionable. I. It will instruct any person, that can speak, and uses to read, in a few hours, by a general rule, contain'd in Two or three lines, and the use of a spelling alphabet, which may be writ on the twelfth part of a sheet of paper, to carry about them. II. Short and easie directions whereby any one may be taught to spell tolerably well in a few days, and in a half a year's time be perfected in the art of true spelling. III. A child, or any person, who can't read or write, may, by the help of this book learn to spell and write perfectly in a small Time. IV. Rules for foreigners, by which they may sweeten their language; and directions how to invent an universal one. Applied to the English tongue.* London

Jones, Rowland (1771). *The Circles of Gomer, or, an essay towards an investigation and introduction of the English, As an universal language, upon the first principles of speech, according to its hieroglyfic signs, argrafic, archetypes, and superior pretensions to originality; a retrieval of original knowledge; and a re-union of nations and opinions on the like principles, as well as the evidence of ancient writers; with an English grammar.* London

___ (1768). *Hieroglyfic; or, a grammatical introduction to an universal hieroglyfic language; consisting of English signs and voices.* London

___ (1764). *The Origin of language and Nations, hieroglyfically, etymologically, and topographically defined and fixed, after the method of an English, Celtic, Greek and Latin English lexicon.* London

___ (1769). *The Philosophy of Words, in two dialogues between the author and Crito; containing, an explanation, with various specimens, of the first language, and thence of all its dialects, and the principles of knowledge; a lexicon of difficult names and passages in the bible, and ancient authors; and a plan for a universal philosophical language.* London

Jonson, Ben (1640). *The English Grammar . . . For the benefit of all strangers, out of his observations of the English language now spoken, and in use.* London

___ *Timber: Or, Discovery* (1640). London

Kenrick, William (1773). *A New Dictionary of the English Language: containing, not only the explanation of words, with their orthography, etymology, and idiomatical use in writing; but likewise, their orthoepia or pronunciation in speech, according to the present practice of polished speakers in the metropolis . . . To which is prefixed, a rhetorical grammar.* London

Kersey, John (1715). *Dictionarium Anglo-Britannicum: or, a general English dictionary, comprehending a brief, but emphatical and clear explication of all sorts of difficult words . . . . To which is added, a large collection of words and phrases.* London

___ (1702). *A New English Dictionary: or, a compleat collection of the most proper and significant words, commonly used in the language; with a short and clear exposition of difficult words and terms of art.* London

Kirkby, John (1746). *A New English Grammar, or, guide to the English tongue, with notes: wherein a particular method is laid down to render the English pronunciation both more fixed among ourselves, and less difficult to foreigners. And a sufficient number of suitable examples are inserted to every figure of speech both grammatical and rhetorical, with an explanation of all the terms. The whole being the result of many years careful observation, as well upon the peculiarities of our own, as its conformity with other languages especially; the Latin.* London

La Serre, Jean Puget de (1673). *The Secretary in Fashion: or, an elegant and compendious way of writing all manner of letters.* London

The Lady's Rhetoric: containing rules for speaking and writing elegantly. In a familiar discourse directed to an honourable and learned lady. Enrich'd with many delightful remarks, witty reparatees, and pleasant stories, both ancient and modern. Done from the French, with some improvements. (1707). London

Lancelot, Claude and Antoine Arnauld (1660). *Grammaire générale et raisonnée.* Paris

Lane, A. (1700). *A Key to the Art of Letters: or, English a learned language, full of art, elegancy and variety. Being an essay to enable both foreigners and the English youth of either sex, to speak and write the English tongue well and learnedly, according to the exactest rules of grammar. After which they may attain to Latin, French, or any other foreign language in a short time, with very little trouble to themselves or their teachers, with a preface shewing the necessity of a vernacular grammar.* London

___ (1695). *Rational, Speedy Method of Attaining the Latine Tongue in two parts. The first containing such precepts as are common to all languages. The second contains what is more peculiar to the Latin tongue. The whole being accommodated to the meanest capacities, not only persons of riper years, but any child that can read English may by this method in a little time arrive at a greater degree of knowledge than is usually attain'd after several years drudgery in the common road. Most logical terms being in this treatise explained, the art of reasoning may be perfectly learned without much further trouble.* London

Leedes, Edward (1685). *English Examples Turned into Latin, beginning with the nominative case and verb, as 'tis varied through all moods and tenses, And after fitted to the rules of the grammar, to which are added some cautions for children to avoid mistakes in making Latin; forms of epistles, themes, and other exercises for the use of young beginners at Bury School.* London

___ (1726). *More English Examples Turned into Latin, beginning with the nominative case and verb, as 'tis varied throughout the moods and tenses, and after fitted to the Rules of the grammar, to which are added some cautions for children to avoid mistakes in making Latin; forms of epistles, themes, and other exercises for the use of young beginners at Bury School.* London

Leigh, Edward (1639). *Critica Sacra: or, philologicall and theologicall observations, upon all the Greek words of the New Testament.* London

Lessons for Children . . . for the use of a charity-school in the country. (1713). London

Lewis, Mark (1674). *An Essay to Facilitate the Education of Youth, by bringing down the rudiments of grammar to the sense of seeing, which ought to be improv'd by syncrisis. Fitted to children's capacities, for the learning, especially of the English, Latin and Greek tongues: but may be as a general grammar, and a foundation to any tongue: in three parts, an accidence, a middle-grammar, and a critical, or idiomatical grammar.* London

___ (1670). *[Intitutio] Grammaticae Puerilis: or the rudiments of the Latin and Greek tongues.* London

___ ([1675?]). *Plain and Short Rules for pointing periods and reading sentences grammatically.* London

___ (1675). *Vestibulum Technicum: or, an artificial vestibulum Wherein, the sense of Janua Linguarum is contained, and most of the leading words chapter by chapter, are compiled into plain, and short sentences, fit for the initiation of children. Each part of speech is distinguished by the character it is printed in (a method never used before) and a sufficient grammar is brought down to the sense of seeing, in regard of the thing signified, contained in two pages.* London

Lily, William (1567). *A shorte Introduction of Grammar.* London

___ (1527). *Joannis Coleti Theologi, olim Decani divi Pauli, aeditio, una cum quibusdam G. Lilii grammatices rudimentis.* Antwerp

Locke, John (1975). Peter H. Nidditch, ed. *An Essay Concerning Human Understanding.* 1790. Oxford: Clarendon Press

___ (1693). *Some Thoughts Concerning Education.* London

Lodowyck, Francis (1647). *A common writing: whereby two, although not understanding one the others language, yet by the helpe thereof, may communicate their minds one to another.* Oxford

___ (1652). *The Ground-Work, or foundations laid, (or so intended) for the framing of a new perfect language and an universal or common writing.* Oxford

Loughton, William (1734). *A Practical Grammar of the English Tongue: or, a rational and easy introduction to speaking and writing English correctly and properly; peculiarly adapted to the nature and genius of the language, and free from the hard and unnecessary terms of the Latin Rudiments.* London

Lowe, Solomon (1721). *A Compendious Way of Teaching the Learned Languages.* London

___ (1737). *English Grammar Reformed.* London

___ (1726). *A Grammar of the Latin Tongue.* London

___ (1728). *The Occasional Critique: on Education, proposing a new scheme of grammar, and method of instruction.* London

Lowth, Bishop Robert (1762). *A Short Introduction to English Grammar with Critical Notes.* London

___ (1767). *A Short Introduction to English Grammar with Critical Notes.* London

Maittaire, Michael (1712). *The English Grammar or an essay on the art of grammar, applied to and exemplified in the English tongue.* London

Makin, Bathsua (1673). *An Essay to Revive the Antient Education of Gentlewomen, in religion, manners, arts, and tongues with an answer to the objections against this way of education.* London

Manson, David (1762). *A New Pocket Dictionary ... to which are prefixed, a practical grammar; with directions for reading; the laws of versification; the explanation of prepositions and terminations; and examples of bad English, to be corrected by the rules of syntax. And a plan for the improvement of children in virtue and learning, without the use of the rod.* Belfast

Marriott, Charles (1780). *The New Royal English Dictionary; or, Complete Library of Grammatical Knowledge.* London

Martin, Benjamin (1737). *Bibliotheca Technologica: or, a philogical library of literary arts and sciences.* London

___ (1749). *Lingua Britannica Reformata: Or, a New English Dictionary, under the following titles, universal ... etymological ... orthographical ... orthoepical ... diacritical ... philological ... mathematical ... philosophical. To which is prefix'd, an introduction, containing a physico-grammatical essay on the propriety and rationale of the English tongue, deduced from a general idea of the nature and necessity of speech for human society; a particular view of the genius and usage of the original mother tongues.* London

Mather, William (1695). *The Young Man's Companion: or, arithmetick made easie. With plain directions for a young man, to attain to read and write to true English, and short-hand, or characters. And also very easie rules for measuring land, globes ... The use of Gunter's quadrant, dialling ... Choice experiments in physick and* chyrugery ... With choice presidents in the law, and advice upon them ... With an alphabetical table, for the ready finding of any matter herein contained. London

Mayne, J. L. (1799). *A Compendious English Grammar, with ungrammatical exercises, to be corrected according to rule: also exercises in false English.* Birmingham

Merriman, Thomas (1750). *A Compendious English Grammar: wherein are comprised all the chief principles, and necessary rules of that art.* Reading

Metcalfe, Theophilus (1645). *Short Writing the most easie exact lineall and speedy method that hath ever yet been obtained or taught by any in this kingdome.* London

Miège, Guy (1688). *The English Grammar setting forth the grounds of the English tongue; and particularly its genius in making compounds and derivatives ... A necessary work in general for all persons desirous to understand the grounds and genius of the English, and very proper to prepare young men for the Latine tongue.* London

___ (1679). *Dictionary of Barbarous French, or a collection, by way of alphabet, of obsolete, provincial, mis-spelt, and made words in French taken out of Cotgrave's dictionary with some additions: a work much desired, and now performed, for the satisfaction of such as read Old French.* London

___ (1688). *The Great French dictionary. In two parts. The first, French and English; the second, English and French; according to the ancient and modern orthography. Wherein each language is set forth in its greatest latitude: the various senses of words, both proper and figurative, are orderly digested; and illustrated with apposite phrases, and proverbs: the hard words explained; and the proprieties adjusted. To which are prefixed the grounds of both languages, in two grammatical discourses; the one English, and the other French.* London

___ (1678). *A New French Grammar; or, a new method for learning of the French tongue. To which are added, for a help to young beginners, a large vocabulary; and a store of familiar dialogues. Besides four curious discourses of cosmography, in French, for proficient learners to turn into English.* London

___ (1685). *A Short Dictionary of English and French, with another French and English according to the present use and modern orthography.* London

___ (1690). *Short French and English Dictionary.* London

Milner, John (1739). *A Practical Grammar of the Latin Tongue. Wherein all the rules for understanding that language, are given in English; those, necessary to be got by heart, made the text, others immediately subjoin'd in the form of notes. The whole establish'd upon rational principles, supported by classical authorities, and consider'd, as to method and length, with all convenience to the learner. To which is added a vocabulary of such particulars as could not well be dispos'd into the analogical part. Being a collection from those very learned masters, Sanctius and Perizonius, Vossius, Oxford annotators, Mr. Johnson, Dr. Shaw, Mr. Blackwall, Mr. Lowe, &c. Drawn up at first to serve a private occasion of life, and now made publick, as a testimony of respect to the British youth.* London

Milton, John (1669). *Accedence Commenc't Grammar, supply'd with sufficient rules, for the use of such (younger or elder) as are desirous, without more trouble than needs to attain the Latin tongue; the elder sort especially, with little teaching, and their own industry.* London

___ (1953–82). Don M. Wolfe, ed. *The Complete Prose Works of John Milton.* 8 vols. New Haven: Yale University Press

___ (1644). *Of Education. To Master Samuel Hartlib.* London

Mitford, William (1774). *Essay upon the Harmony of Languages.* London

Mulcaster, Richard (1582). *The First Part of the Elementarie, which entreateth chefelie of the right writing of our English tung.* London

___ (1581). *Positions Wherein Those Primitive Circumstances Be Examined, Which are Necessarie for the Training up of Children.* London. *The Educational Writings of Richard Mulcaster.* James Oliphant, ed. (1903). Glasgow: James Maclehose and Sons

Murray, Lindley (1795). *English Grammar, adapted to the different classes of learners. With an appendix, containing rules and observations for promoting perspicuity in speaking and writing.* York

Newbery, John (1745). *An easie Introduction to the English Language; or, a compendious grammar for the use of young gentlemen, ladies, and foreigners.* London

New English Accidence, by way of short question and answer, built upon the plan of the Latin grammar, so far as it agrees with and is consistent with the nature and genius of the English tongue. Designed for the use and benefit, and adapted to the capacity of young lads at the English school. In order to teach them the grounds of their mother tongue, and fit them for the more easy and expeditious attaining the grammar of the Latin, or any other language. (1736). London

Newton, John (1693). *The English Academy: or, a brief introduction to the seven liberal arts. Grammar, arithmetick, geometrie, musick, astronomie, rhetorick, & logick. To which is added. The necessary arts and mysteries of navigation, dyaling, surveying, mensuration, gauging & fortification, practically laid down in all their material points and particulars, highly approved to be known by the ingenious, and as such are desirous to profit, or render themselves accomplished. Chiefly intended for the instruction of young scholars, who are acquainted with no other than their native language; but may also be very useful to other persons that have made some progress in the studies of the said arts.* London

___ (1669). *School Pastime for Young Children: or the rudiments of grammar an easie and delightful method, for teaching of children to read English distinctly, and to write it truly. In which, by way of preface, a new method is propounded, for the fitting of children first for trades, and then for the Latin, and other languages.* London

Oldmixon, John ([1712]). *Reflections on Dr. Swift's Letter to the Earl of Oxford, about the English tongue.* London

Oliphant, R. (1781). *A Compendium of English Grammar drawn up for the use of the young ladies at the boarding school.* Newcastle

Osborn, Thomas (1688). *A Rational Way of Teaching.* London

Pape, Daniel (1790). *A Key to English Grammar, by which it has been proved, by experience, that a boy, with a tolerable capacity, and of ten years of age only, may, in a few months, be taught to write the English language properly and correctly, though totally unacquainted with the Latin and Greek languages.* Newcastle

Perottus, Nicholas (1473). *Rudimenta Grammatices.* 1468. London

Perry, William (1776). *The Only Sure Guide to the English Tongue; or, new pronouncing spelling-book . . . to which is added, a comprehensive grammar of the English language.* Edinburgh

___ (1775). *The Royal Standard English Dictionary; in which the words are not only rationally divided into syllables, accurately accented, their part of speech properly distinguished, and their various significations arranged in one line, but likewise by a key to this work, . . . to which is prefixed a comprehensive grammar of the English language.* Edinburgh

Phillips, Edward (1658). *The New World of English Words: or, a General Dictionary: containing the interpretations of such hard words as are derived from other languages . . . Together with all those terms that relate to the arts and sciences . . . To which are added the significations of proper names, mythology, and poetical fictions, historical relations, geographical descriptions of most countries and cities of the world . . . as also all other subjects that are useful, and appertain to our English language.* London

___ (1696). *The New World of English Words: or, a General Dictionary: containing the interpretations of such hard words as are derived from other languages . . . Together with definitions of all those terms that conduce to the understanding of any of the arts and sciences . . . To which is added, the interpretations of proper names, derived from the ancient and modern tongues; also the sum of all the most remarkable mythology and history, deduced from the names of persons eminent in either; and likewise the geographical descriptions of the chief countries and cities in the world, especially of these three nations.* London

___ (1720). *The New World of English Words: or, universal dictionary.* London

Philipps, Jenkin Thomas (1721). *Compendius Way of Teaching the Learned Languages, and some of the liberal sciences at the same time . . . Propos'd to the consideration of parents, and guardians of children. To which is annex'd, Mr. Locke's Judgment of Latin Exercises.* London

___ (1726). *An Essay towards an Universal and Rational Grammar.* London

The Pleasing Instructor: Or, Entertaining Moralist. Consisting of Select Essays, Relations, Visions and Allegories (1756). Newcastle Upon Tyne

A Pocket Dictionary or Complete English Expositor: Shewing readily the part of speech to which each word belongs; its true meaning, when not self-evident; its various senses . . . and the language, from whence it is deriv'd . . . To which is prefix'd an

introduction containing an history of the English language, with a compendious grammar. (1753). London

Poole, Josua (1646). *The English Accidence: or, a short, plaine, and easie way, for the more speedy attaining to the Latine tongue, by the help of the English set out for the use and profit of young children, & framed so, as they may bee exercised in it, as soon as they can but indifferently read English.* London

Pope, Alexander (1964). William K. Wimsatt, Jr, ed. *The Rape of the Lock. Alexander Pope: Selected Poetry & Prose.* New York: Holt, Rinehart and Winston

Priestly, Joseph (1762). *A Course of Lectures: On the Theory of Language, and Universal Grammar.* Warrington

___ (1761). *The Rudiments of English Grammar; adapted to the use of schools. With notes and Observations, For the use of those who have made some proficiency in the Language.* London

Priscian (1855). Martin Hertz, ed. *Institutiones grammaticae.* 2 vols. Leipzig

Quintilian (1920). H. E. Butler (trans.) *Institutio Oratoria.* 4 vols. Cambridge, Massachusetts.: Loeb Classical Library

Ramus, Peter (1559). *Scholae grammaticae.* Paris

Raue, Christian (1648). *A Discourse of the Orientall Tongues viz. Ebrew, Samaritan, Calde, Syriac, Arabic, and Ethiopic. Together with a generall grammar of the said tongues.* London

A Real English Grammar; in which the nature of the several parts of speech, and of their dependence on each other is set forth in a plain and familiar manner fitted for the use of boy, &c. which will enable them to speak and write their native language with grammatical propriety. (1764). Dublin

Reisch, Gregorovius de (1504). "The Complete Epitome of Philosophy, or the Philosophical Pearl, treating of every kind of known thing: with additions such as are to be found nowhere else," in *Margarita Philosophical.* Heidelberg

Rhodes, Benjamin (1795). *Concise English Grammar.* Birmingham

Rice, John (1765). *An Introduction to the Art of Reading with Energy and Propriety.* London

Richardson, Alexander (1657). *The Logician's School-Master: or, a comment upon Ramus logicke.* London

Richardson, Edward (1677). *Anglo-Belgica. The English and Netherdutch Academy. In three parts. Containing the exactest grammar-rules, most usefull discourses and letters, with a copious vocabulary, fitted to the capacities of all sorts of persons. Being a work brought to greater perfection than any ever formerly extant; whereby men may, with a little pains, speedily attain to the compleat knowledge of both the languages.* Amsterdam

Ridpath, George (1687). *Short-hand yet shorter: or, the art of short-writing advanced in a more swift, easie, regular, and natural method than hitherto. Whereby the former difficulties in placing the vowels are removed; they, the dipthongs and* consonants, further contracted; the particles, pronouns, degrees of comparison, persons, moods, tenses, contrarieties, repetitions, sentences negative and interrogatory, are shortned. The rules are plain, easie to be remembred and applied to any other short-hand, that such as have learned other authors may have hence a very considerable help to write more swiftly without altering their foundations.* London

Right Spelling Very much Improved. Teaching the Speediest and Surest way to Write True English; By Rule and not by Rote. With Particular Tables, of the most Material Exceptions, clearly explained, to the meanest Capacity. For the benefit of Foreigners, and all such as desire to Write True English with Ease and Certainty. (1704). London

Robertson, W. ([1654?]). *Sha'ar Ha Rivshon'o Petach Hechivson 'el L 'Shon Hakodesh The first gate, or The outward door to the holy tongue, opened in English.* London

Rodriquez, Alfonso (1697). *The Practice of Christian Perfection.* London

R. R. [Ralph Robinson] (1641). *An English Grammar or, a plain Exposition of Lilies Grammar in English, with easie and profitable Rules for parsing and making Latine: Very usefull for all young Scholars, and others, that would in a short time learn the Latine tongue. Which may serve as a Comment for them that learn Lilies' Grammar.* London

Saxon, Samuel (1737). *The English Schollar's Assistant: or, the rudiments of the English tongue.* Reading

Shaw, Samuel (1678). *Words Made Visible: or grammar and rhetorick accommodated to the lives and manners of men.* London

Sheridan, Thomas (1756). *British Education; or, the source of the disorders or Great Britain.* London

___ (1780). *A General Dictionary of the English Language, one main object of which is to establish a plain and permanent standard of pronunciation, to which is prefixed a rhetorical grammar.* London

___ (1775). *Lectures on the Art of Reading.* Dublin

___ (1781). *A Rhetorical Grammar of the English Language. Calculated solely for the purposes or teaching propriety of pronunciation, and justness of delivery, in that tongue, by the organs of speech.* London

Smetham, Thomas (1774). *The Practical Grammar; or, an easy way to understand English. In which the rules are laid down in a manner entirely new; and the whole rendered so easy, familiar, and entertaining, that a child of only eight years of age may be perfectly initiated into a knowledge of the English tongue, with the greatest expedition and pleasure. To which is added, a poetical epitome of grammar, for the help of the memory, with a supplement, containing examples of bad English to be turned into good, with the good opposite, in order to illustrate every rule of syntax, or the composition of sentences; and a short English grammar, upon the plan of the Latin, for the use of such as are designed for the study of that language.* London

Smith, Adam (1971). John M. Lothian, ed. *Lectures on rhetoric and belles lettres.* 1963. Carbondale: Southern Illinois Press

Smith, J. (1674). *Grammatica quadrilinguis, or, brief instructions for the French, Italian, Spanish, and English tongues. With the proverbs of each language, fitted for those who desire to perfect themselves therein.* London

Smith, James (1778). *A Compendium of English Grammar . . . the whole designed principally for children before they enter upon Latin grammar and for such as have not the advantage of a classical education.* Norwich

Snell, George (1649). *The Right Teaching of Useful Knowledg, to fit scholars for some honest profession; shewing so much skil as anie man needeth (that is not a teacher) in all knowledges, in one schole, in a shorter time in a more plain waie, and for much less expens than ever that been used, since of old the arts were so taught in the Greek and Romane empire.* London

Spelling-Dictionary of the English Language . . . To Which is prefixed a compendious English Grammar (1757). London

Stackhouse, Thomas (1731). *Reflections on the Nature and Property of Language in General, on the advantages, defects, and manner of improving the English tongue in particular.* London

Stirling, John (1735). *A Short View of English Grammar. In a method intirely new.* London

___ (1740). *A System of Rhetoric, in a method entirely new.* London

Story, Joshua (1783). *An Introduction to English Grammar; to which is annexed a treatise on rhetorick.* London

Strong, Nathaniel (1697). *England's Perfect School Master.* London

Swift, Jonathan (1712). *Proposal for Correcting, Improving and Ascertaining the English Tongue.* London

Trapnel, Anna (1654). *The Cry of a Stone, or a relation of something spoken in Whitehall, by Anna Trapnel, being in the visions of God.* London

The True Method of Learning the Latin Tongue by the English, and of obtaining the more perfect knowledge of the English by the Latin; containing a grammar for both the languages in a short, sure and easie way. (1696). London

Tryon, Thomas (1700). *Compleat School-Master, or Childs Instructor: being a new method of teaching children at three years old to read and write English, also to understand Latin or French in 12 months time as well as he can understand English.* London

___ (1695). *A New Method of Education of Children: or rules and directions for the well ordering and governing them, during their young years. Shewing that they are capable, at the age of three years, to be caused to learn languages, and most arts and sciences; which, if observed by parents, would be of greater value than a thousand pounds portion. Also, what methods is to be used by breeding women, and what diet is most proper for them, and their children, to prevent wind, vapours, convulsions, &c.* London

Turner, Daniel (1739). *Abstract of English Grammar and Rhetoric.* London

An Universal Dictionary of the English Language . . . to which is prefixed a grammar of the English Language (1763). Edinburgh

Vives, Juan (1912). *The Instruction of a Christian Woman.* In *Vives and the Renascence Education of Women,* Foster Watson, ed. New York: Longmans, Green and Co.

___ (1592). Richard Hyrde (trans.) *Instruction of a Christian Woman.* (1524). London

Vossius, G. J. (1635). *De Arte Grammatica Libri Septem.* Amsterdam

W. P. (1678). *A Flying Post, with a Packet of Choice new Letters and Compliments: containing variety of examples of witty and delightful letters, upon all occasions both of love and business, and is of very great use and help to all such as have a desire to learn to endite, and write letters, after the best and most elegant manner now used in court, city, or country, being both pleasant and profitable.* London

Walker, Obadiah (1673). *Of Education, especially of young gentlemen.* Oxford

___ (1659). *Some Instruction concerning the Art of Oratory.* Oxford

Walker, William (1686). *English Examples of the Latin Syntaxis.* London

___ (1670). *The Royal Grammar Explained, commonly called Lylly's Grammar, explained in the rules of it which concern the genders and irregular declinings of nouns; and the preterperfect tenses and supines of verbs; ordinarily called, propria quae maribus; quae genus; and as in praesenti. By way of question and answer, opening the meanings of the rules with great plainness to the understanding of children of meanest capacity. With choice critical observations on the same, from the best extant authours and grammarians. For the amending of the mistakes, and supplying of the defects thereof.* London

___ (1669). *Some Improvements to the Art of Teaching especially in the first grounding of a young scholar in grammar learning.* London

___ (1686). *A Treatise of English Particles, shewing much of the variety of their significations and uses in English: and how to render them into Latin according to the propriety and elegancy of that language.* London

Wallis, John (1653). *Grammatica lingua Anglicanae.* London

Ward, John (1758). *Four Essays upon the English Language.* London

Ward, William (1765). *An Essay on Grammar.* London

Wase, Christopher (1676). *Methodi practicae specimen. An essay of a practical grammar; or, an enquiry after a more easie and certain help to the construing and pearcing of authors; and to the making and speaking of Latin. Containing a set of Latins answerable to the most fundamental rules of grammar, and delivered in an easie method for the first beginners to make Latin, at their entrance on the rules of construction.* London

Waterland, Daniel (1730). *Advice to a Young Student.* London

Watts, Isaac (1721). *The Art of Reading and Writing English: or, the chief principles and rules of pronouncing our mother-tongue, both in prose and verse; with a variety of instructions for true spelling. Written at first for private use, and now published for the benefit of all persons who desire a better acquaintance with their native language.* London

Webbe, Joseph (1622). *An Appeale to Truth, in the Controversie betweene Art, & Use; about the best and most expedient course in languages.* London

Welsted, Leonard (1724). *Epistles, odes, &c. written on several subjects. With a translation of Longinus' treatise on the sublime. By Mr. Welsted. To which is prefix'd, a dissertation concerning the perfection of the English language.* London

Wesley, John (1753). *The Complete English Dictionary.* London

Wharton, Jeremiah (1654). *The English-Grammar: or, the institution of letters, syllables, and words in the English-tongue. Conteining all rules and directions necesary to bee known for the judicious reading, right-speaking, and writing thereof. Very useful for all, that desire to bee expert in the foresaid properties. More especially profitable for scholars, immediately before their entrance into the rudiments of the Latine-tongue. Likewise to strangers that desire to learn our language, it will bee the most certain guide, that ever yet was extant.* London

Wheeler, Maurice (1695). *The Royal Grammar Reformed into a more easie method, for the better understanding of the English: and more speedy attainment of the Latin tongue.* London

Willis, John (1621). *The Art of Memory.* London

___ (1602). *The Art of Stenographie; or, Short Writing by Spelling Characterie.* London

Wilkins, John (1646). *Ecclesiastes, Or, a Discourse Concerning the Gifte of Preaching as It Falls under the Rules of Art.* London

___ (1668). *Essay Towards a Real Character and a Philosophical Language.* London

Wilson, M. W. (1724). *Descartes.* London: Routledge & Kegan Paul

Wilson, Sir Thomas (1962). Robert Hood Bowers, ed. *The Arte of Rhetorique.* 1553. Gainesville, Florida: Scolar's Facsimiles & Reprints

Wilson, Thomas (1724). *Many Advantages of a Good Language to any nation with an examination of the present state of our own, as also, an essay towards correcting some things that are wrong in it.* London

Wiseman, Charles (1764). *A Complete English Grammar on a new plan. For the use of foreigners, and such natives as would acquire a scientifical knowledge of their own tongue.* London

Wit and Eloquence: or the Accomplish'd Secretary's Vade Mecum. Containing instruction to write epistles; with many curious examples of letters, and answers, suited to love, business, friendship, and other matters, in a most elegant stile (1697). London

The Writing Scholar's Companion Or, Infallible Rules for Writing True English With Ease and Certainty: drawn from the grounds and reasons of the English tongue. Comprehending in a full, plain and exact method, whatever is necessary to be observed in writing true English. In three parts. Composed for the benefit of all such as are industriously ambitious of so commendable an ornament as writing true English is generally esteemed. Recommended especially to the youth of both sexes, and to be taught in schools. (1695). London

Wynne, Richard (1775). *An Universal Grammar, for the use of those who are unacquainted with the learned languages, and are desirous of speaking and writing English, or any other modern language, with accuracy and precision.* London

Young, E. (1680). *The Compleat English Scholar in spelling, reading, and writing: containing plain and easie directions for spelling, and reading English, according to the present pronunciation. With several tables of common words and proper names in the bible and elsewhere, from one to six and seven syllables, both in whole words and divided into syllables. And directions for true writing of English, with several copies of the most usual hands engraven in copper. Also examples of the different writing and pronouncing of the same words in the English tongue. Lastly, how to spell words as are alike in sound, but differ in their sence and spelling; with the use of all stops and points in spelling and writing, and the interpretation of English Christian names, and many other things of use to learners.* London

Secondary Sources

Aaron, R. I. (1971). *John Locke.* 1937. Rpt. Oxford: Clarendon Press

Aarsleff, Hans (1964). "Leibniz on Locke on Language." *American Philosophical Quarterly* 1: 165–88

___ (1983). *The Study of Language in England: 1780–1860.* Princeton: Princeton University Press

Adolph, Robert (1968). *The Rise of Modern Prose Style.* Cambridge: MIT Press

Allen, D. C. (1949). "Some Theories of the Growth and Origin of Language in Milton's Age." *Philological Quarterly* 28: 5–16

Alston, R. C. (1965–72). *A Bibliography of the English Language from the Invention of Printing to the Year 1800.* Leeds: for the author by E. J. Arnold

Amussen, Susan Dwyer (1988). *An Ordered Society: Gender and Class in Early Modern England.* Oxford: Basil Blackwell

Ayers, M. (1991). *Locke.* Volume I: Epistemology and Volume II: Ontology. London: Routledge

Baldwin, T. W. (1944). *William Shakespeare's Small Latine and Lesser Greeke.* 2 vols. Urbana: University of Illinois Press

Barber, Charles (1976). *Early Modern English.* London: Andre Deutsch

___ (1965). *The Story of Speech and Language.* New York: Thomas Y. Crowell

Baron, Dennis (1982). *Grammar and Good Taste.* New Haven: Yale University Press

Bately, J. (1983). "Miège and the development of the English dictionary." In E. G. Stanley and D. Gray (eds.) *Five hundred years of words and sounds.* For E. J. Dobson. Woodbridge: Boydell & Brewer

Baugh, Albert C. and Thomas Cable (1994). *A History of the English Language.* 3rd edn. Englewood Cliffs, N.J.: Prentice-Hall

Bizzell, Patricia and Bruce Herzberg (1990). *The Rhetorical Tradition: Readings from Classical Times to the Present*. Boston: Bedford Books
Bowen, James (1967). Introduction to *Orbis sensualiumpictus*. 1–33. Sydney: Sydney University Press
Brekle, Herbert E. (1975). "The Seventeenth Century," in *Current Trends in Linguistics: Historiography of Linguistics 13*, ed. T. A. Sebeok, 277–382. The Hague: Mouton
Brengelman, F. H. (1980). "Orthoepists, printers and the rationalization of English spelling." *Journal of English and Germanic Philology* 79: 332–54
Brewer, John and Roy Porter, eds. (1993). *Consumption and the World of Goods*. New York: Routledge
Brink, J. R. (1980). "Bathsua Makin: Educator and Linguist (English, [1608?–1675?])" in *Female Scholars: A Tradition of Learned Women before 1800*, ed. J. R. Brink. Montreal: Eden
Bryan, W. F. (1923). "Notes on the Founders of Prescriptive English Grammar," in *Manly Anniversary Studies*. 383–93. Chicago: University of Chicago Press
Burchfield, Robert (1996). *The New Fowler's Modern English Usage*. Oxford: Clarendon
___ (1987). *Studies in Lexicography*. Oxford: Clarendon
___ (1991). *Unlocking the English Language*. U.S.: Hill and Wang
Breva-Claramonte, M. (1983). *Sanctius' theory of language*. Amsterdam: Benjamins
Burnham, William H. (1926). "Comenius, The Prince of Schoolmasters," in *Great Teachers and Mental Health*. 141–63. New York: D. Appleton and Co.
___ (1926). "The Theoretical Contribution of Comenius," in *Great Teachers and Mental Health*. 164–88. New York: D. Appleton and Co.
Butler, Nicholas Murray (1915). "The Place of Comenius in the History of Education," in *The Meaning of Education*. 283–96. New York: Charles Scribners' Sons
Butler, S. (1982). *The Story of British shorthand*. London: Pitman
Campbell, Gordon (1976). "Milton's *Accedence Commenc't Grammar*," *Milton Quarterly* 10: 39–48
Cannon, Garland H. (1979). "English Grammars of the Seventeenth and Eighteenth Centuries." *Semiotica*: 121-49
Čapková, Dagmar (1992). "Comenius: An Alternative." *Paedagogical Historica* 28: 187–97
___ (1994). "Comenius and His Ideals: Escape from the Labyrinth," in *Hartlib and the Advancement of Learning in the Seventeenth Century*. Eds. Timothy Raylor and Mark Greengrass, 75–91. Cambridge: Cambridge University Press
___ (1970). "J.A. Comenius's *Orbis pictus* in Its Conception as a Textbook for the Universal Education of Children." *Paedagogica Historica* 10: 5–27

___ (1987). "The Reception Given to the *Prodromus pansophiae*, and the Methodology of Comenius." *Acta Comeniana* 7: 37–59

Carr, Thomas M., Jr. (1990). *Descartes and the Resilience of Rhetoric: Varieties of Cartesian Rhetorical Theory*. Carbondale: Southern Illinois University Press

Charlton, Kenneth (1965). *Education in Renaissance England*. London: Routledge & Kegan Paul

Chomsky, Noam (1966). *Cartesian Linguistics: A Chapter in the History of Rationalist Thought*. New York: Harper and Row

Clark, Alice (1968). *Working Life of Women in the Seventeenth Century*. 1919. Rpt. London: Frank Cass and Co.

Clark, Donald Leman (1948). *John Milton at St. Paul's School: A Study of Ancient Rhetoric in English Renaissance Education*. New York: Columbia University Press

Clarke, M. L. (1959). *Classical Education in Britain, 1500–1900*. Cambridge: Cambridge University Press

Clark, Peter (1976). "The Ownership of Books in England, 1560–1640: The Example of Some Kentish Townsfolk," in *Schooling and Society: Studies in the History of Education*, ed. Lawrence Stone, 95–111. Baltimore: Johns Hopkins University Press

Clauss, S. (1982). "John Wilkins' *Essay Towards a Real Character*: its place in the seventeenth-century episteme. *Journal of the History of Ideas;* 43: 531–53

Cohen, Murray (1977). *Sensible Words: Linguistic Practice in England 1640–1785*. Baltimore: Johns Hopkins University Press

Conley, Thomas M. (1990). *Rhetoric in the European Tradition*. New York and London: Longman

Constantinescu, I. (1974). "John Wallis (1616–1703): a reappraisal of his contribution to the study of English." *Historiographia Linguistica* 1: 297–311

Cope, Jackson I. (1971). "Seventeenth-Century Quaker Style," in *Seventeenth-Century Prose: Modern Essays in Criticism*, ed. Stanley E. Fish, 200–35. New York: Oxford University Press

Copeland, Rita (1991). *Rhetoric, Hermeneutics and Translation in the Middle Ages, Academic Tradition, and Vernacular Text*. Cambridge: Cambridge University Press

Corbett, Edward P. J. (1992). *Classical Rhetoric for the Modern Student*. New York: Oxford University Press

Cornelius, Paul (1965). *Languages in Seventeenth and Early Eighteenth-Century Imaginary Voyages*. Geneva: Librairie Droz

Corcoran, Rev. T., S. J. (1911). *Studies in the History of Classical Teaching: Irish and Continental 1500–1700*. Dublin: Educational Company of Ireland

Craig, Hardin (1966). "The Sixteenth Century Grammar School in England in Relation to the English Renaissance," in *English Studies Today*, eds. Ilva Cellini and Giorgio Melchiori, 131–38. Roma: Edizioni Di Storia E Letteratura, 129–35

Cram, D. (1985). "Language universals and 17th-century universal language schemes. In K. Dutz and L Kaczmarek (eds.); *Rekonstruktion und Interpretation: Problemgeschichtliche Studien zur Sprachtheorie von Ockham bis Humboldt*. Tübingen: Narr
___ (1980) "George Dalgarno on *Ars signorum* and Wilkins' *Essay*." In K. Koerner, ed. *Progress in linguistic historiography*. Papers from the International Conference on the history of language sciences (Ottawa, 28–31 August 1978). Amsterdam: Benjamins
Cressy, David (1976). "Levels of Illiteracy in England, 1530–1730," in *Historical Journal*
Cressy, David (1980). *Literacy and the Social Order: Reading and Writing in Tudor and Stuart England*. New York: Cambridge University Press
___ (1993). "Literacy in Context: Meaning and Measurement in Early Modern England," in *Consumption and the World of Goods*, eds. John Brewer and Roy Porter, 305–19. New York: Routledge
Crowley, Sharon (1994). *Ancient Rhetorics For Contemporary Students*. New York: Macmillan
Daunton, M. J. (1978). "Towns and Economic Growth in Eighteenth-Century England," in *Towns in Societies*: Essays in Economic History and Historical Sociology, eds. Philip Abrams and E. A. Wrigley. 245–77. Cambridge: Cambridge University Press
Davies, W. J. F. (1973). *Teaching reading in early England*. London: Pitman
DeMaria, Robert (1986). *Johnson's Dictionary and the Language of Learning*. Chapel Hill: University of North Carolina Press
DeMott, Benjamin (1955). "Comenius and the Real Character in England." *PMLA* 70: 1068–81
___ (1958). "The Sources and Development of John Wilkins' Philosophical Language." *Journal of English and Germanic Philology* 57: 1–13
Dictionary of National Biography (1885–1900). Ed. Leslie Stephens. 63 vols. London
Dolezal, Fredric (1984). "The construction of entries in John Wilkins' and William Lloyd's 'Alphabetical dictionary.'" *Lexicographia*: Series Major, 1. Tübingen: Niemeyer.
___ (1985). *Forgotten But Important Lexicographers: John Wilkins and William Lloyd: A Modern Approach to Lexicography before Johnson*. Tübingen: Max Niemeyer Verlag
___ (1999). *Pedagogical lexicography today: a critical bibliography on learners' dictionaries with special emphasis on language*. Tübingen: Niemeyer
Dorian, Donald C. (1953–82). Introduction to *On Education* in vol. 2 of *The Complete Prose Works of John Milton*, ed. Don M. Wolfe, 357–415. New Haven: Yale University Press
Emery, C. (1947–48). "John Wilkins' Universal Language" *Isis* 38: 174–85

Emma, R. D. (1964). *Milton's Grammar*. Kastovsky Dieter Studies. The Hague: Mouton

Emsley, Bert (1933). "James Buchanan and the Eighteenth Century Regulation of English Usage." *PMLA* 48: 1154–1166

Enkvist, N. E. (1975). "English in Latin guise: a note on some Renaissance textbooks. *Historiographia Linguistica* 2: 283–98

Ezell, Margaret J. M. (1987). *The Patriarch's Wife: Literary Evidence and the History of the Family*. Chapel Hill: University of North Carolina Press

___ (1993). *Writing Women's Literary History*. Baltimore: Johns Hopkins University Press

Finegan, Edward (1980). *Attitudes Toward English Usage: The History of a War of Words*. New York: Teachers College Press, Columbia University

___ (1994). *Language: Its Structure and Use*. 2nd edn. New York: Harcourt Brace

___ (1992). "Style and Standardization in England: 1700–1900," in *English in Its Social Contexts: Essays in Historical Sociolinguistics*, eds. Tim William Machan and Charles T. Scott, 102–30. New York: Oxford University Press

Fisher, Walter R. (1962). The Importance of Style in Systems of Rhetoric." *The Southern Speech Journal* 27: 173–82

___ (1961). "Rhetoric: A Pedagogic Definition." *Western Speech* 25: 168–70

Forie, J. E. (1981). "Secularization, the language of God and the Royal Society at the turn of the seventeenth century." *History of European Ideas* 2: 221–35

Fraser, Antonia (1984). *The Weaker Vessel: Women's Lot in Seventeenth-century England*. London: Weidenfeld & Nicolson

Freeman, Donald C., ed. (1981). *Essays in Modern Stylistics*. London: Methuen

___ (1970). *Linguistics and Literary Style*. New York: Holt, Rinehart and Winston

French, David P. (1953–82). Introduction to *Accedence Commenc't Grammar* in vol. 8 of *The Complete Prose Works of John Milton*, ed. Don M. Wolfe, 32–83. New Haven: Yale University Press

French, J. Milton (1961). "Some Notes on Milton's *Accedence Commenc't Grammar*," in *Milton Studies* 60: 641–50

Gewirth, Alan (1967). "Clearness and Distinctness in Descartes," in *Descartes*, ed. Willis Doney, 250–77. Garden City, New York: Doubleday

Gleason, H. A. (1965). *Linguistics and English Grammar*. New York: Holt, Rinehart and Winston

Gooch, G. P. (1954). *English Democratic Ideas of the Seventeenth Century*. Cambridge: Cambridge University Press

Green, Lawrence D. (1994). "Canonicity and the Renaissance Cicero," in *Composition in Context*, eds. W. Ross Winterowd and Vincent Gillespie, 17–27. Carbondale: Southern Illinois University Press

Grundy, Isobel and Susan Wiseman, eds. (1992). *Women, Writing, History 1640–1740*. Athens: University of Georgia Press

Gustafson, Thomas (1993). *Representative Words: Politics, Literature, and the American Language, 1776-1865*. Cambridge, Massachusetts: Cambridge University Press
Hans, Nicholas (1955). *New Trends in Education in the Eighteenth Century*. London: Routledge
Harrington, Dana. "Hume's concept of taste in the context of epideictic rhetoric and 18th-century ethics." *Scottish rhetoric and its influences*. ed. Lynee Lewis Gaillet. Davis, CA: Hermagoras Press, 1998. 17-30
Harris, Randy Allen (1993). *The Linguistic Wars*. New York: Oxford University Press
Hartmann, R. R. K. (1986). *The History of Lexicography*. Amsterdam: John Benjamins
Hayashi, Tetsuro (1978). *The Theory of English Lexicography 1530-1791*. Amsterdam: John Benjamins
Heath, Terrence (1971). "Logical Grammar, Grammatical Logic, and Humanism in Three German Universities." *Studies in the Renaissance* 18: 9-64
Hexter, J. H. (1950). "The Education of the Aristocracy in the Renaissance." *Journal of Modern History* 22: 1-20
Horgan, A. D. (1994). *Johnson on Language*. New York: St. Martin's Press
Houston, R. A. (1988). *Literacy in Early Modern Europe: Culture and Education 1500-1800*. New York: Longman
Howell, Wilbur Samuel (1971). *Eighteenth-Century British Logic and Rhetoric*. Princeton: Princeton University Press
___ (1956). *Logic and Rhetoric in England: 1500-1700*. Princeton: Princeton University Press
Hüllen, Werner (1999). *English Dictionaries 800-1700: The Topical Tradition*. Oxford: Clarendon Press.
___ (1989). "In the Beginning was the Gloss," in *Lexicographers and Their Works*, ed. Gregory James, 100-116. Exeter: Exeter University Press
___ (1993). "*Picturae sunt totius mundi icones*. Some deliberations on lexicography, ars memorativa and the *Orbis sensualium pictus*." Acta Comeniana 10: 129-40
___ (1987). "Style and Utopia. Sprat's Demand For a Plain Style, Reconsidered," in *Papers in the History of Linguistics: Proceedings of the Third International Conference on the History of the Language Sciences*, 249-62. Amsterdam: John Benjamins
___ (Ed.) (1994). *The World in a List of Words*. Tübingen: Niemeyer
Jakubec, Jan (1971). *Johannes Amos Comenius*. New York: Arno Press and *The New York Times*
Jelinek, Vladimir (1953). *The Analytical Didactic of Comenius*. Chicago: University of Chicago Press
Jones, Bernard (1983). "William Barnes on Lindley Murray's *English Grammar*." *English Studies* 64: 30-35

Jones, Richard Foster (1932). "Science and Language in England of the Mid-Seventeenth Century." *Journal of English and Germanic Philology* 31: 315–31

___ (1953, rpt. 1974). *The Triumph of the English Language: A Survey of Opinions Concerning the Vernacular from the Introduction of Printing to the Restoration.* Stanford: Stanford University Press

Jordan, Constance (1990). *Renaissance Feminism: Literary Texts and Political Models.* Ithaca: Cornell University Press

Joseph, John Earl (1987). *Eloquence and Power: Rise of Language Standards and Standard Languages.* London: Francis Pinter

Kamm, Josephine (1965). *Hope Deferred: Girls' Education in English History.* London: Methuen and Co.

Kaster, Robert A. (1988). *Guardians of Language: The Grammarian and Society in Late Antiquity.* Berkeley: University of California Press

___ (1987). "Islands in the Stream: The Grammarians of Antiquity," in *The History of Linguistics in the Classical Period*, ed. Daniel J. Taylor, 149–68. Amsterdam: Benjamins

Katz, D. S. (1981). The language of Adam in seventeenth-century England." In H. Lloyd-Jones, V. Pearly and B. Worden (eds.). *History and imagination. Essays in honour of H. R. Trevor-Roper.* London: Duckworth

Kelly, Louis G. (1969). *Twenty-Five Centuries of Language Teaching.* Rowley, Massachusetts: Newbury House Publishers

Kennedy, Arthur G. (1926). "Authorship of *The British Grammar*," *Modern Language Notes* 41: 388–91

Kennedy, George A. (1963). *The Art of Persuasion in Greece.* Princeton: Princeton University Press

Kenny, Anthony (1967). "Descartes on Ideas," in *Descartes*, ed. Willis Doney, 250–77. Garden City, New York: Doubleday

Kernan, Alvin (1987). *Samuel Johnson and the Impact of Print.* Princeton: Princeton University Press

Kintgen, Eugene R., Barry Kroll, and Mike Rose, eds. (1988). *Perspectives on Literacy.* Carbondale: Southern Illinois University Press

Knowles, Gerry (1997). *A Cultural History of the English Language.* Arnold: New York.

Knowlson, James (1975). *Universal Language Schemes in England and France 1600–1800.* Toronto and Buffalo: University of Toronto Press

Knox, Dilwyn (1994). "Order, Reason and Oratory: Rhetoric in Protestant Latin Schools," in *Renaissance Rhetoric*, ed. Peter Mack, 63–80. London: St. Martin's Press

Kohn, George C. (1999). *Dictionary of Wars.* New York: Checkmark

Kohonen, V. (1978). "On the development of an awareness of English syntax in early (1550–1660) descriptions of word-order by English grammarians, logicians and rhetoricians." *Neuphilologische Mitteilungen* 79: 44–58

Kroll, Richard, W. F. (1991). *The Material Word: Literature and Culture in the Restoration and Early Eighteenth Century.* Baltimore and London: Johns Hopkins University Press

Lares, Jameela A. (1993). "Christian Knights and the Rhetoric of Religious Controversy, 1500–1800," in *Rhetoric in the Vortex of Cultural Studies: Proceedings of the Fifth Biennial Conference, Rhetoric Society of America,* ed. Arthur Walzer, 131–39. Minneapolis: Burgess

___ (2000). *Milton and the Preaching Arts.* Pittsburgh: Duquesne University Press

Lass, Roger, ed. (1999). *The Cambridge History of the English Language 1476–1776.* Vol. III. Cambridge: Cambridge UP.

Laver, J. (1978). "The concept of articulatory settings: an historical survey." *Historiographia Linguistica* 5: 1–14

Law, Vivian (1987). "Late Latin Grammars in the Early Middle Ages: A Typological History," in *The History of Linguistics in the Classical Period,* ed. Daniel J. Taylor, 193–206. Amsterdam: John Benjamins

___ (1975). "The Grammatical Tradition and the Rise of the Vernaculars," in *Current Trends in Linguistics,* vol. 13. *Historiography of Linguistics,* ed. T. A. Sebeok. The Hague: Mouton

___ and Werner Hüllen, eds. (1996). *Linguists and Their Diversions.* A Festschrift for R. H. Robins on His 75th Birthday. Münster, Germany: Nodus Publikationen.

Leith, Dick (1983). *A Social History of English.* London: Routledge

Leonard, Sterling Andrus (1962). *The Doctrine of Correctness in English Usage, 1700–1800.* 1929. Rpt. New York: Russell and Russell

Locker, Kitty O. (1987). "'As *Per* Your Request': A History of Business Jargon," *Journal of Business and Technical Communication,* 1.1: 27–47

___ (1985). "'Sir, This Will Never Do': Model Dunning Letters, 1592–1873," *Studies in the History of Business Writing,* eds. George H. Douglas and Herbert W. Hildebrandt. 179–200. Champaign, IL: Association for Business Communication

Lynch, Jack. "'The ground-work of stile': Johnson on the History of the Language" *Studies in Philology.* Fall 2000. Vol. 97 no. 4: 454–72

Lyons, John (1982). *Language and Linguistics.* Cambridge: Cambridge University Press

Matchinske, Megan (1998). *Writing, gender and state in early modern England: Identity formation and the female subject.* Cambridge, England: Cambridge University Press

McIntosh, Carey (1986). *Common and Courtly Language: The Stylistics of Social Class in Eighteenth-Century Literature.* Philadelphia: University of Pennsylvania Press

McKnight, George H. (1956). *Modern English in the Making.* 1928. Reissued as *The Evolution of the English Language.* New York: Dover Publications

McQuade, Donald A., ed. (1986). *The Territory of Language: Linguistics, Stylistics, and The Teaching of Composition.* Carbondale: Southern Illinois University Press

Mendelson, Sara and Patricia Crawford (1998). *Women in Early Modern England.* Oxford: Oxford University Press

Michael, Ian (1988). "Early Teachers of Reading: Their Struggles and Methods from the Sixteenth Century," in C. Anderson, ed. *Reading: the ABC and Beyond.* UK: Macmillan. 226-236

___ (1993). *Early Textbooks of English: A Guide.* University of Reading: Colloquium on Textbooks, Schools and Society

___ (1970). *English Grammatical Categories and the Tradition to 1800.* Cambridge: Cambridge University Press

___ (1987). *The Teaching of English: From the Sixteenth Century to 1870.* Cambridge: Cambridge University Press

Miller, P. J. (1973). "Women's Education, 'Self-Improvement,' and Social Mobility – A Late Eighteenth Century Debate," *British Journal of Education Studies* 20: 302–14

Milroy, James and Lesley Milroy (1985). *Authority in Language: Investigating Language Prescription and Standardization.* London: Routledge

Mitchell, Linda C. (1999). "Anne Fisher and Literacy Training in 18th-Century England." ERIC (Educational Resources Information Center)

___ (1997). "Comenius: A Redefinition of a Seventeenth-Century European Mind and the Quest for Education Identity." *Studies in Early Modern Philosophy*, vol. 4, ed. by Stanley Tweyman and David Freeman. Delmar, NY: Caravan Books. 31–42

___ (1994). "Inversion of Grammar Texts and Dictionaries in the Seventeenth and Eighteenth Centuries," in *Euralex '94 Proceedings*, ed. Willy Martin *et al*, 548–54. Amsterdam: Euralex

___ (1998). "Pedagogical Practices of Lexicographers in 17th- and 18th-Century England." Euralex. ed. W. Martin *et al.*, Liége, Belgium

___ "The Use of Rhetoric in Seventeenth-Century Writing Pedagogy." *Proceedings of the Canadian Society for the Study of Rhetoric 94–97* eds. David Goodwin and Jill Tomasson Goodwin. 153–63. Vol. 6. Waterloo, Ontario

Mittens, W.H. "A Grammatical 'Battle Royal.'" *Durham University Journal* 11(1970):110–120

Moore, J. L. (1910). *Tudor-Stuart Views on the Growth, Status, and Destiny of the English Language.* Halle: Max Niemeyer

Moss, Jean Dietz, ed. (1986). *Rhetoric and Praxis: The Contribution of Classical Rhetoric to Practical Reasoning.* Washington, D.C.: The Catholic University of America Press

Murphy, Daniel (1995). *Comenius: a Critical Reassessment of His Life and Work.* Portland, Oregon: Blackrock, Co.

Murphy, James J. (1974). "*Ars dictaminis*: The Art of Letter-Writing," in *Rhetoric in the Middle Ages; A History of Rhetorical Theory from Saint Augustine to the Renaissance*, 194–268. Berkeley, Los Angeles and London: University of California Press
___ ed. (1990). *A Short History of Writing Instruction: From Ancient Greece to Twentieth-Century America*. Davis, California: Hermagoras Press
___ ed. (1971). *Three Medieval Rhetorical Arts*, ed. James J. Murphy. Berkeley: University of California Press
Murray, (Sir) James A. H. (1900). *The Evolution of English Lexicography*. Oxford: Clarendon Press
Myers, Mitzi, (1985). "Domesticating Minerva: Bathsua Makin's 'Curious' Argument for Women's Education," in *Studies in Eighteenth-Century Culture*, vol. 14, ed. O. M. Brack, 173–92. Madison, Wis.: University of Wisconsin Press
O'Day, Rosemary (1982). *Education and Society 1500–1800: The social foundations of education in early modern Britain*. New York: Longman
Ong, Walter J. (1982). *Orality and Literacy: The Technologizing of the Word*. New York: Methuen
___ (1958). *Ramus: Method, and the Decay of Dialogue. From the Art of Discourse to the Art of Reason*. Cambridge, Massachusetts: Harvard University Press
Padley, G. A. (1976). *Grammatical Theory in Western Europe: 1500–1700: the Latin Tradition*. Cambridge: Cambridge University Press
___ (1985). *Grammatical Theory in Western Europe: 1500–1700: Trends in Vernacular Grammar I*. Cambridge: Cambridge University Press
___ (1988). *Grammatical Theory in Western Europe: 1500–1700: Trends in Vernacular Grammar II*. Cambridge: Cambridge University Press
___ (1983). "La Norme dans la tradition des grammairiens." In E. Bédard and J. Maurais, *La Norme linguistique*. Quebec & Paris: Gouvernement du Québec
___ (1982). "L'Importance de Thomas Linacre." *Langues et Linguistique* (Université Laval) 8:17–56
Percival, W. Keith (1986). "Renaissance linguistics: the old and the new," in *Studies in the history of Western linguistics*, ed. Theodora Bynon and F. R. Palmer, 56–68. Cambridge: Cambridge University Press
Piaget, Jean (1967). *John Amos Comenius on Education*. New York: Teachers College Press, Columbia University
Poldauf, Ivan (1948). *On the History of Some Problems of English Grammar Before 1800*. Prague: Facultas philosophica Universitatis Carolinae Pragensis 55
Pollard, A.W. & G. R. Redgrave (1986–91). *A Short-Title Catalogue of Books Printed in England, Scotland and Ireland and English Books Printed Abroad, 1475– 1640*. 2nd ed. Rev. W. A. Jackson, F. S. Ferguson, and Katharine F. Pantzer. 3 vols. London: Bibliographical Society
Porter, Roy (1982). *English Society in the Eighteenth Century*. London: Penguin Books

Poster, Carol and Linda C. Mitchell, eds. *Letter-Writing Manuals from Antiquity to the Present*. Columbia, SC: University of South Carolina Press, forthcoming

Pyles, Thomas and John Algeo (1993). *The Origins and Development of the English Language*. 4th edn. New York: Harcourt Brace Jovanovich

Reynolds, Myra (1920). *The Learned Lady in England, 1650–1760*. Boston: Houghton-Mifflin

Riddell, James Allen (1979). "Attitudes toward English Lexicography in the Seventeenth Century." *Papers on Lexicography in Honor of Warren N. Cordell* ed. by James Edmund Congleton, John Edward Gates and Donald Hobar, 83–91, Terre Haute: Indiana State University, The Dictionary Society of North America

___ (1974). "The beginning: English dictionaries of the first half of the seventeenth century," *Leeds Studies in English*, new series, 7: 117–153

___ (1974). "The Reliability of Early English Dictionaries," *The Yearbook of English Studies* 4: 1–4

Sadler, John Edward (1966). *J. A. Comenius and the Concept of Universal Education*. London: George Allen and Unwin

Salmon, Vivian (1986). "Effort and Achievement in Seventeenth-Century British Linguistics," in *Studies in the history of Western linguistics*, eds. Theodora Bynon and F. R. Palmer, 69–95. Cambridge: Cambridge University Press

___ (1961). "Joseph Webbe: Some Seventeenth-Century Views on Language-Teaching and the Nature of Meaning," *Bibliotheque d'humanisme et renaissance* 23: 324–40. Rpt. in Salmon 1979

___ (1996). *Language and Society in Early Modern England*. The Netherlands: John Benjamins

___ (1966). "Language-Planning in Seventeenth-Century England: Its Context and Aims," from *In Memory of J. R. Firth*, ed. C. E. Bazell *et al.*, 370–97. London: Longman

___ (1964). "Problems of Language Teaching; A Discussion among Hartlib's Friends." *Modern Language Review* 59: 13–24

___ (1979). *The Study of Language in Seventeenth-Century England*. Amsterdam: John Benjamins

___ (1972). *The Works of Francis Lodowyck*. London: Longman

Scheurweghs, G. and E. Vorlat (1959). "Problems of the History of English Grammar," *English Studies*, 60: 135–43

Schofield, R. S. (1968). "The measurement of literacy in pre-industrial England." In J. Goody, ed. *Literacy in Traditional Societies*. Cambridge: Cambridge University Press. 317–24

Seigal, J. P. (1969). "The Enlightenment and the evolution of a language of signs in France and England." *Journal of the History of Ideas* 30: 96–115

Shapiro, Barbara (1969). *John Wilkins, 1614–1672: An Intellectual Biography*. Berkeley: University of California Press

Shayer, David (1972). *The Teaching of English Schools, 1900-1970*. London: Routledge
Sheard, J. A. (1966). *The Words of English*. New York: W. W. Norton
Skulsky, Harold (1992). *Language Recreated: Seventeenth-Century Metaphorists and the Act of Metaphor*. Athens: University of Georgia Press
Slaughter, M. M. (1982). *Universal Languages and Scientific Taxonomy in the Seventeenth Century*. Cambridge: Cambridge University Press
Sledd, James and Wilma R. Ebbitt, eds. (1962). *Dictionaries and THAT Dictionary: A Casebook on the Aims of Lexicographers and the Targets of Reviewers*. Chicago: Scott, Foresman
Smith, Hilda L. (1982). *Reason's Disciples: Seventeenth-Century English Feminists*. Urbana: University of Illinois Press
Spufford, Margaret (1981). *Small Books and Pleasant Histories: Popular Fiction and Its Readership in Seventeenth-Century England*. Athens: University of Georgia Press
Starnes, DeWitt Talmage and Gertrude E. Noyes (1991). *The English Dictionary from Cawdrey to Johnson: 1604–1755*. Chapel Hill: University of North Carolina Press
Stone, Lawrence (1977). *The Family, Sex and Marriage in England, 1500–1800*. London: Weidenfeld & Nicolson
Stone, Lawrence, ed. (1976). *Schooling and Society: Studies in the History of Education*. Baltimore: Johns Hopkins University Press
Strauss, Gerald (1976). "The State of Pedagogical Theory c. 1530: What Protestant Reformers Knew about Education," in *Schooling and Society: Studies in the History of Education*, ed. Lawrence Stone, 69–94. Baltimore: Johns Hopkins University Press
Struever, Nancy (1985). "The Conversable World: Eighteenth-Century Transformations of the Relation of Rhetoric and Truth," in Brian Vickers and Nancy Struever, *Rhetoric and the Pursuit of Truth: Language Change in the Seventeenth and Eighteenth Centuries*, 77–119. Los Angeles: William Andrews Clark Memorial Library
Subbiondo, Joseph L. (1977). "John Wilkins' theory of meaning and the development of a semantic model." *Cahiers linguistiques d'Ottawa*, 5: 41–61
___ (1992). "New Science and English Grammar," in *Diversions of Galway: Papers on the History of Linguistics*, ed. Anders Ahlqvist, 183–90. Amsterdam: John Benjamins
Sugg, R. S. Jr. (1964). "The Mood of Eighteenth-Century English Grammar," *Philological Quarterly* 43: 239–52
Sweetser, Eve (1990). *From Etymology to Pragmatics: Metaphorical and Cultural Aspects of Semantic Structure*. Cambridge: Cambridge University Press
Sylvester, D. W. (1970). *Educational Documents: 800–1816*. London: Methuen
Travitsky, Betty S. and Adele F. Seeff, eds. (1994). *Attending to Women in Early Modern England*. Newark: University of Delaware Press

Treip, Mindele (1970). *Milton's Punctuation and Changing English Usage 1582–1676*. London: Methuen and Co. Ltd
Trentman, J. A. (1976). "The Study of logic and language in the early 17th century." *Historiographia Linguistica* 3: 179–201.
Tucker, Susie I. (1961). *English Examined: Two Centuries of Comment on the Mother-Tongue*. Cambridge: Cambridge University Press
___ (1967). *Protean Shape: A Study in Eighteenth-Century Vocabulary and Usage*. University of London: The Athlone Press
Turnbull, G. H. (1920). *Samuel Hartlib: A Sketch of His Life and His Relations to J. A. Comenius*. London: Oxford University Press
___ (1947). *Hartlib, Dury and Comenius: Gleanings from Hartlib's Papers*. Liverpool: University Press of Liverpool
Ulman, H. Lewis (1994). *Things, Thoughts, Words, and Actions: The Problem of Language in Late Eighteenth-Century British Rhetorical Theory*. Carbondale: Southern Illinois Press
Vancil, David E. (1992). *Catalog of Dictionaries, Word Books, and Philological Texts, 1440–1900*. Inventory of the Cordell Collection, Indiana State University. Westport, Conn.: Greenwood Press
Vickers, Brian (1988). *In Defence of Rhetoric*. Oxford: Clarendon Press
___ (1985). "The Royal Society and English Prose Style: A Reassessment," in Brian Vickers and Nancy Struever, *Rhetoric and the Pursuit of Truth: Language Change in the Seventeenth and Eighteenth Centuries*, 3–76. Los Angeles: William Andrews Clark Memorial Library
Vincent, W.A.L. (1969). *The Grammar Schools: Their Continuing Tradition, 1660–1714*. London: Cox and Wyman
Vorlat, Emma (1979). "Criteria of grammaticalness in 16th and 17th century English grammar." *Leuvense Bijdragen* 68: 129–40
___ (1975). *Development of English Grammatical Theory: 1586–1737*. Leuven: Leuven University Press
Watson, Foster (1909). *The Beginnings of the Teaching of Modern Subjects in England*. Cambridge: Cambridge University Press
___ ed. (1922). *The encyclopaedia and dictionary of education; a comprehensive, practical and authoritative guide on all matters connected with education, including educational principles and practice, various types of teaching institutions, and educational systems throughout the world. With articles by about nine hundred eminent authorities*. London: Waverly Book Company
___ (1968). *The English Grammar Schools to 1660: Their Curriculum and Practice*. 1908. Rpt. London: Frank Cass
___ (1967). *English Writers on Education, 1480–1603*. Gainesville, Florida: Scholars' Facsimiles and Reprints
___ (1968). *The Old Grammar Schools*. 1916. Rpt. London: Frank Cass

___ (1912). *Vives and the renascence education of women.* Stanford U. microfilm and book MFILM N.S. 1508
Watson, George, ed. (1970). *Literary English Since Shakespeare.* London: Oxford University Press
Webber, Joan (1968). *The Eloquent "I": Style and Self in Seventeenth-Century Prose.* Madison: University of Wisconsin Press
Webster, Charles, ed. (1974). *The Intellectual Revolution of the 17th Century.* London: Routledge
___ (1970). *Samuel Hartlib and the Advancement of Learning.* Cambridge: Cambridge University Press
Wells, Ronald (1973). *Dictionaries and the Authoritarian Tradition: A Study in English Usage and Lexicography.* The Hague: Mouton
Willey, Basil (1934). *The Seventeenth-Century Background.* Garden City, New York: Doubleday Anchor Books
Williams, Joseph (1992). "'O! When Degree is Shak'd': Sixteenth-Century Anticipations of Some Modern Attitudes Toward Usage," in *English in Its Social Contexts: Essays in Historical Sociolinguistics,* ed. Tim William Machan and Charles T. Scott, 69–101. New York: Oxford University Press
Wing, Donald, ed. (1972–88). *Short-Title Catalog of Books Printed in England, Scotland, Ireland, Wales, and British American and of English Books Printed in Other Countries, 1641–1700.* 2nd ed. 3 vols. New York: Modern Language Association
Woodward, William Harrison (1965). *Studies in Education During the Age of the Renaissance.* New York: Russell and Russell
Woolhouse, R.S. (1983). *Locke.* Minneapolis: University of Minnesota Press
Wrightson, Keith (1982). *English Society 1580–1680.* London: Hutchinson
Wrigley, E. A. (1978). "A Simple Model of London's Importance in Changing English Society and Economy 1650–1750," in *Towns in Societies: Essays in Economic History and Historical Sociology,* eds. Philip Abrams and E. A. Wrigley, 215–43. Cambridge: Cambridge University Press
Yates, Frances A. (1966). *The Art of Memory.* Chicago: The University of Chicago Press
Young, Robert Fitzgibbon, ed. (1932). *Comenius in England*

Index

References to illustrations are displayed in italics.

Académie Française, 30, 41
The Academy of Eloquence (Blount), 74–75, 144–45
Accedence Commenc't Grammar (Milton), 67, 86–87
The Accidence (Devis), 3
acculturation of foreigners, 133–41
acquisition of language and universal language/grammar, 108–9
Aickin, Joseph, 27, 66, 140
Alton, R. C., 136
analogy
    constructing universal language by, 123–26, 128
    teaching language by, 20–21, 46–54
Ancilla grammaticae, 91
A New English Grammar, prescribing as certain rules as the language will bear, for forreners to learn English (Howell), 138–39
apprenticeships and Latin vs. English grammar, 26
architectural metaphors, 46–54, 128
Aristarchus (Bowles), 4
aristocratic approach to writing instruction, 74–76
    See also upper class
Aristotle, 87, 91
arithmetic numbers as universal characters, 113–15
Ars signorum (Dalgarno), 115–18
Arte of Rhetorique (Wilson), 142

artificial language schemes, 8, 110–24, 131*n*6
artificial memory, 48
The Art of Memory (Yates), 48
Art of Reading and Writing (Watts), 159–60
The Art of Reading (Sheridan), 161
Ascham, Roger, 18
Ash, John, 43
Astell, Mary, 163*n*18
authority, prescriptive, and rise of lexicography, 38–44, 166–67

Bailey, Nathan, 41
Barclay, James
    on composition and grammar, 98–100, 102–3
    moral education through literacy, 160
    rise of lexicography, 43
    standardization issue, 24
    women's education, 151–52
Beattie, James, 129–30
Beck, Cave, 13, 109, 113–15
Besnier, Pierre, 131*n*10
Bibliotheca Technologica (Martin), 3
bilingual dictionaries, 38
bilingual text, Latin vs. English in grammar teaching, 19
blank slate theory of knowledge acquisition, 108–9
Blount, Thomas, 74–75, 144–45
Botley, Samuel, 123
Bowles, Thomas, 4
Brady the Younger, Nicholas, 3–4
Brekle, Herbert E., 9–10

INDEX 209

Brightland, John, 6
Brinsley, John, 18
British Education (Sheridan), 160–61
The British Grammar (Buchanan), 81, 149
Brooke, John, 10
Brown, George, 5, 82–83
Brown, Richard, 33
Buchanan, James, 70, 81, 149
Bullokar, William, 10
business writing, 76–78, 83–85
Butler, Charles, 2

Care, Henry, 5, 27–28, 135
Catholicism vs. Protestantism, and literacy education, 154–56
Cawdrey, Robert, 40
Čapková, Dagmar, 7
children's education, women's role in, 142, 143, 145
Chinese as universal language, 110
Christian education. *See* religious education
Cicero, 87
Circles of Gomer (Jones), 129
Clarke, John
  composition and grammar, 70, 94
  literacy for middle class, 160
  standardization issue, 23, 28–29
  women's education, 146–47
class, social. *See* social position
Cocker, Edward, 41
Cockeram, Henry, 40
Cocker's English Dictionary (Cocker), 41
cognition, writing skills as acts of, 89
Cohen, Murray, 11
Coles, Elisha, 20, 39, 51, 123, 154
Colet, John, 48
Collyer, John, 101–2
Comenius, Johann Amos
  artificial language schemes, 8, 9

  commentary on, 62–66
  dictionaries, 39
  emphasis on religious and moral education, 50
  vs. Milton on educational reform, 66–71
  as reformer, 54–56, 72*n*17
  standardization issue, 26
  visible language method, 7, 59, 60–61
  on women's education, 145
commerce as impetus for universal language, 113
Common and Courtly Language: The Stylistics of Social Class in Eighteenth-Century Literature (McIntosh), 158
A Common Writing (Lodowyk), 110–13
The Compleat English Scholar (Young), 78, 83–84
Compleat School-Master (Tryon), 135, 145, 154–55
A Complete and Universal English Dictionary on a New Plan (Barclay), 43
The Complete Art of Writing Letters (Johnson), 81–82
The Complete Letter-Writer, 83
composition
  definitional issues, 107*n*20
  vs. grammar, 67–69, 88–89, 90–106
Congestorium Artificiose Memorie (Romberch), 48, *49*
The Construction of the Westminster Grammar (Brady), 3–4
Cooke, Thomas, 83
Cooper, Christopher, 6, 139
Coote, Edmund, 5
Cordemoy, Geraud de, 157
Cotgrave, Randle, 50

A Course of Lectures: On the Theory of Language, and Universal Grammar (Priestley), 37, 127
cultural vs. linguistic issues, 13
  See also social position
custom and usage
  descriptive vs. prescriptive approaches, 37, 43
  and standardization, 2–3, 6
  universal language, 125, 126

Dalgarno, George, 115–18
Day, Angel, 106n3
Defoe, Daniel, 30, 124
DeMott, Benjamin, 9
Descartes, Renè, 108–9
descriptive vs. prescriptive approach. *See* prescriptive vs. descriptive approach
Devis, Ellin, 3
dictionaries, 38–44, 89–90, 166–67
A Dictionary of the English Language (Johnson), 38
Dilworth, Thomas, 34–35, 156, 158
Discourse Concerning Speech (Cordemoy), 157
Dissertation of Reading the Classics (Felton), 87–88
Dissertations Moral and Critical (Beattie), 129–30
divine knowledge. *See* religious education
double negative, 35, 45n19
Dury, John, 57, 59
Dyche, Thomas, 2, 4, 42

Eachard, John, 63
empirical approach to universal language, 118–21
The English Accidence, 33–34
English as second language, 137–41
The English Dictionarie (Cockeram), 40

English Examples of Latin Syntaxis (Walker), 154
English examples to be turned into Latin (Leedes), 78–80
English Exercises for School-Boys to Translate into Latin (Garretson), 156
The English Grammar (Aickin), 27, 66, 140
English Grammar (Butler), 2
English Grammar (Jonson), 6, 19, 134–35
The English Grammar (Maittaire), 88–89, 92, 96–97, 101–2, 145
The English Grammar (Miège), 6, 95–96, 136
An English Grammar (Robinson), 86
English Grammar (Wharton), 20, 25, 135
English Grammatical Categories (Michael), 1–2
English language
  interest in history of, 131n1
  vs. Latin, 17–38
  and national identity, 124–25
The English Scholar Compleat, 155
English School-Master (Coote), 5
English School Reformed (Brown), 33
English Secretary (Day), 106n3
The English Teacher (Cooper), 6
Entick, John, 43
An Essay on Grammar (Ward), 4
An Essay to Revive the Antient Education of Gentlewomen (Makin), 65–66, 142, 149
An Essay Towards an Universal and Rational Grammar (Philips), 125
An Essay Towards a Practical English Grammar (Greenwood), 2, 140
Essay Towards a Real Character and a Philosophical Language (Wilkins), 9, 10, 50–51, 118–23

An Essay Upon Several Projects
(Defoe), 30, 124
Essay Upon Study (Clarke), 28–29, 94,
146–47, 160
An Essay Upon the Education of Youth
(Clarke), 23
Ezell, Margaret J. M., 163*n*13,
163*n*17

Farnaby, Thomas, 17, 86
Farro, Daniel, 126
Felton, Henry, 87–88
Fenning, Daniel, 95, 104–5, 140, 152
The First Part of the Elementarie
(Mulcaster), 134, 142
*The First Six Books of Paradise Lost
rendered into Grammatical
Construction* (Buchanan), 70
Fisher, Ann, 69–70, 80–81, 103–4,
152–53
Fisher, George, 32, 85
Fleming, Abraham, 48
foreigners, acculturation through
language, 20, 133–41
French-English Dictionary (Cotgrave),
50
French language and nationalism, 124

Garretson, John, 156
The General Principles of Grammar
(Collyer), 101–2
Gildon, Charles
    on composition and grammar, 80,
    88, 92–93, 97–98
    definition of grammar, 4
    standardization issue, 21
    on women's education, 151
Gill, Alexander, 6, 19, 134
glossing, 79–80
Gordon, William, 85
grammar
    vs. composition, 67–69, 88–89,
    90–106

definitions, 1–5, 89
vs. lexicography, 38–44
separation of philosophy and
practice, 10
A Grammar of the English Tongue
(Gildon)
    composition and grammar, 4, 80,
    88, 92–93, 97–98
    standardization issue, 21
    women's education, 151
grammar texts
    overview of, 12–13
    vs. rhetoric on women's education,
    143–44
Grammatica Anglicana (Greaves), 134
*Grammatica est recte scribendi et
loquendi ars* (Quintilian), 3
Grammatical Categories (Michael),
125–26
Grammatical Commentaries (Gildon),
4
Grammatical Commentaries (Johnson),
22, 33, 125, 155
Grammatica lingua Anglicanae
(Wallis), 19, 139
Grammatica Linguae Anglicanae
(Cooper), 139
*Grammatical Theory in Western
Europe: 1500-1700: the Latin
Tradition* (Padley), 9
*Grammatical Theory in Western
Europe: 1500-1700: Trends in
Vernacular Grammar II*
(Padley), 9
*Grammatical Theory in Western Europe:
1500-1700: Trends in
Vernacular Grammar* (Padley),
9
The Great Didactic (Comenius), 55
The Great French Dictionary (Miège),
136
Greaves, Paul, 134
Greenwood, James, 2, 6, 140

The Grounds & Occasions of the Contempt of the Clergy and Religion (Eachard), 63

habits of speaking. *See* custom and usage
hard-word lists, 38
Harris, James, 125–26, 135
Hartlib, Samuel
   breadth of interests, 13
   as reformer, 54–56, 59, 71n13
   standardization issue, 19–20
   on women's education, 143
Hayashi, Tetsuro, 10
Hebrew as universal language, 110
Hermes: A Philosophical Enquiry Concerning Universal Grammar (Harris), 125–26
hieroglyphic system for artificial language, 111–13
Hill, J., 77–78, 84
history of language, early interest in, 131n1
Hoole, Charles, 3, 19, 58–59, 64, 86
Howell, James, 3, 11, 138–39
humanities, Milton's emphasis on, 67–69
Hyrde, Richard, 142

ideal character language scheme, 8
   See also universal language/grammar
incremental competence. *See* pedagogy
innate nature of knowledge, 108–9
Introduction to English Grammar (Story), 105
Introduction to Grammar (Lily), 18, 38–39
An Introduction to the Art of Reading (Rice), 140–41, 161

James I, King of England, 142

Janua linguarum reserata (Comenius), 9, 53, 65
Johnson, Charles, 81–82
Johnson, Ralph
   background of, 13
   on composition and grammar, 87–88, 91–92, 95
   letter writing, 77
   pedagogical application of work, 166
   vocational focus of, 5
   on women, 143
Johnson, Richard, 4, 22–23, 33, 125, 155
Johnson, Samuel, 13, 38, 41
Jones, Rowland, 129
Jonson, Ben, 6, 13, 19, 134–35

Kenrick, William, 43, 105–6
Kersey, John, 41
A Key to the Art of Letters (Lane), 4, 21, 124, 140, 157–58
Knowlson, James, 8

Labyrinth of the World (Comenius), 55
The Lady's Rhetoric, 143
Lane, Archibald
   definition of grammar, 4
   English for foreigners, 140
   grammar as key to social mobility, 157–58
   standardization issue, 20–22
   universal grammar, 124
   women's education, 143–44
language acquisition and universal language/grammar, 108–9
   See also pedagogy
Language and Society in Early Modern England (Salmon), 8
language instruction. *See* pedagogy
Latin
   and ascendancy of English, 6
   decline of, 109

difficulties in learning, 72n17, 115
English as gateway to, 135–36
and grammar vs. lexicography, 40
merits of, 125
Milton's style of teaching, 68
modifications in teaching of, 86
proliferation of grammar texts in, 13
and Protestantism, 155
role in standardization, 17–38
teaching method controversy, 7
as universal language, 108
The Latine Grammar (Hoole), 3, 19, 86
The Latine Grammar of P. Ramus (Ramus), 3
Lectures on Rhetoric and Belles Lettres (Smith), 94–95
Leedes, Edward, 78–80, 104, 154
Leigh, Edward, 50
Leith, Dick, 11–12, 34
letters, writing instruction, 74–85, 106n3, 166
lexicography, 38–44, 136, 166–67
Lily, William
  architectural metaphor, 48
  authority of, 13, 38–39
  definition of grammar, 3, 4
  focus on Latin, 18
  modifications to grammar of, 86–87
Lingua Britannica Reformata (Martin), 36, 126
literacy
  and lexicography, 41
  as religious education, 139
  and social class, 46, 153–62, 164n32
literature, Milton's emphasis on, 67–69
  See also composition
Locke, John, 74, 108–9
Lodowyck, Francis, 8, 109–13

logic
  definitions, 89
  and grammar definition, 3–4
  in grammar texts, 85, 87, 88, 93
Logomia Anglica (Gill), 6, 19, 134
Loughton, William, 10–11
Lowth, Bishop Robert
  background of, 13
  definition of grammar, 3
  importance of learning English first, 24
  as prescriptivist, 35–36
  on universal grammar, 127–28, 129
Lubinus, Eilhardus, 56, 57, 59, 72n18
Ludus Literarius (Brinsley), 18
Luther, Martin, 142

Maittaire, Michael
  background of, 13
  on composition and grammar, 88–89, 92, 96–97, 101–2
  definition of grammar, 6
  on women's education, 145
Makin, Bathsua, 65–66, 142–43, 149–50
Many Advantages of a Good Language (Wilson), 87–88
Margarita Philosophica (Reisch), 48
marriage and women's education, 147, 150
Martin, Benjamin, 3, 36, 126
Mather, William, 84–85, 150
Maximo in Minimo (Botley), 123
McIntosh, Carey, 158
Mercury (Wilkins), 110
Methodi practicae specimen (Wase), 50
Michael, Ian, 1–2, 7, 107n20, 125–26
middle class
  composition and grammar, 90–106
  letter writing, 76–85
  literacy for, 153–62

214   GRAMMAR WARS

    need for linguistic security, 38, 166
    rhetoric vs. grammar, 85–90
    women's education, 143–45
    See also vocational education
Miège, Guy, 6, 95–96, 135, 136–37
Milner, John, 2
Milton, John, 66–71, 86–87
model of grammar, definition, 18
moral education
    Comenius's focus on, 50, 56–57
    and fragility of women, 141, 143, 144, 145
    and literacy in middle class, 153–56, 160–61
    See also religious education
More English Examples Turned into Latin (Leedes), 104
Mulcaster, Richard, 134, 142, 149–50
Murphy, James, 7
musical notes as universal language, 110, 131*n*10

national identity
    and language acculturation of foreigners, 133–41
    and primacy of vernacular, 25, 124–25
The New and Complete Dictionary of the English Language (Ash), 43
A New Dictionary of the English Language (Kenrick), 43
New Discovery of the Art of Teaching (Hoole), 64
A New English Dictionary (Kersey), 41
New English Examples Turned into Latin (Leedes), 154
The New English Grammar (Howell), 3
The New English Letter-Writer (Brown), 5, 82–83
A New French Grammar (Miège), 136
A New General English Dictionary (Dyche and Pardon), 2, 4, 42

A New Grammar (Fisher), 80–81, 104, 152–53
A New Grammar of the English Language (Fenning), 95, 104
A New Guide to the English Tongue (Dilworth), 34–35, 156, 158
A New Method of Educating Children (Tryon), 145
The New Spelling Book (Fisher), 32, 85
The New Spelling Dictionary (Entick), 43
Newton, John, 26–27, 51, 64–65
Nolens Volens: or you shall make Latin whether you will or no (Coles), 39, 154
Nouvelle méthode pour apprendre l'Anglais (Miège), 136

Of Education (Milton), 67–68
Of Education (Walker), 92
Oldmixon, John, 30–31, 151
On the History of Some Problems of English Grammar Before 1800 (Poldauf), 6
Opera Didactica Omnia (Comenius), 55
Orbis sensualium pictus (Comenius), 9, 39, 58–59, 72*n*20, 145

Padley, Gerald A., 9
pansophism, 55–56
Paradise Lost (Milton), 69–70
Paradise of the Heart (Comenius), 55
Pardon, William, 4
parental responsibility for education, 48–49
passions, moving the, 91–92, 152
patriotism. See national identity
patterns vs. judgment, 10
pedagogy
    architectural metaphors, 46–54
    commentary on Comenius, 62–66

Hartlib and Comenius's reforms,
    54–56
  historical lessons for contemporary,
    166
  Milton vs. Comenius, 66–71
  overview, 3–4
  and religious education, 56–57
  and rise of lexicography, 41–42
  scholarship review, 6–7
  visible language method, 57–62
  women's education, 141–53
  See also standardization
  universal language/grammar
  writing instruction
personal letter writing, 74–76, 78–80
persuasive writing, 91–92, 93
  See also rhetoric
Philips, Jenkin Thomas, 125
Phillips, Edward, 89
philosophical languages
  eighteenth century, 124–31
  seventeenth century, 109–24
  See also universal language/grammar
pictorial method of language learning,
    7, 57–62
The Pleasing Instructor, 29
*The Pleasing Instructor: Or,
    Entertaining Moralist*, 148–49
poetry, grammarians' over-correcting
    of, 69–70
Poldauf, Ivan, 6, 134
Pope, Alexander, 163n21
Practical English Grammar (Fisher),
    69–70, 103–4
*A Practical Grammar of the English
    Tongue* (Loughton), 10–11
A Practical Guide to the Latin Tongue
    (Milner), 2
prescriptive vs. descriptive approach
  and grammar definition, 3
  middle class need for rules, 157,
    158
  and rise of lexicography, 38–44,
    166–67
  and standardization, 35–38
  and universal grammar, 127–28,
    129
  See also standardization
Priestley, Joseph, 13, 36–37, 100–101,
    104, 126–27
printing, effect on grammar texts,
    13–14
privileged classes. *See* upper class
*Proposal for Correcting, Improving, and
    Ascertaining the English Tongue*
    (Swift), 30, 150–51, 156
Protagoras, 48
Protestantism vs. Catholicism, and
    literacy education, 154–56

Quintilian, 3, 48, 145

Ramus, P., 3
*A Rational and Speedy Method of
    Attaining the Latin Tongue*
    (Lane), 4, 20–22, 124
rationalism and universal language
    schemes, 115, 118, 123,
    129–30, 131n10
reading. *See* literacy
real character languages, 8, 115–18
reason and religion, 56
Reflections on Dr. Swift's Letter
    (Oldmixon), 30–31, 151
Reformation of Schooles (Comenius),
    53–54, 58
Reformed School (Dury), 57
reform of education. *See* pedagogy
Reisch, Gregorovius de, 48
religious education
  Biblical metaphors for learning,
    49–50
  and Comenius, 55–57, 62–63
  literacy, 139, 164n24
  social class, 76, 153–56

universal language, 59, 62, 109–10, 113, 118
Renaissance period, architectural metaphor for education, 48
research issues
    scholarship review, 5–12
    theoretical issues, 165
rhetoric
    definitions, 89
    vs. grammar, 12, 67–71, 85–90
    in lexicography, 167
    as purview of upper classes, 74–76
    sexism of, 142–43, 151
    timing of study for, 107*n*11
    See also composition
A Rhetorical Grammar of the English Tongue (Kenrick), 105–6
Rhetorical Grammar (Walker), 107*n*23
Rhetoric (Aristotle), 87, 91
Rice, John, 140–41, 161
Right Spelling Very Much Improved, 4, 52
The Right Teaching of Useful Knowledg (Snell)
    letter writing, 76–77
    on lexicography, 39
    religious motivations for literacy education, 153–54
    school reform, 57
    standardization issue, 25, 32
Robinson, Ralph, 86
Romberch, Johann, 48
rote memorization, Comenius's criticism of, 55
The Royal English Dictionary (Fenning), 140, 152
Royal Grammar (Lily), 3, 4
Royal Grammar Reformed, 21
The Royal Universal British Grammar (Farro), 126
Rudiments of English Grammar (Priestly), 36–37, 100–101, 104, 126–27

rule-based grammar. *See* prescriptive vs. descriptive approach

Salmon, Vivian, 8
The Scholar's Guide (Johnson), 5, 77, 87–88, 91–92, 143
scholarship review, 5–12
The Scholemaster (Ascham), 18
School of Infancy (Comenius), 56–57
The School of Skill (Fleming), 48
School Pastime for Young Children: or the Rudiments of Grammar (Newton), 26–27, 51, 64–65
science
    and literacy, 157
    and universal language, 109, 118–21
secret language, 8
self-help manuals, 83–85
Sensible Words: Linguistic Practice in England (Cohen), 11
sensory knowledge as basis for pedagogical technique, 57
Sheridan, Thomas, 160–61
Shorte Introduction to Grammar (Colet and Lily), 48
A Short History of Writing Instruction: From Ancient Greece to Twentieth-Century America (Murphy), 7
A Short Introduction to English Grammar (Lowth), 24, 35–36, 127–28
Short Introduction to Grammar (Lily), 13, 86
Short Introduction to Grammar (Lowth), 3
Smith, Adam, 91, 94–95
Snell, George
    letter writing, 76–77
    on lexicography, 39
    religious motivations for literacy education, 153–54

school reform, 57
standardization issue, 25, 32
A Social History of English (Leith), 11–12, 34
social position
 acculturation of foreigners, 133–41
 class and lexicography, 41–42
 composition vs. grammar, 90–106
 drive for standard grammar, 166
 grammar focus for working class, 19, 25, 157
 language acquisition theories, 108–9
 lexicography, 43
 overview, 5
 religious education, 76, 153–56
 rhetoric vs. grammar, 85–90
 scholarship review, 10–12
 upper class writing instruction, 74–76
 and vocational education, 57
 women's education, 141–53
 See also middle class; upper class
social reconstruction, 56
social role of language as communication, 124, 127
Some Improvements to the Art of Teaching (Walker), 51
standardization
 English and Latin models, 17–38
 lexicography's rise to authority, 38–44
 overview, 2–3
 scholarship review, 6
 See also universal language/grammar
Story, Joshua, 105
The Study of Language in Seventeenth-Century England (Salmon), 8
style in composition, 95–101
Supplement to Dr. Harris's Dictionary, 5

Swift, Jonathan
 background of, 13
 religious education, 156
 standardization issue, 30, 36
 universal language, 128
 on women's education, 150–51
Syncrisis, Or The Most Natural and Easie Method of Learning Latin (Coles), 20, 51, 123, 154
Systema grammaticum (Farnaby), 17, 86

A Table Alphabetical (Cawdry), 40
teaching of grammar. *See* pedagogy
temple of wisdom metaphor, 53
text vs. word focus of grammarians, 66–71
theoretical considerations, 165
thou, rejection of by middle class, 158
Topics (Cicero), 87
Tower of Knowledge metaphor, *47*, 48
transitions, compositional, 104
Treatise on Education (Barclay), 24, 98–100, 102–3, 151–52, 160
The True and Readie Way to Learne the Latine Tongue (Hartlib), 19–20, 54, 56, 62
Tryon, Thomas, 135, 145, 154–55
Tutor to True English (Care), 5, 27–28, 135

The Universal Character (Beck), 113–15
universal characters for artificial language schemes, 110–13
An Universal Etymological English Dictionary (Bailey), 41
universal language/grammar
 and architectural metaphor for language learning, 50–51
 eighteenth century schemes, 124–31

English as, 134
English vs. Latin, 23–24
language acquisition, 108–9
Latin promoted as, 33
overview, 4
and religious education, 59, 62
scholarship review, 7–10, 12–13
seventeenth century schemes, 109–24
and spiritual wisdom, 53–54
as validation of English, 21, 23–24
Universal Language Schemes in England and France 1600-1800 (Knowlson), 8
The Universal Letter-Writer (Cooke), 83
upper class
grammatical flexibility of, 157
as privileged language acquirers, 108
rhetoric for women, 142–43
writing instruction for, 74–76, 91–92

Via Lucis (Comenius), 9
visible language method, 7, 57–62
visual learning, 48
A Vocabulary or Pocket Dictionary, 4, 42–43
vocational education
Comenius's emphasis on, 54, 57, 67
and language acquisition, 108–9
and Latin vs. English grammar, 26
writing instruction, 73–74, 76–77, 91–92
See also middle class; working class
Vorlat, Emma, 10

Walker, John, 107n23
Walker, Obadiah, 92
Walker, William, 51, 154

Wallis, John, 6, 10, 13, 19–20, 127, 139
Ward, Seth, 110
Ward, William, 4
Wase, Christopher, 50
Watts, Isaac, 159–60
The Way of Light (Comenius), 55
Webbe, Joseph, 10, 59
Wharton, Jeremiah, 20, 25–26, 135-136
Wilkins, John
scientific approach of, 13
universal language schemes, 9, 10, 50–51, 110, 115, 118–23
Wilson, Thomas, 87–88, 142
Wit and Eloquence, 75–76
women's education, 75–76, 141–53, 162n11, 163n17–21
word vs. text focus of grammarians, 66–71, 128
working class, 19, 25, 157
See also vocational education
World of Words (Phillips), 89
Wrightson, Keith, 164n24, 164n32
writing instruction
composition and grammar, 90–106
introduction, 73–74
letters, 74–85
overview, 4
rhetoric vs. grammar, 85–90
scholarship review, 7
The Writing Scholar's Companion, 52, 96

Yates, Francis, 48
Young, E., 78, 83–84
The Young Man's Companion (Gordon), 85
The Young Man's Companion (Mather), 84–85, 150
The Young Secretary's Guide, or, a Speedy Help to Learning (Hill), 77–78, 84